Advance Praise for
Educational Leadership for Ethics and Social Justice:
Views from the Social Sciences

"Out of the fray of fortified academic silos and rampant myopic policymaking come Brooks and Normore who, along with a luminary group of contributors, model the way toward looking at challenges and opportunities in educational leadership from multiple perspectives. Pithy and refreshing!"

—Dr. Leslie Hazle Bussey
Georgia Leadership Institute for School Improvement

"Anthony Normore and Jeffrey Brooks have done it again! This is a timely, much needed work to keep the educational social justice agenda front and center with new research and innovation to do so."

—Dr. Noelle Witherspoon Arnold
Associate Professor of Educational Leadership at the University
of Missouri-Columbia and Executive Committee Member, University Council
for Educational Administration

"A great step forward in the discourse and practice of social justice and leadership. This is not just a great read, but also a need work for application in both the academy and in PK–12 contexts."

—Dr. Judy A. Alston
Professor and Chair of the Department of Leadership Studies,
Ashland University

"*Educational Leadership for Ethics and Social Justice* provides prospective school leaders with essential historical and conceptual underpinnings that shape how they can think and act as leaders for social justice. From across different fields, the authors shine a light on the social, political, philosophical, ethical, and pedagogical context in which injustice occurs in our educational institutions. This allows school leaders to develop a principled framework from which they can begin enacting justice-oriented policies and practices.

—Madeline M. Hafner, PhD
Executive Director, Minority Student Achievement Network
Associate Scientist, Wisconsin Center for Education Research
University of Wisconsin–Madison

"Professors Normore and Brooks do an outstanding job presenting a timely and important edited volume that examine lessons learned from social justice and its impact on leadership. This book is a must read for any school leader interested in rethinking the way theories of social justice influence educational leadership and school systems."

—Dr. David A. Gomez
Executive Director of the California Association of Latino Superintendents and Administrators; retired US Army Officer, retired superintendent of Santa Paula Union High School District and former State President of the Association of California School Administrators

"Drs. Normore and Brooks have produced a long overdue book about how to increase and improve "social justice" in our schools, based on many fields and disciplines. Great news. Taking a wide angle view, based on a number of key definitions of justice, the book rightly places the concept and practices in both highly personal *and* societal perspectives. Critically, the book relates the *just practices* of education with the *fair and equitable* outcomes—that in turn help to make schooling more just and effective for all our children, regardless of their background, race, or socio-economic standing. Vital for all educators—not to mention leaders, and parents, and politicians—to read, learn, and act!"

—Bruce S. Cooper
Professor at Fordham University, New York City

"In their new book, Drs. Normore and Brooks have captured key elements of interdisciplinary learning about ethics and social justice for school leaders who work in public, private and charter school positions. It's a must read for leaders faced with modern day challenges and opportunities."

—Robert Fraisse
Distinguished Educator in Residence Graduate School of Education; Former Superintendent of California School Districts including Conejo Valley Unified School District, Hueneme Elementary School District, and Laguna Beach Unified School District

"At a time when poverty rates continue to rise and there are persistent resource inequalities across schools, school leaders must be pillars of advocacy for social justice. Editors Normore and Brooks offer the necessary step of re-examining social justice through multiple lenses. They have assembled a collection of distinguished scholars who each provide a slice of this very complex topic. Their multi-disciplinary framework promises to strengthen school leadership by providing new avenues that promote equity for all."

—Sharon Conley
Professor at University of California Santa Barbara

"We will never achieve equality of access and opportunity for all of our children until school supervisors and those who prepare them come to terms with the political, ethical and moral ramifications of their leadership practices. Normore and Brooks have masterfully put together a collection of readings to better prepare practicing and aspiring school leaders with lessons that can lead to a more just society."

—Eric Nadelstern
Professor of Educational Leadership & Director
of the Summer Principals Academy at Teachers College Columbia University;
former Deputy Chancellor of Division of School Support and Instruction
for New York City Department of Education

"*Educational Leadership for Ethics and Social Justice: Views from the Social Sciences* is a thought provoking collection of works focused on the convergence of leadership as a practical and logistical matter while contextualized in an array of issues connected to justice. The term social justice, like many others in the educational sphere, has taken on sometimes myopic, specified political, and polarizing baggage. Normore and Brooks provide a text that challenges the reader to stop and re-think social justice from multiple vantage points and to take these new frames into the day to day work of educational leadership."

—John Puglisi
Superintendent of RIO Unified School District, Oxnard, California

"Drs. Normore and Brooks have a deep understanding of the dynamic environment in which educational leaders find themselves today. This book provides specifics on how to rethink our leadership approach to ethics and social justice and the best chance for us to advance this most worthy of causes."

—Dr. Dan Stepenosky
Superintendent, Las Virgenes Unified School District, Las Virgenes, California

"*Educational Leadership for Ethics and Social Justice: Views from the Social Sciences* is at once sweeping and focused. Tony Normore and Jeff Brooks furnish new insights about how educational leaders can work with others across a multitude of disciplines to dramatically transform the field. The result is both an inspirational and insightful compilation of interdisciplinary perspectives about the role of leadership in the context of ethics, morality, and social justice. It's a must read for all who have a vested interest in the reciprocal nature of social sciences and educational leadership."

—Jacqueline A. Stefkovich, EdD, JD
Professor of Law and Ethics, The Pennsylvania State University

Educational Leadership for Ethics and Social Justice

Views from the Social Sciences

A volume in
Educational Leadership for Social Justice
Jeffrey S. Brooks, Denise E. Armstrong, Ira Bogotch, Sandra Harris,
Whitney Sherman, and George Theoharis, *Series Editors*

Educational Leadership for Ethics and Social Justice

Views from the Social Sciences

edited by

Anthony H. Normore
California State University Dominguez Hills

Jeffrey S. Brooks
University of Idaho

INFORMATION AGE PUBLISHING, INC.
Charlotte, NC • www.infoagepub.com

Library of Congress Cataloging-in-Publication Data

Educational leadership for ethics and social justice : views from the social
sciences / edited by Anthony H. Normore, California Lutheran University,
Jeffrey S. Brooks, University of Idaho.
    pages cm. – (Educational leadership for social justice)
 ISBN 978-1-62396-535-8 (pbk.) – ISBN 978-1-62396-536-5 (hardcover) –
ISBN 978-1-62396-537-2 (ebook) 1. Educational leadership–Moral and
ethical aspects. 2. Social ethics. 3. Social justice. 4. Social sciences.
I. Normore, Anthony H.
 LB2806.E4225 2014
 371.2–dc23

                                                    2013040812

CONTENTS

SERIES EDITOR'S PREFACE

Jeffrey S. Brooks

I am pleased to serve as series editor for this book series, Educational Leadership for Social Justice, with Information Age Publishing. The idea for this series grew out of the work of a committed group of leadership for scholars associated with the American Educational Research Association's (AERA) Leadership for Social Justice Special Interest Group (LSJ SIG). This group existed for many years before being officially affiliated with AERA and has benefitted greatly from the ongoing leadership, support, and counsel of Dr. Catherine Marshall (University of North Carolina–Chapel Hill). It is also important to acknowledge the contributions of the LSJ SIG's first Chair, Dr. Ernestine Enomoto (University of Hawaii at Manoa), whose wisdom, stewardship, and guidance helped ease a transition into AERA's more formal organizational structures. This organizational change was at times difficult to reconcile with scholars who largely identified as nontraditional thinkers and push toward innovation rather than accept the status quo. As the second Chair of the LSJ SIG, I appreciate all of Ernestine's hard work and friendship. Moreover, I also thank Drs. Gaetane Jean-Marie and Whitney Sherman Newcomb, the third and fourth Chairs of the LSJ SIG for their visionary leadership, steadfast commitment to high standards, and collaborative scholarship and friendship.

I am particularly indebted to my colleagues on the LSJ SIG's first publications committee, which I chaired from 2005–2007: Dr. Denise Armstrong, Brock University; Dr. Ira Bogotch, Florida Atlantic University; Dr. Sandra

Educational Leadership for Ethics and Social Justice, pages vii–viii
Copyright © 2014 by Information Age Publishing
All rights of reproduction in any form reserved.

Harris, Lamar University; Dr. Whitney Sherman, Virginia Commonwealth University; and Dr. George Theoharis, Syracuse University. This committee was a joy to work with and I am pleased we have found many more ways to collaborate—now as my fellow series editors of this book series—as we seek to provide publication opportunities for scholarship in the area of leadership for social justice.

This book, *Educational Leadership for Ethics and Social Justice: Views from the Social Sciences*, that I co-edited with Dr. Anthony H. Normore, is the twelfth in the series. The book, as we explain in the introduction, is devoted to looking deeper into the social sciences to advance our understanding of issues related to leadership, ethics, and social justice.

Again, welcome to this seventh book in this Information Age Publishing series, Educational Leadership for Social Justice. You can learn more about the series at our web site: http://www.infoagepub.com/series/Educational-Leadership-for-Social-Justice. I invite you to contribute your own work on equity and influence to the series. We look forward to you joining the conversation.

—**Dr. Jeffrey S. Brooks**
University of Idaho

FOREWORD

Gary L. Anderson
New York University

The study of leadership, like most specific areas of study, is riven with quandaries. As a field of study it draws on multiple disciplines for its methodologies and theoretical frameworks. Few scholars are well grounded in more than one discipline, let alone several. Add to this complexity the question of whether we are scholars in the social sciences doing "leadership studies" or faculty in professional schools attempting to both generate knowledge and bring knowledge to bear on the preparation of leaders. Add to this the problem that leadership is an amorphous concept that lends itself to either easy prescription or pontification "from the trenches" of leadership[1]. After all, virtually every CEO has written a book on leadership. Who needs interdisciplinary scholars?

And then there is "social justice," which outside the discipline of philosophy is an even more amorphous concept. I suspect it would be hard to find anyone who is against "social justice," and it has become omnipresent in some fields, such as education. In an age in which economic inequalities are rivaling or surpassing those of the 1920s, and we are experiencing a "new Jim Crow" (Alexander, 2012), it is curious that educational researchers and even venture philanthropists and hedge fund managers are using the language of social justice. Ironically, school choice is promoted as the legacy of the civil rights movement, even though it was school choice that allowed Southern Whites to avoid racial integration.

Educational Leadership for Ethics and Social Justice, pages ix–xii
Copyright © 2014 by Information Age Publishing
All rights of reproduction in any form reserved.

All of this is to say that this is a courageous book. In attempting to bring some clarity to both educational leadership and social justice from a multi-disciplinary perspective, we may at least get clearer about how we are using these terms when we use them. It may also be that the terms have outlived their usefulness. From a critical linguistic view (I would have added a chapter by a linguist), we might ask what ideological work these terms are currently doing. In other words, by using the language of "leadership," do we risk being absorbed into a new common-sense world of neoliberal modalities of governance? Particularly at the level of urban superintendents (or, CEOs, as Broad graduates are called), leadership is becoming a key modality for leveraging current reforms, promoting some scholars to replace leadership with "leaderism."

Educational leadership has been caught up in the neoliberal discourse of new public management (NPM). It has been heavily influenced by total quality management gurus, the Wallace Foundation and venture philanthropists like Eli Broad. At the organizational level, neoliberalism intersects with NPM. To the extent that neoliberal models aim at the privatization and marketization of the public sector, NPM represents a set of management principals that are congruent with those aims (Ward, 2011). NPM primarily promotes

- A shift from a focus on inputs to the system to results (mainly quantitative) in the name of efficiency, effectiveness, and quality of service
- Decentralization of management, in which decisions on resource allocation and provision of services are made closer to the point of delivery, often resulting in the outsourcing of auxiliary services, and accompanied by new technologies of control that steer the organization from a distance (Kickert, 1995)
- The introduction of internal and external competition, customer service, public relations and corporate marketing techniques within the public sector

Terms that some associate with social justice are often part of this NPM discourse—more "autonomy" for school principals, more "participation" in decision-making, more "transparency" through publishing test scores, more "accountability" through competition, and so on. Without the kind of in-depth disciplinary analysis that this book provides, we have few tools for deconstructing these discourse practices. While traditionally the domain of analytic philosophy, all disciplines have developed a small set of critical scholars who pay attention to such things. While functionalism and "what works" utilitarianism have made a comeback in most disciplines, as well as educational leadership, the genie of critical theory and post-structuralism won't be going back in the bottle anytime soon.

In this sense, the fact that educational researchers have landed on "social justice" as a cover term for a plethora of ideas itself should be a topic of study. Unfortunately, scholars in education too often sprinkle social justice terms like "emancipatory" or "hegemonic" or "empowering" into their writing. Does this mean they have a deep understanding of how Habermas uses "emancipatory" or how Gramsci used "hegemonic"? And to return to an earlier theme, is it realistic in this age of knowledge proliferation to expect this level of interdisciplinary knowledge of any scholar—especially scholars who are also expected to be former or current practitioners of leadership? Many scholars of educational leadership in schools of education, like myself, had previous careers as teachers and educational administrators. When younger social science scholars were reading John Rawls, we were chaperoning the kids building the homecoming float.

So what is the utility of a book like this? Perhaps it is to clear the air a bit. To, as the editors say, take a step back, in order to take a step forward. Perhaps it will remind scholars of educational leadership that thinking deeply and carefully about the language and concepts we use and their disciplinary origins, can lead not only to better scholarship, but also to better practice. When Mayor Bloomberg tells principals they have more "autonomy," what does he mean? What kinds of things do principals have control over and what don't they and what should they?

We live in a world in which the knowledge base of our field is more heavily influenced by new public management ideology than interdisciplinary scholarship. Given the savvy and well-funded policy networks promoting NPM, we will need to do more than shore up our knowledge base. We will also need to take some lessons from scholarship in community organizing, political advocacy, new social media, and policy framing. Disciplinary knowledge can help us think more clearly, but it should also help us act more effectively in a world that is changing rapidly.

NOTE

I should note here that I believe that through participatory action research, we can produce important knowledge about educational leadership from "the trenches." Here I am referring to a naïve approach to "experience" that fails to understand that experience needs to be interpreted and problematized.

REFERENCES

Alexander, M. (2012). *The new Jim Crow: Mass incarceration in the age of colorblindness.* New York, NY: New Press.

Kickert, W. (1995). Steering at a distance: A new paradigm of public governance in Dutch higher education. *Governance, 8,* 135–157.

Ward, S. (2011). The machinations of managerialism: New public management and the diminishing power of professionals. *Journal of Cultural Economy, 4*(2), 205–215.

INTRODUCTION

Anthony H. Normore and Jeffrey S. Brooks

The purpose of this edited volume is to examine and learn lessons from the way leadership for social justice is conceptualized in several disciplines and to consider how these lessons might improve the preparation and practice of school leaders. In particular, we examine philosophy, Black studies, anthropology, sociology, law, economics, interdisciplinary studies, political science, public policy, and psychology. It is important first, however, to point out certain assumptions about social justice that together form a framework for this book. *First, social justice is both individual and collective* (Bogotch, Beachum, Blount, Brooks, & English, 2008; Normore, 2008). Justice has both personal and collective dimensions, and it can be enacted and experienced as one person and as a collective or subcollective. Accordingly, while educational leaders can (and should) be conceived as advocates for social justice, especially those with positional power and formal influence, it is also appropriate to consider leaders as advocates for individual justice. *Second, social justice has both conceptual and empirical qualities.* While research on justice often necessarily begins with abstract conceptualizations, it is also manifest as tangible and observable activities and behaviors. Thus, it follows that justice can be studied through a variety of methodological approaches. Depending on the epistemological and/or methodological orientation of a study, justice may be a measurable or observed event, a purely theoretical construct, or more likely a combination of the two. *Third, school leaders' individual values and ethics are critical because they are uniquely positioned to influence socially just processes and outcomes in schools.* These leaders have the

Educational Leadership for Ethics and Social Justice, pages xiii–xvii
Copyright © 2014 by Information Age Publishing
All rights of reproduction in any form reserved.

moral imperative to address important questions about morality, including concepts such as right versus wrong, virtue versus vice, and good versus evil (Brooks & Normore, 2005). Of equal importance to educational leaders is how to navigate complex ethical dilemmas, how to respond to situations where personal and professional codes of ethics collide, and how to best engage in the decision-making processes while keeping the best interest of students at the fore (Normore, 2004; Starratt, 2004).

Our contention is that the field of educational leadership might consider taking a step backward in order to take several forward. That is, educational leadership researchers might reexamine social justice, both in terms of social and individual dynamics and as disciplinary-specific, multidisciplinary and interdisciplinary phenomenon. By adopting this approach, we can connect and extend long-established lines of conceptual and empirical inquiry and thereby gain insights that may otherwise be overlooked or assumed. This holds great promise for generating, refining, and testing theories of social justice in educational leadership and will help strengthen already vibrant lines of inquiry. That is, rather than citing a single work or a few works out of their disciplinary context, it might be more fruitful to situate educational leadership for social justice research in their respective traditions. This could be carried out by extending extant lines of inquiry in educational leadership research and then incorporating lessons gleaned from this work into innovative practice. For example, why not more clearly establish lines of educational leadership and justice research into the philosophy of social justice, economics of social justice, political studies of social justice, sociology of social justice, anthropology of social justice, and the public policy of social justice as focused and discrete areas of inquiry?

Once this new orientation toward the knowledge base of social justice and educational leadership is laid, we might then seek to explore some of the natural connections between traditions before ultimately investigating justice in educational leadership through a free association of ideas as the worlds of practice and research co-construct a "new" language they can use to discuss educational leadership. Such an endeavor *may* demand reconceptualization of both the processes and products of collaborative research and the communication of findings, but it *will* demand a breaking down of methodological and epistemological biases and a more meaningful level and type of engagement between primary and applied knowledge bases.

The book is organized into 10 chapters. Each chapter focuses on a specific perspective from the social sciences. Accordingly, authors provide a historical perspective on social justice in individual disciplines as it relates to both society and schooling; key theories, concepts, and debates are identified in relation to the study of social justice in the discipline, paying special attention to those used to explore society and schooling; given these perspectives, authors discuss how school leadership influences (or can influence) the way these dynamics are manifest in schools, paying special attention to the role that values and ethics play in promoting socially just processes and outcomes in schools (Starratt, 2004); and recommendations are made for improving the preparation and practice of school leadership are proposed in relation to how that are grounded in the various disciplinary perspective.

In Chapter 1, "The Strategic Merging of Political Orientation and Social Justice Leadership" authors Sarah Diem and Bradley W. Carpenter argue that educational leaders desirous of enacting an agenda based upon the ideals of social justice must develop a politically oriented identity. Specifically, leaders must acquire a refined understanding of the institutions and actors operating within the educational policy arena, allowing them to better respond to conflicts pertaining to educational governance, political ideologies, and the competing interests shaping education reform. Chapter 2, "Positive Psychology as a Foundation for Social Justice Leadership," is presented by Derik Yegar-Elloriaga and Paula T. McWhirter. These authors examine and learn lessons from the way psychology conceptualizes leadership for social justice, with an emphasis on positive psychology. Based on these lessons, the chapter concludes with psychology-based recommendations and tools for improving the preparation and practice of school leadership. In Chapter 3, Gaetane Jean-Marie and T. Elon Dancy present "Pedagogy of the Discipline: How Black Studies Can Influence Educational Leadership." They examine the intellectual tradition of Black studies to offer a lens on how social justice can improve the preparation and practice of educational leaders. The chapter concludes with implication for leadership preparation and practice as the field of educational leadership continues to grapple with issues of social justice. In Chapter 4, Nancy Erbe discusses "What School Leaders Do Not Know about Law Will Hurt Them and Others: The Importance of Quality Legal Counsel and Collaborative Skills." The author argues that leadership for social justice within legal studies in the United States is primarily conceptualized as constitutional, judicial and statutory, or technical. Erbe recommends that all schools employ quality trustworthy legal counsel and staff and all leaders and their team (administrators, counselors, teachers, parents, students, etc.) learn the ethical and effective collaborative skills that show success with bullying and dramatically reduce violent behavior.

Chapter 5 is presented by Genevieve Siegel-Hawley, titled "Bending Toward Justice: What Public Policy Can Tell Us about Leadership for Social Justice." Siegel-Hawley explores the arc of education policy in the aftermath of Brown versus Board of Education and illuminates key tensions that have shaped its evolution. Understanding how this macro-level history should influence contemporary policy efforts to ensure equity in schools is a critical component of leading for social justice. In Chapter 6, "In Pursuit of Social Justice: The Influence of Anthropology in Facilitating Models of

Participation, Agency, and Equity in Education," Diane Rodriguez-Kiino and George J. Petersen, illustrate the critical role that anthropology has played in supporting social justice frameworks in education that seek to increase student participation, build and develop human agency, and ensure equitable resource distribution. A distinctive contribution of this chapter includes a collection of strategies rooted in anthropology to bolster the development of educational leaders in pursuit of social justice in K–12 schooling. Lynn Ilon and JuYoung Lee present Chapter 7, "Changing Views of Economics of Inequality and Implications for Leadership and Learning." These authors argue that the manner in which inequality is viewed is one of the shifts from neoclassical economics to knowledge economics. They review the dominant theory of economics and its view of equality and then contrast this view with the new view of knowledge economics. In Chapter 8, "A Philosophical Deconstruction of Leadership and Social Justice Associated with the High-Stakes Testing and Accountability System," Tawannah G. Allen, Fenwick W. English, and Rosemary Papa argue that the current high-stakes testing and accountability system used in public education is too narrowly defined, applies only to certain schools and to some students, and is not applicable to the larger social system in which schools are embedded. To this end, the authors suggest various metrics to provide social justice within the testing and accountability system. Chapter 9, "Sociology and Social Justice: Prospects for Educational Leaders in the United States," by Mark Berends, examines the roots of sociology, particularly the sociology of education, and its perspectives on social justice and provides specific examples from the sociology of education to inform educational leaders about those aspects of schools and schooling processes that have implications for social justice—for students, teachers, parents, and leaders. Chapter 10, "I've Done My Sentence, but Committed No Crime: An Interdisciplinary Perspective on Violence Exposure, Urban Male Adolescents, and Educational Leadership," concludes the volume. Nicole Limperopulos provides educational leaders with critical insights into the pernicious effects that chronic violence exposure has on the physiological, psychological, and emotional development of urban male adolescents. The chapter represents an interdisciplinary approach, calling upon essential theories in psychology, urban studies, education leadership, and adolescent development, to illustrate the ways in which chronic violence exposure is contributing to the underachievement of African American and Latino males in urban settings.

The implications of the interdisciplinary orientation of *Educational Leadership for Ethics and Social Justice: Views from the Social Sciences* are as much of interest to practitioners as it is researchers. Faculty teaching in educational leadership preparation programs might, for example, create an interdisciplinary strain of justice research or organize program curricula, course content, and student experiences on this framework. P–12 educational leaders might consider that social justice, as we have described them here, entail both (1) a sensitivity toward and understanding of the ways these concepts are theoretically and empirically manifest in educational settings, and, more importantly and (2) an understanding of how to influence change in each of these domains. It is simply not sufficient to identify achievement gaps using standardized testing data, although that is certainly a useful point of departure. Instead, we would argue that practitioners should be attuned to the various disciplinary manifestations and conceptualizations of justice and be trained in techniques that allow them to positively influence these phenomena. Only then will we begin not only to rethink the way theories of justice and practice inform educational leadership, but also to reconsider how leaders can influence systems and practices to offer a new vision of social justice for their students.

Finally, a book is a monumental and at times frustrating project, one that requires much assistance and support if it's ever to reach completion. We would be remiss not to acknowledge the many people involved with this project. First and foremost, our sincere gratitude goes to each of our authors who relentlessly wrote to meet deadlines. This book would not have been possible without their commitment to the project, motivation to strengthen their work, understanding and endless patience, and intrinsic desire to share their message of hope and inspiration with the world. Our hope is that their leadership work will serve as catalysts for important interdisciplinary dialogue throughout the various professions. We are equally indebted to many of our local, national, and international friends and colleagues who offered invaluable suggestions. Finally, to the Information Age Publishing team we offer our sincere gratitude for their ongoing diligence and support throughout the publication process.

REFERENCES

Bogotch, I., Beachum, F. Blount, J., Brooks, J. S., & English, F. W. (2008). *Radicalizing educational leadership: Toward a theory of social justice.* Rotterdam, the Netherlands: Sense Publishers.

Brooks, J. S., & Normore, A. H. (2005). An Aristotelian framework for the development of ethical leadership. *Journal of Values and Ethics in Educational Administration, 3*(2), 1–8

Normore, A. H. (2004). Ethics and values in leadership preparation programs: Finding the North Star in the dust storm. *Journal of Values and Ethics in Educational Administration, 2*(2), 1–7.

Normore, A. H. (2008). *Leadership for social justice: Promoting equity and excellence through inquiry and reflective practice.* Charlotte, NC: Information Age Publishers.

Starratt, R. (2004). *Ethical leadership.* San Francisco, CA: Jossey-Bass.

CHAPTER 1

THE STRATEGIC MERGING OF POLITICAL ORIENTATION AND SOCIAL JUSTICE LEADERSHIP

Sarah Diem and Bradley W. Carpenter

ABSTRACT

While over the course of the past decade the field of educational leadership has placed a more purposeful focus on exposing practitioners to the importance of social justice leadership, beginning principals are often ill-prepared to address the diverse range of political complexities associated with public schooling in today's society (Brown, 2004; Cambron-McCabe & McCarthy, 2005; Dantley, 2002; Grogan & Andrews, 2002; Hawley & James, 2010; Jean-Marie, 2010; López, 2003; Marshall & Oliva, 2006; McKenzie et al., 2008; Tillman, 2004). Subsequently, educational leaders frequently fail to cultivate the skillsets necessary to engage in the policymaking processes that can be used to help realize equitable educational systems. In this chapter, we argue that educational leaders desirous of enacting an agenda based upon the ideals of social justice must develop a politically oriented identity. Specifically, leaders must acquire a refined understanding of the institutions and actors operating within the educational policy arena, allowing them to better respond to conflicts pertaining to educational governance, political ideologies, and the

Educational Leadership for Ethics and Social Justice, pages 1–22
Copyright © 2014 by Information Age Publishing
All rights of reproduction in any form reserved.

competing interests shaping education reform. We conclude the chapter by offering recommendations on how to strategically merge the fields of political science and social justice in order to develop a new line of inquiry that will facilitate the preparation of politically-oriented school leaders able to fulfill their role as advocates for social justice for their schools and communities.

INTRODUCTION

Over the course of the past several years, there has been a noticeable crescendo in the politics of education (Cooper, Cibulka, & Fusarelli, 2008; Glass, 2008). Specifically, an increasing number of interests have focused their political energies toward influencing the debates surrounding school improvement (Kaestle & Lodewick, 2007) and school turnaround reform efforts (Murphy & Meyers, 2008). Debray-Pelot and McGuinn (2009) offer their insights on the current education reform environment and what they consider to be the establishment of a "new politics" of education asserting, "New policy has created a new politics of education, in the sense that the law (NCLB) has spurred the mobilization of established interest groups, induced the creation of new entrants, and pushed these groups into new and often cross cutting coalitions" (p. 25).

This influx of new entrants in the school improvement and school turnaround debates contribute to what Hajer (2006) labels as institutional ambiguity, a complex policy environment that lacks a specific "constitution that pre-determines where and how a legitimate decision is to be taken" (p. 43). Subsequently, as is the case in the current school reform environment, diverse policy actors are forced to compete when categorizing the policy solutions deserving of the most attention. This complex and shifting environment contributes to what Hajer (2006) describes as the policymaking phenomenon of multisignification, a situation in which actors conceive of policy issues in different terms, and thus the very meanings at stake are often unclear. While the concept of sensemaking in the policy realm is not a new idea (Allison, 1971; Stone, 1997), Hajer's (2006) conceptualization is helpful when considering a new era of education politics inhabited by a wide array of interests, each attempting to make sense of the significance of low-performing public schools, and each entering the school improvement debate operating from a unique and politically oriented perspective. This is especially true for school level leaders, who, in this political environment, must establish a sophisticated understanding of the various political perspectives as they attempt to solidify the coalitional support necessary to facilitate contextually specific school improvement efforts.

Engaging in this political environment can be intimidating, particularly for leaders who have not been prepared with the skills necessary to address the dire conditions facing many schools and communities across the country. While a growing number of educational leadership preparation programs recognize the need to critically examine issues of social justice and diversity, and have thus committed themselves to preparing leaders as change agents that can interrogate the policies continuing to marginalize certain subgroups of students, a large number of programs continue to lack a curriculum that provides a critical discourse focused on issues of diversity and social justice (Dantley, 2002; Hawley & James, 2010; Rusch, 2004; Singleton & Linton, 2005; Tillman, 2004). This is particularly concerning given the current inequities existent within public schools.

We feel in order to move the field of educational leadership forward and better prepare aspiring leaders to find their political voice, preparation programs must "begin to challenge the status quo and search for viable solutions" to issues of injustice and "create an agenda to do something about it" (Gooden & Dantley, 2012, p. 244). Further, more effort needs to be put forth in utilizing research from other disciplines that are examining similar issues but from different frameworks. In this chapter, we argue that educational leaders desirous of enacting an agenda based upon the ideals of social justice must develop a politically oriented identity. Specifically, leaders must develop a sophisticated understanding of the various institutions and actors operating within the educational policy arena and how they relate to each other (Baumgartner & Leech, 1998), thus allowing them to better respond to conflicts pertaining to educational governance, political ideologies, and the competing interests shaping education reform. We believe that the field of political science can offer leadership preparation programs many insights surrounding political processes, systems, and behaviors within education and help illustrate how education policies are developed and implemented. Further, by being more aware and knowledgeable of the relationship between education and political science, school leaders can become more empowered to participate in policy conversations and challenge those making decisions that are not in the best interests for all students. We conclude the chapter by offering recommendations on how to strategically merge the fields of political science and social justice in order to develop a new line of inquiry that will facilitate the preparation of politically oriented leaders able to fulfill their role as advocates for social justice for their schools and communities.

HISTORICAL PERSPECTIVES ON THE POLITICS OF EDUCATION AND SOCIAL JUSTICE

American education, historically, has been rooted in the local control of schools. Initially, policy, management, and finances were decentralized and local officials were the ultimate decision makers in the daily operation of local education agencies (Kirst & Wirt, 2009). It was not until the 1950s that confidence in local school officials began to erode with the failure of local leaders to faithfully implement federal policies addressing issues of equity. Public confidence in local control continued to decline in the 1960s and 1970s when local and state policymakers continued to ignore the federal government's push for equal educational opportunities via desegregation. Thus, equity would serve as the driving force in President Johnson's Elementary and Secondary Education Act (ESEA) of 1965, forever changing the federal government's role in education (Kirst & Wirt, 2009).

With the passage of the ESEA of 1965, equity as a policy value would be centered at the "heart of federal education policy," as the federal government made a considerable commitment to provide supplemental funds in the "hope of equalizing educational opportunity for poor and minority students" (DeBray-Pelot & McGuinn, 2009, p. 17). At a time when racial and socioeconomic tensions were growing across the country, the ESEA progressively expanded, eventually including programs that would, in conjunction with federal court rulings, provide categorical assistance to children with disabilities and English language learners, among others. Indeed, in the 1970s, federal courts led the way in fighting segregation and establishing the right of disabled children to an appropriate and free education (Kirst & Wirt, 2009).

As the 1970s progressed, the growing interconnectedness of global economies and the perpetual threat of economic instability began to shape all public policy debates in the United States. International events such as the Organization of the Petroleum Exporting Countries' (OPEC) dramatic increase in the price of crude oil during the Carter presidency undermined the authority of once sovereign polities by destabilizing domestic economies and facilitating the rearrangement of institutional politics. Hajer (2006) described this political reorganization as "institutional ambiguity" (p. 43). Offering further explanation, Hajer (2006) asserted, "Established institutions often lack the powers to deliver the required or requested policy results on their own. They therefore have to interact in 1) multi-party, 2) polycentric (and often trans-national) and, almost by necessity, 3) intercultural networks of governance" (p. 43).

Although Hajer's insights speak to the rearrangement of European politics, the concept of institutional ambiguity captures how the threat of economic crisis and a globally connected marketplace can dislocate the traditional rules guiding educational policymaking in the United States. Due to an interdependent and rapidly evolving global economy, legitimate decision making in the United States no longer resides under the constitutional authority of the states or federal government. Consequently, during an era where the regulatory boundaries for a global marketplace are still being developed, rules for educational policymaking and decision making cannot be made in advance, and are thus continually reinterpreted and renegotiated in the deliberative enactment of politics.

Hence, due to the emergence of a globally interdependent economy, issues such as trade, energy, environment, labor, health care, welfare, taxation, and education often appear as credible responses to the procurement of economic growth and stability (Dean, 1999) in order to secure top billing on the political agendas of federal policymakers. Although each of these issues has received recognition at different points in U.S. history, education has since emerged as an emblematic issue, one that serves as an effective metaphor for the nation's economic crisis (Brooks & Normore, 2010).

It is with this understanding that the context of federal education policy in the 1980s should be considered. In 1983, the first challenges to the equity approach to education established by ESEA were made through the publication of *A Nation at Risk*. The report indicted education officials and school leaders, claiming, "Our society and its educational institutions seem to have lost sight of the basic purposes of schooling, and of the high expectations and disciplined effort needed to attain them" (National Commission on Excellence in Education, 1983, p. 9). The report outlined indicators of risks, most of which centered on international comparisons of student achievement, the inability of gifted students to meet their tested abilities, low college graduation rates, and the overall economic impact low student achievement would have for the country in a globalized economy. As a result, a new policy regime began to emerge, one that promoted school reforms focused on improving academic achievement for all students, as the fiscally responsible course of action.

By the late 1980s, the standards-based reform movement became a powerful national movement. Proponents of this movement claimed the procurement of a sound fiscal future could be obtained via accountability for student outcomes, regulation, standardization, alignment of curriculum, and more effective teaching (Deschenes, Cuban, & Tyack, 2001). This particular movement has attracted support from liberals and conservatives alike over the last two decades: liberals view data-driven reform and accountability measures as ways to identify and assist disadvantaged students, while conservatives, still wary about increased state and federal influence on local schools, developed an alternative policy agenda including parental choice and market-based education efforts intended to limit the role of the federal government in education (Kaestle & Lodewick, 2007).

In its original iteration, ESEA was popular within the education arena, state capitols, and Washington, D.C., in large part because federal dollars were allocated to every congressional district with minimal provisions attached and minimal accountability regarding student achievement (DeBray-Pelot & McGuinn, 2009; Kirst & Wirt, 2009). While interest groups on both the right and left differed philosophically and politically on education, there was no significant policy formulation role for interest groups from either side until the late 1990s. This resulted in an incremental expansion of federal education spending, programs, and regulations for 30 years, all under the guise of ESEA's original equity framework. The role of educational interest groups between 1965 and 1994 was minor in regards to the formulation of federal education policy, and the larger policymaking environment saw more consensus than conflict. However, by the end of the 1990s, this consensus around ESEA and its financial equity approach waned as Congress became increasingly bipartisan in a new era of standards, testing, and accountability reforms (DeBray-Pelot & McGuinn, 2009; Manna, 2006; Vinovskis, 2009; Wong, 2008).

Propelled by the standards-based reform movement of the 1990s, the passage of No Child Left Behind (NCLB) in 2002 fundamentally shifted the focus and goals of federal education policy initially set forth in the original ESEA legislation. Shifting the statutory emphasis from equity and access towards accountability, NCLB placed value on outputs rather than inputs. One example of this shift was NCLB's focus on imposing harsher sanctions on schools failing to meet Adequate Yearly Progress (AYP) on state-administered assessments (McGuinn, 2006).

The implementation of NCLB created new political dynamics among education interest groups. As a result, the political debates surrounding federal education policy today are debated in a different political environment than those proceeding NCLB. According to DeBray-Pelot and McGuinn (2009), NCLB has fundamentally changed the national politics of education in three ways: (a) the conversation and context within school reform debates that occur at the federal level are now different; (b) "traditional" educational interest groups have shifted their policy positions and advocacy activities to accommodate this new context; and (c) new interest groups have formed to challenge established patterns of influence. Indeed, within today's post-NCLB, Race to The Top (RT2) political environment where federal education policy is now, more than ever, placing teachers and administrators at the center of the accountability movement, it is crucial for leaders to develop politically oriented skills so they, too, can be part of the conversation.

The history of education policy and politics highlights what many scholars consider to be the global reconfiguration of educational purposes (e.g., Ball, 2008; Blackmore, 2007; Lingard, 2009; Torres, 2009). Drawing from the works of Ball (2008), Jensen and Walker (2008), and Levin (1998), Carpenter (2011) developed a framework for the three primary narratives constructing the discourse of educational globalization: (a) *market/choice*, which promotes parents as savvy consumers able to choose the appropriate provider for their children's education and thus, through the principles of competition, facilitate the dramatic improvement of school outcomes;

(b) *management/surveillance*, which promotes local school authorities and parents as self-governing entities who, through state and federal monitoring, can better achieve the centralized objectives of increased standards; and (c) *performativity/accountability*, which promotes the reconfiguration of local school governance, the narrowing of pedagogical offerings in response to standardized testing, and the performance-driven regulation of students, teachers, and local administrators. This framework captures the dominant discourse most often used to structure the current policies being used to guide school improvement reforms and is used to critique the current neoliberal ideology that currently shapes the tenor and scope of federal education policy. Furthermore, the predominance of these discourses within educational policies allude to the neoliberal replacement of traditional liberal values, as the government has become an active partner in the creation of policies that promote individual freedoms via consumer choice and the enactment of market-based transactions.

Secretary of Education Arne Duncan offered a preview of this reasoning during his Senate confirmation hearing when he stated: "The President-elect views education as both a *moral obligation and an economic imperative.* In the face of rising *global competition,* we know that education is the *critical,* some would say the only, road to *economic security*" (Confirmation of Arne Duncan, 2009, para. 9, emphasis added). Though Duncan's testimony also cited issues of social justice as the moral justification for education reform, the global reconfiguration of educational purposes begin to emerge through Duncan's rhetorical linking of urgency ("imperative," "critical"), global competition, education reform, and economic security. According to Ginsberg and Lyche (2008), in the current political environment, the

> constant promotion of a culture of fear regarding the failure of education at both pre-K–12 and higher education levels, involving speculative conclusions drawn about the sorry state of affairs in education and their scary potential outcomes, . . . has become the dominant means for projecting issues on to the educational policy agenda. (p. 13)

Indeed, scaring the public to believe students will not be prepared to compete globally is a fear tactic used to promote the Administration's agenda of developing more punitive education policies to increase achievement and sanction those that are not helping to meet specific academic goals. Thus, Secretary Duncan's Senate confirmation testimony served as an effective introduction for the discourse of educational globalization, which has functioned as the dominant discourse in the Obama/Duncan school reform agenda.

Therefore, the current politics of education appear to operate upon a discursive chain of reasoning that suggests the following: If the collective citizenry had the courage to make difficult decisions and do what is morally necessary to improve the public school system, then the United States could provide the educational opportunities necessary to secure its dominant position in the global economy. Consequently, for the purposes of this chapter, it is important to consider how and why the preparation of socially just school leaders is needed to counteract the dominant discourses guiding educational reform. Specifically, how can school leaders be adequately prepared to use their agency and better position themselves politically as social justice advocates? In the following section, we discuss traditional theories of political science that have long been applied to examining education politics and policy and then offer more critically oriented theories that we believe leaders should consider in reframing analyses of education politics and policy with a focus on social justice.

TRADITIONAL POLICY STUDIES AND THE CRITICAL RESPONSE

Harold Lasswell (1936), often referred to as the founder of policy sciences, defined policy analysis as an attempt to discover "who gets what, when, how." Frustrated by the unproductive nature of public policy debate in the post-World War II era, Lasswell established an applied social science that could provide empirical solutions for the problematic social issues of his time (Fischer, 2003; Torgerson, 1985). Lasswell's desire was to create a "policy science of democracy" founded upon both quantitative and qualitative methods, the contextual consideration of problems, and a normative orientation based upon human values (Fischer, 2003, p. 3).

The rise of policy sciences in the late 1960s and early 1970s can be attributed to several era-specific stimuli. First, societal issues such as environmental pollution, racial discrimination, poverty, and national security placed pressure upon policy sciences to develop applicable solutions. Second, there was a movement within policy sciences to look beyond the political composition of policy decisions and instead acknowledge the importance of socioeconomic factors such as income and education. Additionally, inspired by the intellectual framework of David Easton (as cited in Sabatier, 1991), policy sciences began to consider the entire policymaking process, from the initial articulation of policy demands to the final stages of collecting feedback on the effects of chosen policy solutions.

Sabatier (1991) categorized the initial era of policy sciences into four general typologies explaining the analytical tasks of policy sciences: (a) *substantive area research* is the analysis of the politics of a specific policy area; (b) *evaluation and impact studies* are the interrogation of policy outcomes; (c) *policy process* is the analysis of factors affecting policy formulation, implementation, and effect; and (d) *policy design* is the analysis of policy research instruments and their efficacy. However, in the decades following this initial period, the understanding of what policy analysis *is* and what policy analysis is supposed to *do* has been muddled, as the definition of policy analysis has been shaped and reshaped by an assortment of theories and specialized vocabularies (Theodoulou, 1995). In an effort to provide operational clarity to the understanding of contemporary policy studies, Theodoulou (1995) highlights five common elements and ideas most often used to define policy analysis: (a) public policy includes what governments intend to do and what they actually do; (b) public policy is shaped by the actions of formal and informal actors; (c) public policy goes beyond legislative and executive orders, beyond rules and regulations; (d) public policy focuses on an intentional course of action defined by specific goals and objectives; and (e) public policy is concerned by both short- and long-term effects. Although each of these elements contributes to Lasswell's (1936) ideal of a "policy science of democracy," the contemporary dominance of traditional policy–science frameworks differs significantly from the multidisciplinary approach Lasswell envisioned.

Informed by the assumptions of scientific reasoning, traditional frameworks are based upon positivistic rationalities and thus attempt to identify the objective existence of a problem by formulating the goals and objectives meant to provide optimal success, determining the relevant consequences and probabilities of alternative solutions, and quantifying the costs and benefits of chosen solutions. Consequently, the purpose of such frameworks is to select the most effective and efficient policy solutions for the future based upon the objective analysis of empirical data (Fischer, 2003). Studies based upon such rationalities dismiss the contested arena of policymaking. Instead, they attempt to navigate the "messiness" of political interaction through the use of standardized measures (Patton, 1990), thus failing to provide insight as to how varied formations of power shape the actors and practices that guide policy making.

Traditional policy frameworks have contributed valuable insights into political behaviors (public opinion, participation rates, and voting percentages) and have offered an empirical understanding of campaigns, elections, and the workings of Congress (Pierson, 2007). However, these research efforts are limited by reliance on direct correlations to the construction of policy solutions and the interactions of varied interests. Additionally, many of these efforts consider the interests of political actors as a priori, meaning the behaviors of interest groups can be empirically defined through the naming of specific beliefs. Despite these limitations, the social sciences, particularly the field of policy studies, continue to be dominated by traditional approaches seeking to provide empirical truths. Pierson (2007) highlights the effects of this domination, claiming that quantitatively based studies of American politics are considered to be "the most sophisticated, advanced, and 'scientific'" (p. 145). Consequently, from 2005–2006, only 6% of articles found within the leading American political journals relied exclusively upon qualitative methodologies (Pierson, 2007).

A Critical, Socially Just Rebuttal

Historically, the field of education politics and policy research has also been bound by methodologies built upon the assumptions of logical positivism (Rorrer & Lugg, 2006). Young and López (2008) claim this history can be attributed to the ways in which scholars within the academy were "enamoured" by the "strong predictive science and felt compelled to adopt methods of positivism in order to develop generalizable theories in the social sciences" (p. 157). The predictive desires of social scientists bound educational policy analyses within what Stone (1988) labeled as the "rationality project" (p. 4). Yet, despite the historically significant dominance of positivistic policy studies, a critical response emerged during early 1980s, as critical scholars began to question the rationality that policy sciences are able to offer value-neutral and empirically objective claims (Hajer & Wagenaar, 2003). Subsequently, over the course of the past several decades a growing number of critical policy scholars have begun to problematize the normative consequences of positivistic empirical efforts by questioning the beliefs, practices, and stated outcomes of traditionally valued frameworks (Young & López, 2008).

We offer three examples of critical theoretical frameworks being increasingly used by education researchers in their analyses of politics and policies. These frameworks are by no means exhaustive, yet we feel that they help provide insight into how scholars are helping to reframe and reshape the way policy problems are defined in contemporary society.

Critical Policy Analysis

Embracing a critical theoretical framework, critical policy analysis (CPA) is an approach to policy studies that focuses on the complexities of policy problems including the role of context, group values, power arrangements, and the differing and often problematic nature of problem definition, research findings, and arguments for solutions (Blackmore, 1997; Fischer, 2003; Marshall, 1999; Rochefort & Cobb, 1994; Young, 1999; Young, Diem, Lee, Mansfield, & Welton, 2010). Critical policy analysts consider the ways policies may "empower and democratize" individuals as well as expose policies that seek to maintain privilege, restrict access to opportunities, and disempower and silence marginalized populations. This approach "acknowledges that political agendas and negotiations over power, resources, and values occur during microinteractions and talk as much as they do in formal policy arenas" (Marshall & Gerstl-Pepin, 2005, p. 91). Scholars engaging in CPA make use of many perspectives that fall under the umbrella of critical theory to interrogate the policy process and the epistemological roots of policy work (Young et al., 2010).

Critical Race Theory

Initially developed by legal scholars in the 1990s (Matsuda, Lawrence, Delgado, & Williams-Crenshaw, 1993), critical race theory (CRT) became a prominent theoretical, conceptual, and analytic framework in the field of education used to unmask and reveal how racism is embedded into our every day lives (Atwood & López, 2013; Delgado & Stefancic, 2001; Ladson-Billings & Tate, 1995; López, 2003). CRT starts with the idea that racism is "normal, not aberrant, in American society" (Delgado, 1995, p. xiv) and, because it is so rooted in the fabric of our society, it is "natural" to people and has thus become a permanent fixture of American life (Ladson-Billings, 1998). Further, CRT scholars posit that racial equality and equity for people of color will only be pursued when it benefits and converges with the interests, needs, and expectations of Whites (Bell, 1980). López (2003) argued that because the larger social order works in the interest of Whites, "Whites will tolerate and advance the interests of people of color only when they *promote the self-interests of* Whites" (p. 84; emphasis added). Thus, CRT can be used as a framework to expose and interrogate how policy perpetuates racism and social injustices in education *and* propose solutions for addressing it (Ladson-Billings, 1998).

Argumentative Discourse Analysis

Argumentative discourse analysis (ADA) and the critical interpretive examination of policy actors can be traced to the release of Fischer and Forester's (1993) *The Argumentative Turn in Policy Analysis and Planning*. The ideas proposed by Fischer and Forester (1993) challenged policy scholars to reconsider the subjective identity of the analyst, how language and modes of representation shape the practices of an analyst, and how discourses ultimately determine the scope of an analyst's focus. Argumentative frameworks differ from discourse-only perspectives, as they push beyond the discursive analysis of political language to examine the deliberative and socially constructed politics of policymaking as well (Fischer & Forester, 1993).

Yanow (2000) addressed the historical significance of argumentation in policy studies: "Interpretative policy analysis rests on a long tradition of philosophical argumentation that stands on its own, without reference to positivist argument. Its hallmark is a focus on meaning that is situated in a particular context" (p. 13). This statement elaborates on the ways in which argumentative discourse policy studies move beyond value-neutral assumptions by placing a focus on the examination of "local knowledge" that originates from the lived experiences of those being investigated (Yanow, 2000, p. 5). Therefore, studies based upon the epistemological assumptions of ADA interrogate the rational observation of political actors in an effort to explore the ideas, values, feelings, and meanings that shape the deliberative creation of policy (Fischer, 2003).

CPA, CRT, and ADA are just a few of the many critical theories scholars are using as alternatives to traditional policy studies. Other critical theoretical frameworks being used to study education politics and policy include feminism (Blackmore, 1997; Ferguson, 1984; Marshall, 1997, 1999), queer theory (Capper, 1999; Lugg, 2003), and social and cultural reproduction theories (Anderson, 1989; Anyon, 1980; Bourdieu, 1991; Bowles & Gintis, 1976; Giroux, 1993; Willis, 1977), among others. At the core of all of these critical theories is a desire to explore how education politics and policies that are "presented as reality are often political rhetoric; how knowledge, power, and resources are distributed inequitably; how educational programs, regardless of intent, reproduce stratified social relations; how schools institutionalize those with whom they come into contact; and how individuals react (e.g., resistance or acquiescence) to such social and institutional forces" (Young et al., 2010, p. 9).

SOCIAL JUSTICE EDUCATIONAL LEADERSHIP

Twenty-five years ago, in an article about democracy, schooling, and educational leadership, Giroux (1992) called for educators "to refashion educational leadership through a language of critique and possibility that expands and deepens the possibility for cultural and political democracy" (p. 1). He emphasized the significance that educational leadership has for addressing educational issues and the social responsibility of these leaders in terms of the wider sociopolitical context in which these problems are situated. As Shapiro (1984) notes, the relationship between democracy and education is often tense as "in no other social institution are notions of hierarchy and equality and democracy and authoritarian control forced to co-exist in quite the same proximity" (p. 37). While schools are essential for democracy, how democracy is envisioned varies depending on who is defining it, allowing the way in which it is pursued to vary, particularly given the current education reform context. Thus, Giroux (1992) argued that the narrative of educational administration and the story of leadership need to be rewritten to ensure that educational leaders are taught how to develop a philosophy whose purpose is to foster a democratic society that advocates for social justice within their schools and communities. He states,

> Put simply, democracy is both a discourse and a practice that produces particular narratives and identities informed by the principles of freedom, equal-

ity, and social justice. It is expressed not only in moral platitudes but also in concrete struggles and practices that find expression in classroom social relations, everyday life, and memories of resistance and struggle. When wedded to its most emancipatory possibilities, democracy encourages all citizens to actively construct and share power over those institutions that govern their lives. At the same time the challenge of democracy resides in the recognition that educators, parents, and others must work hard to ensure that future generations will view the idea and practice of democracy as a goal worth believing in and struggling for. (Giroux, 1992, p. 5)

While over the course of the past decade the field of educational leadership has placed a more purposeful focus on exposing practitioners to the importance of social justice leadership and cultivating the imperatives of democracy and social justice Giroux (1992) championed, beginning principals are often ill-prepared to address the diverse range of social justice and political complexities associated with public schooling in today's society (Brown, 2004; Cambron-McCabe & McCarthy, 2005; Dantley, 2002; Grogan & Andrews, 2002; Hawley & James, 2010, Jean-Marie, 2010; López, 2003; Marshall & Oliva, 2006; McKenzie et al., 2008; Tillman, 2004). Though these concerns have been continually voiced for many years, preparatory programs may not be providing the skills necessary to lead within today's diverse schools. Indeed, oftentimes leadership programs marginalize issues of diversity and social justice to singular course offerings (Hawley & James, 2010). Moreover, students in these programs rarely engage with the curriculum and pedagogical practices focused specifically on issues of social justice and diversity (Herrity & Glasman, 1999; Parker & Hood, 1995; Rusch, 2004). Subsequently, educational leaders frequently fail to cultivate the sophisticated skillsets necessary to engage in discussions around social justice and the realization of equitable educational systems (Jean-Marie, Normore, & Brooks, 2009).

According to Capper, Theoharis, and Sebastian (2006), in preparing leaders for social justice, preparation programs must pay particular attention to critical consciousness, knowledge, and practical skills focused on social justice. In this sense, leaders need to "embody a social justice consciousness within their belief systems or values" (p. 213), be knowledgeable about practices that lead to equitable schools, and possess skills that allow leaders to combine their consciousness and knowledge to enact justice and put policies and systems in place that lead to equity for all students (Capper et al., 2006). Theoharis (2007) argues, and we agree, that "leadership that is not focused on and successful at creating more just and equitable schools for marginalized students is indeed not good leadership" (p. 253).

Social justice discourse calls on school leaders to question the beliefs that drive school policies and practices to create more equitable schooling (Cambron-McCabe & McCarthy, 2005). Leaders for social justice are constantly interrogating the status quo; disrupting and unveiling oppressive structures, policies, and practices; denouncing dominant belief systems inside and outside of their schools; and working toward achieving social change so that equal educational opportunities are provided to all students (Mthethwa-Sommers, 2013). In becoming a leader for social justice, school leaders must be prepared to engage in the political process and help others, particularly marginalized groups, do so as well. This is particularly important in a federal education policy context that makes it harder for educators to focus on issues of social justice within their classroom as they are increasingly pressured to implement NCLB and other related accountability policies (Mthethwa-Sommers, 2013). Thus, in order to meet these political challenges, leadership preparation programs must seek to develop leaders who can critically question the structures, systems, and norms within education that often pose overwhelming barriers for many students' academic success.

TROUBLING THE DEVELOPMENT OF POLITICALLY ORIENTED LEADERS FOR SOCIAL JUSTICE

Critical scholars have argued that education must be seen as a political act. In order to view education through this lens, we must situate the broader educational system within inequitable and historically defined power relations (Apple, 2008). Thus, the educational system as an institutional entity must be viewed through the context of a large and complex society, one shaped by the operationalization of dominant and subordinate relationships. Along these lines, Apple (2008) challenges us to dig deeper into the politics of education by asking critically oriented questions about who benefits from the dominant systems and definitions of knowledge espoused by the dominant discourses of public education. Foucault (2007), within his lectures on security, territory, and population, provides insights as to how educational policy scholars might examine institutional politics, as he challenges critical policy scholars to examine the operation of power at its specific site of application. Thus, we ask: What role should critical scholars and critical practitioners play in the changing of the broader educational system? How can the field of critical educational scholars work with and through varied interests and differences to address existing educational and social inequalities while also better establishing preparation programs that help prepare politically oriented and socially just leaders?

We believe that over the last 30 years, the field of educational leadership has attempted to address such questions, as the political role of the school leader has expanded significantly (Carpenter & Brewer, 2012). Today's school leaders are expected to realize their identities as advocates at the local, state, and federal levels. Much of this shift can be attributed to the ways in which professional leadership standards were re-authored to include the discourses of social justice. As an example, the Interstate School Leaders Licensure Consortium (ISLLC) standards and the Educational Leadership Constituent Council (ELCC) standards have explicitly addressed the intended role of the principal/political advocate. ISLLC Standard 6 challenges leaders to advocate for all students success by "understanding, responding to, and influencing the political, social, economic, legal, and cultural context" (CCSSO, 2008, p. 15). The ELCC standards address this political positionality in Standard 6.3, claiming all principals must by able to influence the larger political context by realizing their advocate identities in a way that promotes "equitable learning opportunities and success for all students" (ELCC, 2011, p. 23). Subsequently, today's school leaders are expected to intervene on the behalf of students, parents, and school community stakeholders (Boyd & Crowson, 2002).

While the re-authoring of professional standards to explicitly address the need for politically oriented school leaders should be viewed as a positive, the question remains: Is it enough? Embedding explicit language into national leadership standards is a start; however, it leaves those working in the trenches with the difficult task of having to develop a politically oriented identity while negotiating the micropolitics of everyday practice. Subsequently, if educational leaders are expected to realize their identities as politically oriented participants in the broader political context the field must refocus on the educational practices and/or vehicles that provide leaders with the best opportunity to promote the civic literacy required to shape local, state, and federal policy. We use the term "refocus" purposefully, as we have previously discussed a diverse range of critically oriented alternatives, both theoretical and empirical, to educational policy research and practice.

CONCLUSIONS AND IMPLICATIONS FOR THE FIELD OF EDUCATIONAL LEADERSHIP PREPARATION

As the demographic makeup of public schools continues to dramatically shift, and the federal government continues to develop and mandate policies intended to heighten accountability standards, scholars within the field of educational leadership must reflect on and examine the ways in which we facilitate the development of socially just leaders. First, part of becoming a social justice leader includes embracing and actualizing a politically oriented identity and thus effectively advocating, both at the district and state level, for the students, schools, and communities we are called on to serve. Social justice leaders are committed to agendas that question and seek to eradicate "past practices anchored in open and residual racism, gender exclusivity, homophobia, class discrimination, and religious intolerance are confronted and changed with time. They challenge exclusion, isolation, and marginalization of the stranger; respond to oppression with courage; empower the powerless; and transform existing social inequalities and injustices" (Brown, 2006, p. 711). Second, social justice leaders must learn how to navigate through contentious policy contexts existent within their schools and communities. Power relations and schooling policies that work to benefit a select few must be examined so leaders can better understand and eventually create opportunities for all students within their sociopolitical and geographic contexts (Brown, 2006).

These two suggestions push against the current state of leadership preparation as programs commonly relegate courses on social justice leadership and policy to special topic courses and/or stand-alone seminars (Hawley & James, 2010). If we fail to provide leaders with the skills necessary to realize their identity as oriented participants in the political contexts of local, state, and federal policymaking, how can we expect for their voices to be included in the policy-oriented conversations impacting the lives of our children? We believe preparation programs must make a more concerted effort when designing curriculum and pedagogical experiences around diversity and social justice to embed the critically oriented scholarship of political science throughout all of the courses offered to aspiring leaders.

Fortunately, there are examples of preparation programs actively engaged in the preparation of socially just and politically oriented leaders. With the financial support provided from a United States Department of Education (USDOE) FIPSE grant, the University Council for Educational Administration (UCEA) recently launched the Leaders to Support Diverse Learners (LSDL) initiative. As a result of this effort, a geographically diverse group of faculty teams from various institutions focused specifically on the development of urban school leaders have crafted six curriculum modules intended to better prepare leaders for diverse settings. Two of the initiative's prerequisites mandate that (1) each of the six modules be infused with critical content knowledge and learning experiences, and (2) each module be developed specifically to assist in strengthening a leader's ability to support the education and development of low-income and diverse student populations. Additionally, expert scholars and leaders of professional organizations participating in the LSDL initiative were tasked with constructing each module via innovative, research-based pedagogies intended to elicit the transfer of researched knowledge to practice. One of the six modules—Developing Advocacy Leadership—is specifically designed to

> develop aspiring leaders' capacity to advocate for or act on behalf of children, families and caregivers, particularly those who are most marginalized in public schools and their communities. The aim of such advocacy and action is to

improve the quality and effectiveness of participant learning by: developing skills to address policies and practices that affect the success of students and schools; learning how to identify and unpack critical issues; analyzing data on emerging trends and initiatives; identifying where and how to act to influence local decisions through direct advocacy or action; and reflecting upon this work. This module gives special attention to how to advocate or act on behalf of and with historically marginalized populations, particularly based on a race, national origin and socio-economic status. (UCEA, 2011, "Developing Advocacy Leadership," para. 1)

Efforts such as those made by UCEA, as well as groups such as the Politics of Education Association, implicitly recognize the "new politics of education" by providing aspiring leaders with the political knowledge and skills necessary to respond to a rapidly shifting and increasingly complex political environment.

Today's leaders must inhabit a politically oriented identity allowing them to recognize, navigate, and capitalize upon the promises and perils of participatory governance. It is our belief that the strategic melding of social justice and political science scholarship will allow preparatory programs to recognize and react to the ways in which the democratic foundations of education are being reconfigured.

REFERENCES

Allison, G. (1971). *Essence of decision: Explaining the Cuban Missile Crisis.* New York, NY: Harper Collins.

Anderson, G. L. (1989). Critical ethnography in education: Origins, current status, and new directions. *Review of Educational Research, 59*(3), 249–270.

Anyon, J. (1980). Social class and the hidden curriculum of work. *Journal of Education, 162*(1), 67–92.

Apple, M. W. (2008). Can schooling contribute to a more just society? *Education, Citizenship, and Social Justice, 3*(3), 239–261.

Atwood, E., & López, G. (2013, April). *Let's be critically honest: Towards a messier counterstory in critical race theory.* Paper presented at the annual meeting of the American Educational Research Association, San Francisco, CA.

Ball, S. (2008). *The education debate.* Bristol, UK: The Policy Press.

Baumgartner, F., & Leech, B. (1998). *Basic interests.* Princeton, NJ: Princeton University Press.

Bell, D. A. (1980). *Brown v. Board of Education* and the interest-convergence dilemma. *Harvard Law Review, 93*(3), 518–533.

Blackmore, J. (1997). Level playing field? Feminist observations on global/local articulations of the re-gendering and restructuring of educational work. *International Review of Education, 43*(5–6), 439–461.

Blackmore, J. (2007). Localization/globalization and the midwife state: strategic dilemmas for state feminism in education? In S. Ball, I. F. Goodson, &

M. Maguire (Eds.), *Education, globalisation and new times* (pp. 21–46). New York, NY: Routledge.

Bourdieu, P. (1991). *Language and symbolic power.* Cambridge, MA: Harvard University Press.

Bowles, S., & Gintis, H. (1976). *Schooling in capitalist America.* New York, NY: Basic Books.

Boyd, W., & Crowson, R. L. (2002). The quest for a new hierarchy in education: From loose coupling back to tight? *Journal of Educational Administration, 40*(6), 521–533.

Brooks, J. S., & Normore, A. H. (2010). Educational leadership and globalization: Toward a glocal perspective. *Educational Policy, 24*(1), 52–82.

Brown, K. M. (2004). Leadership for social justice and equity: Weaving a transformative framework and pedagogy. *Educational Administration Quarterly, 40*(1), 79–110.

Brown, K. M. (2006). Leadership for social justice and equity: Evaluating a transformative framework and andragogy. *Educational Administration Quarterly, 42*(5), 700–745.

Cambron-McCabe, N., & McCarthy, M. M. (2005). Educating school leaders for social justice. *Educational Policy, 19*(1), 201–222.

Capper, C. A. (1999). (Homo)sexualities, organizations, and administration: Possibilities for in(queer)y. *Educational Researcher, 28*(5), 4–11.

Capper, C. A., Theoharis, G., & Sebastian, J. (2006). Toward a framework for preparing leaders for social justice. *Journal of Educational Administration, 44*(3), 209–224.

Carpenter, B. W. (2011). *(Re)Framing the politics of educational discourse: An investigation of the Title I School Improvement Grant Program of 2009.* Unpublished doctoral dissertation, The University of Texas at Austin, Austin, TX.

Carpenter, B. W., & Brewer, C. (2012). The implicated advocate: The discursive construction of the democratic practices of school principals in the USA. *Discourse: Studies in the Cultural Politics of Education.* DOI: 10.1080/01596306.2012.745737

Chief Council of State School Officers (CCSSO). (2008). *Educational Leadership Policy Standards: ISLLC 2008 as adopted by the National Policy Board for Educational Administration.* Retrieved from http://www.ccsso.org/projects/education_leadership_initiatives/ISLLC_Standards/

Cooper, B. S., Cibulka, J. G., & Fusarelli, L. D. (Eds.). (2008). *Handbook of education politics and policy.* New York, NY: Routledge.

Confirmation of Arne Duncan: Hearing of the Committee on Health, Education, Labor, and *Pensions,* 111th Cong., 1st sess. (2009, January 13) (statement of Tom Harkin).

Dantley, M. E. (2002). Uprooting and replacing positivism, the melting pot, multiculturalism, and other important notions in educational leadership through an African American perspective. *Education and Urban Society, 34*(3), 334–352.

Dean, M. (1999). *Governmentality: Power and rule in a modern society.* Thousand Oaks, CA: SAGE Publications Inc.

DeBray-Pelot, E., & McGuinn, P. (2009). The new politics of education: Analyzing the federal education policy landscape in the post-NCLB era. *Educational Policy, 23*(1), 15–42.

Delgado, R. (Ed.). (1995). *Critical race theory: The cutting edge.* Philadelphia, PA: Temple University Press.

Delgado, R., & Stefancic, J. (2001). *Critical race theory: An introduction.* New York, NY: New York University Press.

Deschenes, S., Cuban, L., & Tyack, D. (2001). Historical perspectives on schools and students who don't fit them. *Teachers College Record, 103*(4), 525–547.

Educational Leadership Constituent Council (2011). *Educational leadership program recognition standards: Building level.* Arlington, VA. Author.

Ferguson, K. E. (1984). *The feminist case against bureaucracy.* Philadelphia, PA: Temple University Press.

Fischer, F. (2003). *Reframing public policy.* New York, NY: Oxford University Press.

Fischer, F., & Forester, J. (1993). *The argumentative turn in policy analysis and planning.* New York, NY: Routledge.

Foucault, M. (2007). *Security, territory, population: Lectures at the College de France, 1977–78* (G. Burchell, Trans.). Basingstoke, UK: Palgrave Macmillan.

Ginsberg, R., & Lyche, L. F. (2008). The culture of fear and the politics of education. *Educational Policy, 22*(1), 10–27.

Giroux, H. A. (1983). Theories of reproduction and resistance in the new sociology of education: A critical analysis. *Harvard Educational Review, 53*(3), 258–293.

Giroux, H. A. (1992). Educational leadership and the crisis of democratic government. *Educational Researcher, 21*(4), 4–11.

Glass, G. V. (2008). *Fertilizers, pills, and magnetic strips: The fate of public education in America.* Charlotte, NC: Information Age Publishing, Inc.

Gooden, M. A., & Dantley, M. (2012). Centering race in a framework for leadership preparation. *Journal of Research on Leadership Education, 7*(2), 237–253.

Grogan, M., & Andrews, R. (2002). Defining preparation and professional development for the future. *Educational Administration Quarterly, 38*(2), 233–256.

Hajer, M. A. (2006). The living institutions of the EU: Analysing governance as performance. *Perspectives on European politics and society, 7*(1), 41-55.

Hajer, M. A., & Wagenaar, H. (Eds.). (2003). *Deliberative policy analysis: Understanding governance in the network society.* Cambridge, UK: Cambridge University Press.

Hawley, W., & James, R. (2010). Diversity-responsive school leadership. *UCEA Review, 52*(3), 1–5.

Herrity, V., & Glasman, N. S. (1999). Training administrators for culturally and linguistically diverse school populations: Opinions of expert practitioners. *Journal of School Leadership, 9*(3), 235–253.

Jean-Marie, G. (2010). "Fire in the belly": Igniting a social justice discourse in learning environments of leadership preparation. In A. K. Tooms & C. Boske (Eds.), *Bridge leadership: Connecting educational leadership and social justice to improve schools* (pp. 97–124). Charlotte, NC: Information Age Publishing, Inc.

Jean-Marie, G., Normore, A. H. & Brooks, J. S. (2009). Leadership for social justice: Preparing 21st Century school leaders for a new social order. *Journal of Research on Leadership in Education, 4*(1), 1–31.

Jensen, K., & Walker, S. (2008). *Education, democracy and discourse.* New York, NY: Continuum International Publishing Group.

Kaestle, C. F., & Lodewick, A. E. (Eds.). (2007). *To educate a nation: Federal and national strategies of school reform.* Lawrence, KS: University Press of Kansas.

Kirst, M. W., & Wirt, F. M. (2009). *The political dynamics of American education* (4th edition). Richmond, CA: McCutchan Publishing Corporation.

Ladson-Billings, G. (1998). Just what is critical race theory and what's it doing in a nice field like education? *Qualitative Studies in Education, 11*(1), 7–24.

Ladson–Billings, G., & Tate, W. F. IV. (1995). Toward a critical race theory of education. *Teachers College Record, 97*(1), 47–67.

Laswell, H. D. (1936). *Politics: Who gets what, when, how.* New York, NY: Whittlesey House.

Levin, H. M. (1998). Educational vouchers: Effectiveness, choice and costs. *Journal of Policy Analysis and Management, 17*(3), 373–392.

Lingard, B. (2009). Researching education policy in a globalized world: Theoretical and methodological considerations. In T. Popkewitz & F. Rizvi (Eds.), *Globalization and the study of education* (pp. 226–246). Malden, MA: Wiley-Blackwell.

López, G. R. (2003). The (racially neutral) politics of education: A critical race theory perspective. *Educational Administration Quarterly, 39*(1), 68–94.

Lugg, C. A. (2003). Sissies, faggots, lezzies, and dykes: Gender, sexual orientation, and a new politics of education. *Educational Administration Quarterly, 39*(1), 95–134.

Manna, P. (2006). *School's in: Federalism and the national education agenda.* Washington, DC: Georgetown University Press.

Marshall, C. (1997). Dismantling and reconstructing policy analysis. In C. Marshall (Ed.), *Feminist critical policy analysis: A perspective from primary and secondary schooling* (pp. 1–39). London, UK: The Falmer Press.

Marshall, C. (1999). Researching the margins: Feminist critical policy analysis. *Educational Policy, 13*(1), 59–76.

Marshall, C., & Gerstl-Pepin, C. (2005). *Re-framing educational politics for social justice.* Boston, MA: Pearson Education, Inc.

Marshall, C., & Oliva, M. (2006). *Leadership for social justice: Making revolutions in education.* Boston, MA: Pearson Education.

Matsuda, M. J., Lawrence, C., Delgado, R., & Williams-Crenshaw, K. (1993). *Words that wound: Critical race theory, assaultive speech, and the First Amendment.* San Francisco, CA: Westview Press.

McGuinn, P. J. (2006). *No Child Left Behind and the transformation of federal education policy, 1965–2000.* Lawrence, KS: University Press of Kansas.

McKenzie, K., Christman, D., Hernandez, F., Fierro, E., Capper, C., Dantley, M., Gonzalez, M., Cambron-McCabe, N., & Scheurich, J. (2008). Educating leaders for social justice: A design for a comprehensive, social justice leadership preparation program. *Educational Administration Quarterly, 44*(1), 111–138.

Mthethwa-Sommers, S. (2013). Pedagogical possibilities: Lessons from social justice educators. *Journal of Transformative Education, 10*(4), 219–235.

Murphy, J., & Meyers, C. V. (2008). *Turning around failing schools.* Thousand Oaks, CA: Sage.

National Commission on Excellence in Education. (1983). *A nation at risk: The imperative for educational reform.* Washington, D.C.: Author.

No Child Left Behind (NCLB) Act of 2001, Pub. L. No. 107-110, § 115, Stat. 1425 (2002).

Parker, L., & Hood, S. (1995). Minority students vs. majority faculty and administrators in teacher education: Perspectives on the clash of cultures. *Urban Review, 27*(2), 159–174.

Patton, M. (1990). *Qualitative evaluation and research methods* (2nd ed.). Newbury Park, CA: Sage.

Pierson, P. (2007). The rise and reconfiguration of activist government. In P. Pierson & T. Skocpol (Eds.), *The transformation of American politics: Activist government and the rise of conservatism* (pp. 19–38). Princeton, NJ: Princeton University Press.

Rochefort, D. A., & Cobb, R. W. (Eds.). (1994). *The politics of problem definition: Shaping the policy agenda*. Lawrence, KS: University of Kansas.

Rorrer, A. K., & Lugg, C. A. (2006). Introduction: Power, education, and the politics of social justice. *Educational Policy, 20*(1), 5–7.

Rusch, E. A. (2004). Gender and race in leadership preparation: A constrained discourse. *Educational Administration Quarterly, 40*(1), 14–46.

Sabatier, P. A. (1991). Political science and public policy. *Political Science & Politics, 24*, 143–146.

Shapiro, S. (1984). Crisis of legitimation: Schools, society, and declining faith in education. *Interchange, 15*(4), 26–39.

Singleton, G. E., & Linton, C. (2005). *Courageous conversations about race: A field guide for achieving equity in schools*. Thousand Oaks, CA: Corwin Press.

Stone, D. A. (1988). *Policy paradox and political reason*. Glenview: IL: Scott Foresman.

Stone, D. A. (1997). *Policy paradox: The art of political decision making*. New York, NY: W.W. Norton.

Theodoulou, S. Z. (1995). The contemporary language of public policy: A starting point. In S. Z. Theodoulou & M. A. Cahn (Eds.), *Public policy: The essential readings* (pp. 1–9). Upper Saddle River, NJ: Prentice Hall.

Theoharis, G. (2007). Social justice educational leaders and resistance: Toward a theory of social justice leadership. *Educational Administration Quarterly, 43*(2), 221–258.

Tillman, L. C. (2004). (Un)intended consequences? The impact of the *Brown v. Board of Education* decision on the employment status of black educators. *Education and Urban Society, 36*(3), 280–303.

Torgerson, D. (1985). Contextual orientation in policy analysis: The contribution of Harold D. Lasswell. *Policy Sciences, 18*(3), 241–261.

Torres, C. A. (2009). *Education and neoliberal globalization*. New York, NY: Taylor & Francis.

University Council for Educational Administration. (2011). *Preparing leaders to support diverse learners: LSDL module development project*. Retrieved from http://ucea.org/lsdl-preparation-modules-new/

Vinovskis, M. (2009). *From A Nation at Risk to No Child Left Behind: National education goals and the creation of federal education policy*. New York, NY: Teachers College Press.

Willis, P. (1977). *Learning to labor*. New York, NY: Columbia University Press.

Wong, K. K. (2008). Federalism, equity, and accountability in education. In B. S. Cooper, J. G. Cibulka, & L. D. Fusarelli (Eds.), *Handbook of education politics and policy* (pp. 19–29). New York, NY: Taylor & Francis.

Yanow, D. (2000). *Conducting interpretive policy analysis.* Thousand Oaks, CA: Sage.

Young, M. D. (1999). Multifocal educational policy research: Toward a method for enhancing traditional educational policy studies. *American Educational Research Journal, 36*(4), 677–714.

Young, M. D., Diem, S., Lee, P. L., Mansfield, K. C., & Welton, A. D. (2010, May). *Understanding critical policy analysis.* Paper presented at the annual meeting of the American Educational Research Association, Denver, CO.

Young, M. D., & López, G. D. (2008). Putting alternative perspectives to work in the politics of education. In E. A. Samier & A. G. Stanley (Eds.), *Political approaches to educational administration leadership* (pp. 155–172). New York, NY: Routledge.

CHAPTER 2

POSITIVE PSYCHOLOGY AS A FOUNDATION FOR SOCIAL JUSTICE LEADERSHIP

Derik Yager-Elorriaga and Paula T. McWhirter
University of Oklahoma

ABSTRACT

The field of psychology has broad relevance to societal issues and social justice. By nature, psychologists aim to better understand human behavior. In doing so, the field of psychology is well positioned to provide key insight into social justice, especially with regards to educational leadership. Specifically, the sub-field of positive psychology emphasizes promoting individual strengths and developing institutions that foster positive traits, which can provide leaders in education with tools to better promote social justice within the schooling system. The goal of this chapter is to examine and learn lessons from the way psychology conceptualizes leadership for social justice, with an emphasis on positive psychology. Based on these lessons, the chapter concludes with positive psychology-based recommendations for improving the preparation and practice of school leadership.

Psychology has a strong link to societal concerns and social justice. The field strives to better comprehend human behavior, and in doing so, promotes

Educational Leadership for Ethics and Social Justice, pages 23–42
Copyright © 2014 by Information Age Publishing
All rights of reproduction in any form reserved.

understanding of both psychological and social influences. This places psychology in the unique position to give insight into social justice issues, including those related to education (e.g., Pedrotti, Edwards, & Lopez, 2009; Theoharis, 2007). In this chapter, we explore the links between positive psychology and learning. The influence of strengths-based learning approaches is discussed, along with the importance of the promotion and appreciation of individual interventions. We begin by addressing historical perspectives and connections between psychology and social justice as it has evolved within the context of education. Next, we examine key theories and explore concepts and debates related to the study of social justice, paying particular attention to society and schooling. We then discuss leadership processes and outcomes manifested in schools; we explore the influence of positive psychology on social justice programming currently evident within schools. Finally, we conclude with recommendations for continued social and educational programming grounded in positive psychology.

HISTORICAL PERSPECTIVES: THE EVOLUTION OF POSITIVE PSYCHOLOGY AND SOCIAL JUSTICE

The Inferiority Model and the Deficit Mode

While modern psychologists (e.g., Kenny & Romano, 2009; Vasquez, 2012) have made social justice an emphasis in the field, historically this has not always been the case. As early psychological theories emerged, most theories took a singular approach that ignored the comprehensive and widespread influence of injustices at a systematic level (Kenny & Romano, 2009). The *inferiority model* and the *deficit mode* exemplify the limited and narrow scope of early psychology's conceptualizations. Specifically, these early models viewed racial and ethnic differences as a result of inherent, genealogically specific deficiencies (Pedrotti et al., 2009). The *inferiority model*, for example, considered racial and ethnic difference a result of a natural need to create species variability among humans. The paradigm posited that non-majority racial and ethnic groups were inherently unable to advance in society due to biologically based limitations. Consequently, the concept of adjusting the environment to level the playing field by providing favorable opportunities for racial and ethnic minorities became unnecessary (Pedrotti et al., 2009). Equally simplistic in its conceptualization, the *deficit mode* moved away from biological explanations, maintaining that ethnic and racial differences were due to unchallengeable environmental constructs (Pedrotti et al., 2009). Prejudice, for example, was viewed as an unchallengeable societal condition. As such, prejudice was thought to create stress, adversely affecting any minority group's ability to succeed. The model further maintained that minority members' hostile environments led to higher rates of distress, often resulting in inferior and/or self-destructive coping strategies (Pedrotti et al., 2009).

Concomitantly, psychotherapy was focused on how the individual could enhance functioning by coping to better fit the environment. Thus, emphasis was typically placed on helping individuals adapt, as opposed to changing environments plagued with oppressive and unjust values, and subsequently limiting the advancement of social justice progress (Kenny & Romano, 2009). Furthermore, traditional psychology's reactive, rather than proactive approach to negative events, including ethno-political conflict, helped maintain oppressive societal values (Kenny & Romano, 2009).

Historically, psychology has also focused on culturally bound values deeply embedded in Western-based philosophy, including a focus on the promotion of individual freedom, responsibility, and self-actualization (Kenny & Romano, 2009). Viewing psychology through a culturally limited lens left psychologists at risk of utilizing culturally biased definitions of adjustment and wellbeing. In doing so, psychology undermined and dismissed cultural traditions and history essential to promoting the welfare of underrepresented communities (Kenny & Romano, 2009).

Early psychology's pattern of marginalizing ethnic/racial minorities did not exclude school psychology. As European immigrants and compulsory attendance laws emerged, both the number of students attending school and the range of linguistic, economic, racial, and cultural diversity among the students attending school increased (Newell, Nastasi, Hatzichristou, Jones, Schanding, & Yetter, 2010). Schools were not prepared for the influx in student diversity. Special classes for atypical students were formed to aid students with a broad range of intellectual and social disabilities. These classes also served children identified as "backward," a label frequently given to African American, Latino, southern or eastern European immigrants, and/or the economically disadvantaged (Newell et al., 2010). In order to place students into these special classes, schools became in need of experts who could sort their increasingly diverse student populations. To meet this demand, these experts, along with teachers and other professionals, administered and interpreted mental and intellectual tests (i.e., Binet). These tests often failed to account for cultural differences, and early school psychologists rarely addressed issues related to cultural diversity (Newell et al., 2010). As diversity continued to increase, schools found themselves more radically separating and excluding culturally and linguistically different students. This set the stage for how diversity would be dealt with in the future, and in an era of legal segregation, Native American relocation, and vast immigration, diverse students became "problematic" to school psychologists and other school personnel.

Fortunately, psychology's general view of social justice has evolved considerably. Models on racial and ethnic diversity have shifted from conceptualizing differences as a reflection of deficiency to recognizing value in cultural diversity (Pedrotti et al., 2009). One such emerging model is the "human diversity model." This model recognizes that each person has a unique culture, both independently and connected to the larger society. With this emphasis on the individual and connection to society, the model focuses research beyond racial, ethnic, and cultural issues to include a larger variety of groups and populations with unique differences, strengths, and histories (Pedrotti et al., 2009). In the realm of education, significant legislation such as *Brown v. Board of Education* and the Civil Rights Act began a process that prohibited segregation and the denial of benefits of the educational system based on cultural and linguistic differences of minority children (Newell et al., 2010). Additionally, as the Civil Rights movement continued, an increased focus on multiculturalism (e.g., training and becoming more organizationally diverse) became apparent in major organizations such as the American Psychological Association and the National Association of School Psychologists (Newell et al., 2010).

Tracing through the history of psychology, there are a variety of forerunners of positive psychology that encompassed positive psychology's goal of understanding and accentuating healthy psychological functioning and wellbeing (Waterman, 2013). Leading psychologists who set the theoretical foundation of positive psychological functioning include: Goldstein (1939/1995) on organismic theory, Erikson (1950) on normative stages of psychosocial development, Shoben (1957) on normal personality, Jahoda (1958) on positive mental health, Rogers (1963) on the fully functioning individual, and Maslow (1968) on the nature of motivation and self-actualization and transcendence. Additional researchers who began exploring aspects of positive psychological functioning prior to the formal creation of positive psychology illustrate how positive psychology could be effectively and meaningfully examined. Notably, these include Bandura's (1977) work on self-efficacy, Harter's (1975) exploration of mastery, and Csikszentmihalyi's (1975) studies on flow. Additionally, the body of well-being research (e.g., Diener, 1984; Emmons, 1986; Ryff, 1989; Tesser, 1988) furthered the evolution of research focused on intensively examining positive psychological concepts in a variety of contexts and allowed the successful introduction of positive psychology (Waterman, 2013).

In addition to these forerunners of positive psychology, others, including Alfred Adler, Abraham Maslow, and Albert Ellis, have helped facilitate the link between positive psychology and social justice. Alfred Adler was perhaps the first psychologist to use public education as a way to address community health (e.g., Adler, 1938, 1956). His work on social interest stressed the core values of democracy, including equality, civil rights, mutual respect, and the social determinants of mental health. Adler is sometimes referred to as the first community psychologist, with his focus on community prevention and population health and well-being.

Abraham Maslow examined positive motivation, growth, needs and emotions (e.g., Maslow, 1943, 1954). Maslow's work and humanistic psychology incorporates social welfare and social responsibilities at an individual, group, and community level. While there are fundamental differences between current positive psychology and humanistic psychology, Maslow's work and concern for social justice issues laid a foundation, demonstrating how work on positive psychological functioning relates to social justice.

Like Adler and Maslow, Albert Ellis' work in better understanding human happiness can be linked to positive psychology, specifically, and to social justice efforts more generally (Bernard, Froh, DiGiuseppe, Joyce, & Dryden, 2010). In their discussion of how Ellis' work relates to positive psychology, Bernard and colleagues (2010) presented ways in which many of Ellis' concepts (e.g., self-actualization, purpose of goals of life and happiness, and self-acceptance) are connected to happiness and wellbeing beyond the individual, toward societal and community levels. Further, they establish that the implementation of these concepts and Ellis' ABC-DE model can be used to increase individual happiness with effects that build cyclically within the individual, ultimately reaching beyond the individual. Ellis' work promotes both individual happiness and, if encouraged on a more broad level, can be linked to social justice initiatives (Bernard et al., 2010).

Since Martin Seligman's 1998 APA presidential address, positive psychology has rapidly grown. In his address, Dr. Seligman called for psychology to play a role in leading people to wellbeing, communities to flourish, and societies to be just. In order to achieve this goal, Dr. Seligman called for the field of psychology not only to study what goes wrong in one's wellbeing, but to meaningfully explore what contributes to positive wellbeing. He called for the promotion and appreciation of individual strengths, and a greater understanding of the means that contribute to individuals' flourishing. With this initiative, Dr. Seligman urged that psychologists make life better not only for the mentally ill, but for all people (Seligman, 1998). With these themes of empowering the individual, creating better communities, and promoting just societies, positive psychology's modern birth was interwoven with social justice.

Over the past decades, positive psychology has provided vast amounts of research that can contribute to promoting a just society (Kenny & Romano, 2009). Examples reflect positive psychology's focus on pragmatic, incremental improvement on quality of life and are designed to improve happiness and subjective wellbeing (Lyubomirsky, 2007), promote mindfulness (Germer, Siegel, & Fulton, 2005; Huppert & Johnson, 2010), increase experiences of gratitude (Roffey, 2013), and build character strengths (Proctor,

Tsukayama, Wood, Maltby, Eades, & Linley, 2011). These techniques focus on immediate improvement in individuals, families, and communities, and lead to a continued cycle of increased optimism and future positive change (Waterman, 2013).

Positive Education

As positive psychology flourished, its research and application trickled over to the educational domain, including the initiative known as *positive education* (Seligman, 2011). Positive education is based on the notion that wellbeing can and should be taught in schools. Techniques within positive psychology have influenced many schools, and current research is focused on the benefits of positive education and its successful implementation on a school-wide basis (Seligman, Ernst, Gillham, Reivich, & Linkins, 2009). While we discuss specific school-based techniques in more detail later, most positive psychology techniques, including those utilized in positive education initiatives, emphasize either increasing student wellbeing or utilizing student strengths to promote better learning. Promoting and utilizing strengths is a crucial part of positive psychology, which has resulted in the development of the Values in Action Inventory of Strengths, a measure that identifies 24 character strengths (VIA; Seligman, Park, & Peterson, 2004). Seligman and colleagues (2004) maintain that these character strengths are universally found and considered positive in every culture worldwide. Interestingly, in terms of social justice, early positive psychologists may have largely ignored specific cultural differences, maintaining that because character strengths are universal, cultural differences are already considered.

KEY THEORIES, CONCEPTS AND DEBATES

Despite a wide acknowledgement of the importance of social justice within psychology, there is still no clear consensus on how to implement social justice systematically. For example, within the APA, the largest organization of psychologists in the world, many of its members believe that the organization advocates too much for social justice and societal issues. However, other members maintain that the organization is not doing enough to speak for marginalized communities (Vasquez, 2012). Much of this disagreement stems around specific moral issues that members have failed to reach a consensus on—particularly reproductive health, abortion, and same-sex marriage (Vasquez, 2012).

This disagreement reflects a shift on how society has viewed justice. Around the 1950s, justice theory emerged with the *homo economicus* model

(Skitka, 2009). This model examined social life through a series of nego-tiated exchanges, and how people employ a cost–benefit model to guide their decision making. Further, although this model hypothesized that people are self-interested, they accepted that fairness in material and so-cial exchange is necessary to maximize long-term interests. As researchers found that this model failed to consider that people value more than just the outcome, the *homo socialis* model emerged in the 1970s to factor in this idea (Skitka, 2009). This model focused on procedural characteristics that people use to reach decisions related to resource allocation. Theoretically, the justice perspective shifted from self-interest towards a perspective that held fair procedures as crucial in maintaining people's need to feel that they are respected and valued group members. The most recent shift in justice theory is reflected in the emergence of *homo moralis*, a perspective that focuses on concepts of what should be occurring using a moral frame of reference. This perspective holds that when people have a strong stake in moral outcomes, their fairness reasoning is influenced more by whether their preferred outcome is achieved rather than whether a fair procedure is achieved. Which perspective one takes often is dependent on the situa-tion and context (Skitka, 2009). When taking a *homo moralis* perspective, arguments and reasoning are largely based on morals, which often make conversations heated and emotional. Social justice debates generally fall into this category, making it unlikely that a consensus will be reached when discussing issues related to social justice.

The emphasis on social justice in psychology has resulted in a call for more social justice research within the field. The defining characteristic of social justice research is moving towards a society that allows full and equal participation among all groups, and is equitable in the redistribu-tion of resources (Chapman & Schwartz, 2011). However, how to approach social justice research is not explicitly clear. Traditional research has taken a positivistic or postpositivistic epistemological paradigm approach, which assumes that the social world can be studied with the same methodologi-cal rigor applied to the study of the biological or natural world (Chapman & Schwartz, 2011). In this paradigm, researchers are able to take a value-free approach to their research questions and remain objective in defining research concepts or uncovering "universal truths." Whether or not this traditional approach can be taken in social research is up to debate. How-ever, most social justice researchers recognize that it is nearly impossible to achieve value-free research when looking at action research (Morrow, Rakhsha, & Castañeda, 2001; Trickett, 1992). For example, even the best-intentioned researchers from a dominant social/cultural group cannot help but find difficulty in recognizing oppressive features of their own cul-tural beliefs and practices when conducting action research (Chapman & Schwartz, 2011). Given the difficulties taking a value-free approach, social justice researchers (e.g., Chapman & Schwartz, 2011) argue for moving away from studying dominant groups to studying historically underserved groups and view participants as an agent of change. This approach gives researchers a different position—that of community consultant who determines the goals and agenda of research, rather than that of a primary researcher (Chapman & Schwartz, 2011).

Within positive psychology, much of the debate centers on this idea: whether or not social justice research can be done while remaining objective (e.g., Pedrotti, 2011; Seligman et al., 2004). This debate has been especially prominent in the study of character strengths. Two camps have arisen in this debate: the culture-free perspective and the culture-embedded perspective. While both these perspectives hold that all cultures have strengths, the culture-free side argues that strengths are universal, while the culture-embedded side argues that what is determined to be a strength or virtue is determined by context and cultural values (Pedrotti, 2011). As mentioned previously, when identifying character strengths, Seligman and colleagues (2004) determined that certain attributes exist across several cultures and that these attributes are universally viewed as beneficial across all cultures and society. Furthermore, those on the culture-free side maintain that a researcher's own culture and associated values do not enter into his/her profession work, as scientists should and are able to move beyond personal biases by using validated and reliable methods of research (Pedrotti et al., 2009). Those on the culture-embedded side argue differently, holding that cultural values impact professional work, and that researchers operating within a multicultural framework can view human functions within an isolated vacuum. Thus, it is impossible to separate culture and context. Furthermore, this camp maintains that strengths can only be viewed within a cultural context (Pedrotti et al., 2007). Thus, while strengths can be found within all cultures and societies, how these strengths appear is different based on the cultural lens they are being viewed through.

Similarly to the general debate about the study of social justice in psychology in general, there is conversation about the link between positive psychology and social justice. With many psychologists arguing that those within the field have an emerging responsibility about social justice issues, a key debate focuses on the avenues to research and implement interventions. Some researchers see the link between positive psychology and social justice clearly, holding that positive psychology emphasizes the role of the individual and contextual assets that facilitate and promote human flourishing (Kenny & Romano, 2009). According to these researchers, positive psychology calls for the enhancement of families, schools, the corporate world, and broader society to participate in a strength-fostering environment, one that promotes justice (Kenny & Romano, 2009). Others (e.g., Becker & Marecek, 2008) see the positive psychology movement as having striking resemblance to previous movements that focused on fostering the positive in the individual while ignoring the contextual factors (e.g., mental hygiene movement; history in the remaking). For example, Becker and Marecek (2008) argue that positive psychology encourages individual flourishment and to research what avenues led to this flourishment, it ignores how societal context impacts access to flourishing, often limiting it to only privileged members of society. Thus, this camp argues that positive psychology does not recognize key aspects of social justice, such as power, privilege, and social hierarchy (Becket & Maracek, 2008).

Another current debate concerns the influence of character strengths, which directly relates to the potential effectiveness of positive psychology in the educational domain. For example, taking a culture-free approach, the belief is that character strengths are universal, and thus school personnel would not have to pay special attention to culture when identifying or utilizing character strengths in an educational setting. On the other hand, one who takes the culture-embedded approach holds that culture and context are crucial in determining and displaying character strengths, and thus would pay close attention to culture and context when identifying and utilizing character strengths in an educational setting.

SCHOOL LEADERSHIP COMPLEXITIES

Based on a study by Seligman (2011), there appears to be a lack of congruence between what parents want for their children and what the education system is teaching its students. When parents were are asked what they want most for their children, they responded with themes related to wellbeing. However, when asked what schools teach, parents responded with themes related to accomplishment (Seligman, 2011). While accomplishment is important, positive education strives to integrate a curriculum that teaches students both accomplishment and wellbeing.

From a positive psychology perspective, building a positive education system is crucial to not only improve the wellbeing of our students, but to promote communities that flourish. To begin this process of flourishing on a communal level, it is crucial to understand the problems plaguing students. Young people are facing huge amounts of distress, especially from body image issues, substance abuse behaviors, lack of confidence or security, not fitting in, or not performing well enough (Waters, 2011). Furthermore, depression is not only rampant among young people worldwide, but it is occurring sooner than it did before (i.e., shifting from first occurring in adulthood to now appearing first in adolescence; Seligman et al. 2009). While there is debate as to whether this rate is due to an actual increase in depression or an increase in awareness or methodological methods is up to debate, the increase in depression is still a concern, especially considering the progress society has made on technological and social fronts.

With the higher rates of depression plaguing our school (Seligman et al., 2009), it appears that students in this generation not only have to deal with increasingly difficult curricula and national standards, but also with psychological barriers. Given the complexities that are keeping many students from flourishing, school leaders need to understand their influence in promoting socially just processes and outcomes in schools. Currently, school leaders' influence is enormous, as schools are a major provider of mental health services and have an incredible potential for prevention and wellbeing initiatives (Seligman et al., 2009). Children and adolescents in the United States spend a large portion of their time in schools, typically 30–35 hours per week.

Theoharis' (2007) study demonstrates how school leaders can positively influence their schools and communities to promote a socially just educational system. Theoharis carefully selected seven principals committed to social justice, especially in relation to increasing opportunities and removing discrimination for students from typically marginalized groups. He found four successful means by which these principals were able to create more socially just schools: *raising student achievement, improving school structures, recentering and enhancing staff capacity,* and *strengthening school culture and community.*

While the latter three methods increase student achievement, Theoharis found that school leaders also raised student achievement by focusing on more than state standardized testing. These school leaders were critical of standardized testing, but they prepared their students for these tests and also enacted supplemental local testing. Further, they also increased the number of students who were taking the state assessments, particularly increasing the number of minority students. In one example, a school principal reported that the school went from excluding Latinos in their local assessments to having 90% of the Latino students achieve at proficient or advanced level.

These school leaders also aimed to improve school structures by means consistent with positive psychology. Six of the seven principals removed pullout and segregated programs at their schools. For example, they removed ability-tracked programs that resulted in the lower-ability classes being dominated by poor and minority students and moved towards a heterogeneous grouping based on both ability and background characteristics. Further, these leaders integrated special education students into the regular curriculum as fully as possible. In addition to being more inclusive, these school leaders increased the rigor and access to educational opportunities. For example, they introduced more advanced courses, raised expectations that teachers had for themselves and student achievement, and introduced more accountability in school records.

In addition to changing school structures, these school leaders also recentered and enhanced staff capacity by creating new developmental programs. These leaders resisted the assumptions that current staff developmental programs and typical teacher education were sufficient in preparing teachers for a social justice orientation and provided opportunities for personal development. These leaders increased teacher capacity as they provided developmentally grounded training on issues of social and racial equity, encouraged staff members to understand and invest in matters of social justice, made hiring and supervising decisions with consideration of social justice issues, and made concerted efforts to educate and empower staff. Leaders completed these goals as they led staff through examining issues of race, explored existing and historical injustices, offered English language learning (ELL) courses, and gave teachers a greater say in school processes.

Lastly, school leaders strengthened the school culture and community by creating a warmer and safer climate. The leaders described improvement in school safety, and community involvement came through developing personal relationships with students and community members. Further, they went out into the community to develop these relationships, and when parents or community members came to schools, they welcomed them and granted them the respect they deserved. They emphasized the involvement of parents and community members from marginalized groups in school processes. For example, they often encouraged these groups to serve on school communities.

While this intervention focused on increasing social justice from a principal standpoint, teachers are also in an incredibly influential position to promote social justice. Early school failure is an important factor in the development of peer rejection and antisocial behavior, and teachers are in a position to help prevent these things from occurring (Martens & Witt, 2004). Teachers usually have the most interaction with students and can reinforce certain behaviors or means that lead to more just outcomes. However, the makeup of school systems often encourages teachers to engage in a scenario where teachers intend for children to work quietly on completing problems, and they only attend to disruptive behaviors. Without great teaching, students in this, and often other, scenarios are given the responsibility to teach themselves, placing them at the mercy of their individual differences such as family background, innate ability, and socioeconomic status (Martens & Witt, 2004). This process is socially unjust and affects low-achieving or at-risk students most, beginning a process that may lead them to access social and material reinforces other than school (Martens & Witt, 2004).

Martens and Witt (2004) provide three sets of established instructional strategies grounded in positive psychology that promote high levels of academic competence through skill practice. First, they suggest teaching children at their instruction level and monitoring progress. Students working at levels other than their instructional level often become frustrated quickly and frequently become behaviorally problematic, or they lose joy for a subject. Second, Martens and Witt propose teaching students differently as their skills improve through a stage process: *acquisition, fluency, maintenance, generalization,* and *adaptation.* Thus, teachers should teach their students according to their stage. Lastly, they reward success and set goals for students. Contrary to popular belief, rewarding either verbally or tangibly is shown to increase task interest and enjoyment (Martens & Witt, 2004). The problem arises when rewards are given as noncontingent reinforcement—that is, when a reward is given independent of performance.

One of the most fundamental ways positive psychology paradigms promote social justice is through the recognizing of strengths relative to their context. Pedrotti (2011) has introduced five key strategies to infuse cultural strengths in the teaching of positive psychology and influence the conversation about multiculturalism. First, teachers should emphasize culture from the beginning of the course. This allows culture to be an integral part of human strengths and prevents it from becoming partially applied or marginalized by introducing it as a special issue or presenting it at the end of courses. Secondly, teachers are encouraged to explain that culture is a multifaceted concept. Although cultural is typically defined through race and ethnicity, which are very salient in U.S. culture, other factors such as gender, socioeconomic status or social class, and sexual orientation are also cultural facets. Culture does not incorporate just one facet, and personal strengths often arise from one or multiple facets. Thus, understanding how strengths arise and how different cultures determine strengths is important. Third, teachers should strive to challenge students to spot and remedy views that adhere to only one worldview. Pedrotti (2011) identified three key concepts by which one can determine how culturally relevant findings are: *conceptual equivalence* (e.g., do different cultures define constructs the same?), *linguistic equivalence* (e.g., do certain phrases mean the same thing across languages?), and *metric equivalence* (e.g., do different cultures have the same tendency when answering on a Likert-scale?). Fourth, teachers should examine the inclusion of diverse perspective in research theory. In psychology, a lack of proper attention has been given to issues of culture and diversity (Sue & Sue, 2008). This lack of attention includes individual character strengths; however, culturally based strength research is emerging (e.g., Pedrotti et al., 2011). Looking at this research allows new perspectives in strength research. Fifthly and lastly, teachers should encourage discussion on culturally relevant strengths inside and outside the classroom. For example, teachers can urge students to investigate strengths that are more prominent in other cultures. By investigating, or even mimicking these strengths, students can learn more about different cultures, how they view strengths, and how to apply a diverse set of strengths to their lives.

Pedrotti's approach is adaptable to a variety of different settings, and her strategies to infuse multiculturalism are a reminder of how school leaders can influence the conversations inside and outside the classroom. Further, strength-based approaches such as Pedrotti's and those in positive psychology provide an avenue to become more culturally competent in the classroom. Additionally, these approaches can facilitate efforts towards repairing past damage to traditionally marginalized groups by acknowledging their individual and communal strengths (Pedrotti et al., 2011).

RECOMMENDATIONS: IMPROVING PREPARATION AND PRACTICE OF SCHOOL LEADERSHIP

Given the influence of the school system, implementing curricula that include improving wellbeing could be used as a means to combat depression, increase life satisfaction, and to promote better learning and creative thinking (Csikszentmihalyi, 1996; Peterson, 2006; Seligman et al., 2009). In promoting such techniques, the education system can better promote student wellbeing and learning, and thus provide more socially just procedures and outcomes. Introducing positive psychology into schools is not a novel idea, and most schools already employ techniques that are similar, if not the same as techniques grounded in positive psychology (Seligman et al., 2009).

Before discussing specific interventions that can be made to improve both student wellbeing and achievement, the question remains as to whether teaching wellbeing should be included in school curricula. Parents are concerned that wellbeing programs will teach values incongruent with theirs, that these programs will waste money, or that they will lower student achievement by diverting time and money away from strictly academic programs (Seligman et al., 2009). While these concerns are important, Seligman and colleagues (2009) argue that wellbeing programs can promote skills and strengths considered universally relevant, produce tangible improvements in students' behavior, health and safety, and simultaneously boost students' engagement in learning and achievement. Wellbeing is congruent with better learning, with increases likely to produce improvements in learning.

Integrating wellbeing in school curriculums provides a more holistic education. In psychology, the addition of positive psychology has redefined the field, shifting from simply treating the negative to also accentuating the positive. The mere absence of symptoms does not reflect health, and thus applying this strength-based approach to schools can be incredibly beneficial to students, especially those in marginalized groups. Too often, schools are forced to encourage students to just get by, rather than to educate students on how to prosper and flourish. Many current school interventions simply focus on the removal or reduction of negative factors (e.g., anti-bullying, smoking cessation, and depression-reduction), whereas positive psychology interventions add an emphasis to increase positive factors. As researchers gain a better understanding of mental health for children and adolescents, society can move towards a schooling system that cultivates the whole student through emotional, social, and intellectual development.

A positive mood allows broader attention, and increased creative and holistic thinking, where as a negative mood produced narrower attention, and more critical and analytical thinking (Peterson, 2006; Seligman et al., 2009). Further, negative emotions can affect cognitions, and result in action tendencies such as fight or flight. Such emotions can hinder learning and positive coping behaviors in the classroom (Lewis, Huebner, Malone, & Valois, 2011). While all these types of thinking are important, schools often emphasize critical and analytical thinking (Seligman et al., 2009), and with it indirectly promote a negative mood. Additionally, positive emotion reduces some racial biases. At this point, research suggests that a positive education curriculum helps fight depression, promotes learning, and increases creative thinking (Seligman et al., 2009). Promoting an environment where individual and communal strengths are valued is crucial to in increasing students' capacity to handle day-to-day stressing and problems, especially for those in marginalized groups. Given these stressors and the benefits of a wellbeing curriculum, schools should consider employing such a curriculum.

Researchers demonstrate the role that positive psychology constructs play in motivation, academic engagement/achievement, and mental health (Marques, Pais-Ribeiro, & Lopez, 2011; Pajaras, 2001). For example, Pajaras (2001) looked at the relationship between *optimism*, feelings of authenticity (*perceived authenticity*), and beliefs surrounding themselves and others that help form a means for interpreting novel experiences (*invitations*), and motivational concepts: task-goal orientation (engage in tasks to master material and ideas to seek academic challenge), expectancy beliefs (judgments of capability to attain designated types of performance), and value (perceived importance, interest in, and enjoyment of school). Pajaras found that overall, high-achieving students had higher levels of variables associated with positive psychology relative to low-achieving students. Specifically, achievement goals, expectancy beliefs, and value were predicative of positive psychology variables, as task goals were positively associated with optimism and invitations, whereas performance goals were negatively associated with optimism and perceived authenticity.

Student engagement—the degree of active involvement in school through thoughts, feelings, and actions—is crucial to academic success.

Examining the role of life satisfaction in student engagement in 7th and 8th grade middle school students, Lewis and colleagues (2011) found a bi-direction relationship between life satisfaction and student engagement. Specifically, time 1 (fall '08) life satisfaction was significant in predicting changes in cognitive engagement and marginally significant in predicting emotional engagement at time 2 (spring '09). Middle school students who were satisfied with their lives at the beginning (time 1) reported higher levels of believing school is important for their future (even after controlling for demographic variables). Additionally, time 1 level of cognitive engagement, but not behavioral or emotional engagements, predicted changes in time 2 life satisfaction.

In terms of mental health and academic achievement, Marques, Pais-Ribeiro, and Lopez (2011), in Portugal, conducted a two-year longitudinal study to determine the role positive psychology constructs play in predicting mental health and academic achievement. Exploring the predictive role of hope, life satisfaction, and self-worth, the authors found that mental health had moderate to strong correlations with hope, life satisfaction, and self-worth at all times of testing—time 1, time 2 (a year later), and time 3 (two years later). Furthermore, regression analysis revealed that time 1 life satisfaction significantly predicted mental health at time 1 and that hope scores added significant variance beyond life satisfaction scores. Additionally, life satisfaction scores significantly predicted mental health at time 3, and also hope scores added significant variance beyond life satisfaction scores. Lastly, hope at time 1 significantly predicted academic achievement at time 1, time 2, and time 3.

In addition to researching the role of positive psychology constructs in wellbeing, determining the effectiveness of a positive psychology curriculum on a large scale is also important. To date, there are three major projects that have employed a positive psychology school-based curriculum finding promising evidence (Huppert & Johnson, 2010; Proctor et al., 2011; Seligman et al., 2009). The first of these programs is the Penn Resiliency Program (PRP). The PRP's goal is to promote optimism, assertiveness, creative brainstorming, decision-making, relaxation, and other coping and problem-solving skills to allow students to think more realistically and flexibly about problems and stressors they face. Over the last 20 years, there have been 17 students evaluating PRP to a control group—the studies have included over 2,000 children and adolescents between the ages of 8 and 15. These studies included a *diverse set of samples*, including students from a variety of racial/ethnic backgrounds, settings (urban and rural), and countries; *a variety of group leaders*, including teachers, counselors, psychologists, social workers, and graduate students; and *an independent evaluation of the program*. Thus far, the findings are promising, and the PRP has been found to reduce and prevent symptoms of depression, reduce hopelessness, prevent clinical levels of depression and anxiety, reduce and prevent anxiety, and may reduce behavioral problems—there is less research on this, but the few students have look at this have found significant effects. Finally, and importantly, the program has been found to work equally well for children of different racial/ethnic backgrounds. In sum, the research on the PRP indicates that the program produces reliable and positive improvements on students' wellbeing (Seligman et al., 2009).

Next was the implementation and evaluation of the *positive psychology curriculum*, guided by a $2.8 million grant from the U.S. Department of Education. The curriculum's major goals are to help students identify their signature strengths and to increase students' use of their strengths in daily life. The program identified strengths using the VIA classification (Peterson & Seligman, 2004) and promoted student resilience, positive emotions, and sense of meaning or purpose through 20–25 80-minute sessions delivered throughout students' 9th grade year. A majority of the lessons included discussion of the students' strengths, and in-class activity, and a real-world homework assignment that encouraged students to apply concepts and skills to their own lives. Some of the exercises used were *three good things*—write and discussing three good things that happened each day—and *using signature strengths in a new way*—using one's strengths as much as possible in school, in hobbies, and/ or with family and friends. In reviewing the program, researchers found increased *engagement in learning, enjoyment of school, achievement,* and *increased social skills.* However, the program did not improve students' reports of their depression and anxiety symptoms, character strengths, and participation in extracurricular activities (Seligman et al., 2009).

Lastly is Australia the Geelong Grammar School Project, a project infused with a positive psychology curriculum for an entire school. Thus far, anecdotal evidences looks extremely promising, but formal empirical evidence is still being collected. The project involves three major aspects: *teaching positive education, embedding positive education*, and *living positive education*. In the courses at GGS, educators teach the elements of positive psychology (e.g., resilience, gratitude, strengths, meaning, flow, positive relationships, and positive emotion) in stand-alone courses, as well as through existing courses. For more specifics on the project, see Seligman et al. (2009), but the project's apparent success indicates that a positive education curriculum is both possible and effective.

In addition to these large-scale positive psychology programs, smaller-scale programs have showed equally promising evidence for the effectiveness of positive psychology interventions (e.g., Huppert & Johnson, 2010; Ng, 2012; Proctor et al., 2011; Shoshani & Aviv, 2012). In terms of the link between positive psychology and social justice, Schmid, Phelps, Kiely, Napolitano, Body, and Lerner (2011) assessed how hope for one's future and intentional self-regulation skills affect developmental outcomes. Of note, they included the outcome of contribution, a measure that taps into adolescents' thoughts and actions on behaviors that promote social justice. The study found that a hopeful future was the best predictor of favorable outcomes, including contribution, highlighting the role of hope in the promotion of social justice.

In terms of interventions in school, Huppert and Johnson (2010) explored the effectiveness of mindfulness training program. Huppert and Johnson implemented a short classroom program of mindfulness for adolescent boys, and compared intervention and group groups on mindfulness, resilience, and psychological wellbeing measures. While the overall differences on these measures were non-significant, there was a significant positive association between the amount of individual practice outside the classroom and psychology well-being and mindfulness improvements. Further, the authors found that well-being improvements were related to personality variables. The mindfulness program was well received, as 74% of students stated that they would like to continue with it in the future (Huppert & Johnson, 2010).

Additionally, in terms of character techniques, two recent studies have demonstrated some encouraging results (Proctor et al., 2011; Shoshani & Aviv, 2012). Proctor and colleagues (2011) explored the impact of a character-based positive psychological intervention program on adolescent life satisfaction. The study compared student outcomes for life satisfaction, positive and negative affect, and self-esteem for 12–14 year olds who participated in character strength-based exercises infused into the school curriculum to those who did not participate. Compared to students who were not part of the program, students in the program reported significantly increased life satisfactions, providing preliminary support for the application of character strength-based exercises into school curriculums to increase life satisfaction and wellbeing among students. Furthermore, Shoshani and Aviv (2012) examined the relations between parental and children's character strengths and children's school adjustment for first-grade students in Israel. Using parental questionnaires, the Values in Action inventories of strengths, and teacher questionnaires on students' cognitive, social, emotional, and behavioral adjustment, the authors found that parents' intellectual, interpersonal, and temperance strengths were positively related to children's school adjustment. Additionally, children's intellectual, interpersonal, group-interaction, temperance, and transcendence strengths were also positively associated to broad aspects of adjustment (Shoshani & Aviv, 2012).

In sum, the current research on both smaller and larger-scale positive psychology school-based projects suggests that positive psychology techniques and interventions can be effectively incorporated systemically into schools. In addition to these school-wide approaches, at the individual level, school leaders can promote more socially just outcomes by identifying, promoting, and utilizing teacher, student, and community strengths. Understanding and cultivating strengths within the school and community cultural context is essential on the route to an education system that allows students to thrive and flourish.

REFERENCES

Adler, A. (1938). *Social interest: A challenge to mankind* (J. Linton & R. Vaughan, Trans.). London, UK: Faber and Faber Ltd.

Adler, A. (1956). *The individual psychology of Alfred Adler* (H. L. Ansbacher and R. R. Ansbacher, Eds.). New York, NY: Harper Torchbooks.

Bandura, A. (1977). Self-efficacy: Toward a unifying theory of behavioral change. *Psychological Review, 84,* 191–215.

Becker, D., & Marecek, J. (2008). Positive psychology: History in the remaking? *Theory & Psychology, 18,* 591–604.

Bernard, M. E., Froh, J. J., DiGiuseppe, R., Joyce, M. R., & Dryden, W. (2010). Albert Ellis: Unsung hero of positive psychology. *The Journal of Positive Psychology, 5,* 302–310.

Chapman, S., & Schwartz, J. P. (2012). Rejecting the null: Research and social justice means asking different questions. *Counseling and Values, 57,* 24–30.

Csikszentmihalyi, M. (1975). *Beyond boredom and anxiety: Experiencing flow in work and play.* San Francisco, CA: Jossey-Bass.

Csikszentmihalyi, M. (1996). *Creativity: Flow and the psychology of discovery and invention.* New York, NY: Harper Perennial.

Diener, E. (1984). Subjective well-being. *Psychological Bulletin, 95,* 542–575.

Emmons, R. A. (1986). Personal strivings: An approach to personality and subjective well-being. *Journal of Personality and Social Psychology, 51,* 1058–1068.

Erikson, E. H. (1950). *Childhood and society.* New York, NY: Norton.

Germer, C. K., Siegel, R. D., & Fulton, P. R. (Eds.). (2005). *Mindfulness and psychotherapy.* New York, NY: Guilford Press.

Goldstein, K. (1995). *The organism: A holistic approach to biology derived from pathological data in man.* Brooklyn, NY: Zone Books. (Original work published 1939)

Harter, S. (1975). Developmental differences in the manifestation of mastery motivation on problem-solving tasks. *Child Development, 46,* 370–378.

Huppert, F. A., & Johnson, D. M. (2010). A controlled trial of mindfulness training in schools: The importance of practice for an impact on well-being. *The Journal of Positive Psychology, 5,* 264–274.

Jahoda, M. (1958). *Current concepts of positive mental health.* New York, NY: Basic Books.

Kenny, M. E., & Romano, J. L. (2009). Promoting positive development and social justice through prevention: A legacy for the future. In M. E. Kenny, A. M. Horne, P. Orpinas, & L. E. Reese (Eds.), *Realizing social justice: The challenge of preventive interventions* (pp. 17–35). Washington, DC: American Psychological Association.

Lewis, A. D., Huebner, E., Malone, P. S., & Valois, R. F. (2011). Life satisfaction and student engagement in adolescents. *Journal of Youth and Adolescence, 40,* 249–262.

Lyubomirsky, S. (2007). *The how of happiness: A scientific approach to getting the life you want.* New York, NY: Penguin.

Marques, S. C., Pais-Ribeiro, J. L., & Lopez, S. J. (2011). The role of positive psychology constructs in predicting mental health and academic achievement in children and adolescents: A two-year longitudinal study. *Journal of Happiness Studies, 12,* 1049–1062.

Martens, B. K., & Witt, J. C. (2004). Competence, persistence, and success: The positive psychology of behavioral skill instruction. *Psychology in the Schools, 41,* 19–30.

Maslow, A. H. (1943). A theory of human motivation. *Psychological Review, 50,* 370–396.

Maslow, A. H. (1954). *Motivation and personality.* New York, NY: Harper.

Maslow, A. H. (1968). *Toward a psychology of being* (2nd ed.). Princeton,NJ: Van Nostrand.

Morrow, S., Rakhsha, G., & Castañeda, C. (2001). Qualitative research methods for multicultural counseling. In J. G. Ponterotto, J. M. Casas, L. A. Suzuki, & C. M. Alexander (Eds.), *Handbook of multicultural counseling* (2nd ed., pp. 575–603). Thousand Oaks, CA: Sage.

Newell, M. L., Nastasi, B. K., Hatzichristou, C., Jones, J. M., Schanding, G. R., & Yetter, G. (2010). Evidence on multicultural training in school psychology: Recommendations for future directions. *School Psychology Quarterly, 25,* 249–278.

Ng, W. (2012). Neuroticism and well-being? Let's work on the positive rather than negative aspects. *The Journal of Positive Psychology, 7,* 416–426.

Pajares, F. (2001). Toward a positive psychology of academic motivation. *The Journal of Educational Research, 95,* 27–35.

Pedrotti, J. (2011). Broadening perspectives: Strategies to infuse multiculturalism into a positive psychology course. *The Journal of Positive Psychology, 6,* 506–513.

Pedrotti, J., Edwards, L. M., & Lopez, S. J. (2009). Positive psychology within a cultural context. In S. J. Lopez & C. R. Snyder (Eds.), *Oxford handbook of positive psychology* (2nd ed., pp. 49–57). New York, NY: Oxford University Press.

Peterson, C. (2006). *A primer in positive psychology.* New York, NY: Oxford University Press.

Peterson, C., & Seligman, M. E. P. (2004) *Character strengths and virtues: A handbook and classification.* New York, NY: Oxford University Press.

Proctor, C., Tsukayama, E., Wood, A. M., Maltby, J., Eades, J., & Linley, P. (2011). Strengths gym: The impact of a character strengths-based intervention on the life satisfaction and well-being of adolescents. *The Journal of Positive Psychology, 6,* 377–388.

Roffey, S. (2013). Thought you knew about being thankful? Think again!! *The Journal of Positive Psychology, 8,* 79–80.

Rogers, C. R. (1963). The concept of the fully functioning person. *Psychotherapy: Theory, Research, & Practice, 1,* 17–26.

Ryff, C. D. (1989). Happiness is everything, or is it? Explorations on the meaning of psychological well-being. *Journal of Personality and Social Psychology, 57,* 1069–1081.

Schmid, K. L., Phelps, E., Kiely, M. K., Napolitano, C. M., Boyd, M. J., & Lerner, R. M. (2011). The role of adolescents' hopeful futures in predicting positive and negative developmental trajectories: Findings from the 4-H Study of Positive Youth Development. *The Journal of Positive Psychology, 6,* 45–56.

Seligman, M. E. P. (1998). President's column: Building human strength: Psychology's forgotten mission. *APA Monitor, 29,* 1.

Seligman, M. E. P. (2011). *Flourish: A visionary new understanding of happiness and well-being.* New York, NY: Free Press.

Seligman, M. E. P., Ernst, R. M, Gillham, J., Reivich, K., & Linkins, M. (2009). Positive education: Positive psychology and classroom interventions. *Oxford Review of Education, 35,* 293–311.

Seligman, M. P., Park, N., & Peterson, C. (2004). The values in action (VIA) classification of character strengths. *Ricerche Di Psicologia, 27,* 63–78.

Shoshani, A., & Aviv, I. (2012). The pillars of strength for first-grade adjustment— Parental and children's character strengths and the transition to elementary school. *The Journal of Positive Psychology, 7,* 315–326.

Skitka, L. J. (2009). Exploring the "lost and found" of justice theory and research. *Social Justice Research, 22*(1), 98–116.

Shoben, E. J., Jr. (1957). Toward a concept of the normal personality. *American Psychologist, 12,* 183–189.

Sue, D.W., & Sue, D. (2008). *Counseling the culturally diverse: Theory and practice* (5th ed.). New York, NY: Wiley.

Theoharis, G. (2007). Social justice educational leaders and resistance: Toward a theory of social justice leadership. *Educational Administration Quarterly, 43,* 221–258.

Tesser, A. (1988). Toward a self-evaluation maintenance model of social behavior. In L. Berkowitz (Ed.), *Advances in experimental social psychology: Vol. 21. Social psychological studies of the self: Perspectives and programs* (pp. 181–227). San Diego, CA: Academic Press.

Trickett, E. J. (1992). Prevention ethics: Explicating the context of prevention activities. *Ethics & Behavior, 2,* 91–100.

Vasquez, M. T. (2012). Psychology and social justice: Why we do what we do. *American Psychologist, 67,* 337–346.

Waters, L. (2011). A review of school-based positive psychology interventions. *The Australian Educational and Developmental Psychologist, 28,* 75–90.

Waterman, A. S. (2013). The humanistic psychology–positive psychology divide: Contrasts in philosophical foundations. *American Psychologist, 68,* 124–133.

CHAPTER 3

PEDAGOGY OF THE DISCIPLINE

How Black Studies Can Influence Educational Leadership

Gaëtane Jean-Marie
University of Louisville

T. Elon Dancy
University of Oklahoma

ABSTRACT

In this chapter, we examine the intellectual tradition of Black Studies to offer a lens on how social justice can improve the preparation and practice of
educational leaders. Specifically, the chapter is organized in three parts. First,
it examines the origin of Black Studies, depicting how this historic movement
began by chronicling the influential moments and pioneering individuals
that led to the radical change that was sought in educational settings throughout the U.S. Second, it considers how Black Studies and education intersect
in the quest for cultural enlightenment through educational access, situating
its important historical context as a driver for racial and social uplift. Thirdly,

Educational Leadership for Ethics and Social Justice, pages 43–62

the chapter examines the paths and parallels of the Black Studies and social justice leadership movements to draw similarities that align their purpose and commitment to eradicate social injustice. The chapter concludes with implications for leadership preparation and practice as the field of educational leadership continues to grapple with issues of social justice.

INTRODUCTION

Social movements throughout U.S. history depict the complex process of social change that has unfolded over several centuries. These movements have influenced how schools and school leaders ameliorate structural and social systems and practices to achieve social justice (Brooks & Miles, 2008; Dancy & Horsford, 2010; Jean-Marie, 2006; Jean-Marie & Normore, 2008). In particular, the Black Studies movement during the late 1960s depicts the social change and racial progress that can be achieved in the struggle for educational equity in common and higher education (Bell, 2012; Brown & Dancy, 2009; Jean-Marie, 2006; Jean-Marie & Normore, 2008; Williamson-Lott, 2003, 2008). Jennings (2000) contends that "many Black Studies programs in U.S. higher education were established during the 1960s and 1970s not only because of the need to examine race and political economy in urban settings but also to enhance the effectiveness of black civic participation in the interests of social and racial justice" (p. 178). Given its influence on the analysis of political and economic issues facing black communities and other marginalized groups, Black Studies makes theoretical and practical connections between scholarship and social change. We argue this discipline has much to offer the social justice literature in educational leadership.

In this chapter, we examine the intellectual tradition of Black Studies to offer a lens on how social justice can improve the preparation and practice of educational leaders. Specifically, the chapter is organized in three parts. First, it examines the origin of Black Studies depicting how this historic movement began by chronicling the influential moments and pioneering individuals that led to the radical change that was sought in educational settings throughout the U.S. Second, it considers how Black Studies and education intersect in the quest for cultural enlightenment through educational access, situating its important historical context as a driver for racial and social uplift. Thirdly, the chapter examines the paths and parallels of the Black Studies and social justice leadership movements to draw similarities that align their purpose and commitment to eradicate social injustice. We conclude with implications for leadership preparation and practice as the field of educational leadership continues to grapple with issues of social justice.

ORIGINS OF BLACK STUDIES: DEFYING BLACKS' INFERIORITY AND ELEVATING SELF-PRIDE IN SOCIETY

Behind the concept of Black Studies is essentially the Black intellectual tradition, the critical thought and perspectives of intellectuals of African descent and scholars of Black America, and Africa, the Black diaspora (Asante, 1990, 1998; Fenderson, Stewart, & Baumgartner, 2012; Gates, 2000; Karenga, 1988, 1995; Marable, 2000). Among the pioneers of the field were W.E. B. Du Bois, Carter Woodson, Charles Spurgeon Johnson, Allison Davis, Horace Mann Bond, Ralph Bunche, Rayford Logan, Melville Herskovitz, E. Franklin Frazier, John Hope Frankin, Kelley Miller, Irea de Augustine Reid—to name a few of Black Studies intellectuals (Kilson, 2000). These intellectuals have historically occupied a very important role in the field of Black Studies, and their works have also operated as progenitors of social and political change in various facets of American life (Bobo, Hudley, & Michel, 2004; Dancy, 2012; King, 2004; Marable, 2000; Myrdal, 1994; Rooks, 2006; Turner, 1969 West, 1993). Collectively, they set out a vision of building a Black intellectual community in common and higher education, the Black and broader community. Further, within this academic discipline, the voices of African American leaders (e.g., Nannie Helen Burroughs, Mary McLeod Bethune, Anna Julia Cooper, Septima Clark, Fanny Jackson Coppin; Adam Clayton Powell Jr., W. E. B. Du Bois, Paul Robeson, Carter G. Woodson, Whitney Young, Jr., etc.) illuminate their historical and cultural significance in movements for social change imbued with a vision to eradicate racism in society, not only as educators but also as public speakers, community activists, and civil and women's rights advocates (Bloom & Erlandson, 2003; Jean-Marie, 2006; Loder, 2005; Tillman, 2004;).

Efforts to institutionalize Black Studies included development of departments in universities throughout the U.S. As pioneers, the establishment of Black Studies departments was located in five major institutions of higher education in the Connecticut Valley—University of Massachusetts (UMass), Amherst, Smith, Mt. Holyoke, and Hampshire Colleges (Bell, 2012). UMass, the first academic department named in honor of W. E. B. Du Bois, became the basic paradigm for the development of the consortium of Black Studies departments at these institutions (Rojas & Byrd, 2012). Although not as radical as UMass, Cornell, Harvard, San Francisco State University, and other institutions in the north and south became some of the many to institutionalize Black Studies. These departments were outcomes of protests and demands from proponents of the Black Studies movement across the U.S. In addition to development of departments, students' demands also included "the recruitment and retention of black faculty and students in compliance with federal policies to redress historical racial injustice and imbalance in personnel and curriculum by reconstructing a more racially and culturally just, supportive, and diverse system of education" (Bell, 2012, p. 98).

According to Rojas and Byrd (2012), Black Studies represents a political and intellectual mission. The knowledge created with Black Studies programs is meant to capture the African American experience in ways that do not denigrate or marginalize that community. Black Studies sought to provide an alternative to American history books (see e.g., *The History of the United States: Source Readings* [Harris, Rothman, & Thernstrom, 1969]; *Builders of American Institutions: Readings in United States History,* [Freidel, 1963]; *American Higher Education: A Documentary Record* to name a few) that negated or undermined Black people's experiences and their contributions to America's progress (Aptheker, 1971). The deliberate omission of Blacks in mainstream books and history created an impenetrable veil (Aptheker, 1971) that bred a racist society. Since Black Studies' inception, scholars sought to examine the reality of the Black experience from the point of view of Black people themselves (Du Bois, 1996; Karenga, 1995, 2000; Rooks, 2006; Turner, 1969). Through the Black intellectual tradition, Black Studies sought to correct the racist stereotypes and assumptions of cultural inferiority that unfortunately still exist within society (Baum, 2010; Fenderson, Stewart, & Baumgartner, 2012; Murji & Solomos, 2005; Myrday, 1994; Rojas, 2007). Even today, the nation's "intelligentsia (i.e., media, educators, scholars, and cultural leaders) continue to approach black urban communities as pathology, rather than recognize their significant cultural and intellectual contributions to U.S. society reflected in the nation's black community" (Jennings, 2000, p. 178). In response, Black Studies provides examination of major social, political, and economic issues facing Black communities, which include how its leaders should respond to national policies. It brings forth the ongoing quest of people of African descent reaffirming the best of their history and heritage while simultaneously deconstructing oppressive ideological beliefs and practices that endeavor to annihilate or make powerless the Black race.

Karenga (2000) explicates seven fundamental intellectual and social contributions made by Black Studies proving its value as a discipline. First is that Black Studies is a contribution to humanity's understanding itself, using the African experience as a paradigmatic human struggle and achievement. For examples, Aptheker's (1971) exposition on the "Afro American History" in the 20th century and Du Bois' (1939, 1996) influential writings about Blacks along a continuum of social, historical, and political thought accomplished this humanitarian understanding of overcoming. Second, Black Studies is a contribution to the university's realizing its claim of universality, comprehensiveness, and objectivity by demanding and facilitating a holistic approach to the study of truth and the class, race, and sexual contradictions that constrain and distort that truth (Karenga, 2000). Black Studies challenges dominant discourse or various forces of "isms" (i.e., racism, sexism, classism, separatism, etc.) that operate in society. Thirdly, it is a contribution to U.S. society's understanding itself by critically measuring its claim against performance in its variance with the paradigmatic just society. Black Studies not only examines critically the forces of "isms" that have operated historically but also those who are/were the perpetrators and silent bystanders (Whites and Blacks) of social injustice.

A fourth contribution of Black Studies is its contribution to the rescues and reconstruction of Black history and humanity from alien hands and the restoration of African classical culture on and through which we can build a new body of human sciences and humanity (Diop, 1982; Williams, 1993). The fifth is also a contribution to the creation of a new social science and humanities, more critical, more corrective, more holistic, more ethical, and more inclusive. A sixth contribution is its contribution to the creation of a self-conscious body of capable and committed Black intellectuals who self-consciously choose to use their knowledge and skills in the service of a black community and, by consequence and extension, in the interest of a new and better society and the world (Du Bois, 1996; Franklin & Moss, 1969; Strickland, 1975). Finally, Black Studies finds its grounding and meaning in its ongoing contribution to the critique, resistance, and reversal of one of the greatest problems of our time, the progressive Europeanization of human consciousness (Reed, 1997).

The future of Black Studies is tied to past and present political battles. Black Studies emerged as a legitimate area of study that has been devoted to exploring the contours and substance of the historical experience of Blacks in the U.S. and Diaspora (Bell, 2012). The curriculum of Black Studies evolved over time from its initial focus on black realities associated with North American Blacks to a broader curriculum that embraces Black African societies, the Afro-American community, Afro-Caribbean communities, and Afro-Latin communities (Bobo et al., 2004; Fischer, 1971; Franklin & Moss, 1969; Kilson, 2000). Since its start up between the years of 1968 and 1972, Black Studies as a field has experienced transformations to reflect a broader perspective on the social inequities within American society. The formative years of Black Studies encountered political and intellectual upheaval (Fischer, 1971; Kilson, 2000), mainly driven by student activism on university campuses across the country (Bell, 2012; Bobo, et al., 2004; Williamson-Lott, 2003; 2008). Important to our analysis of what Black Studies can tell us about leadership for social justice is an examination of how Black Studies intersects education to fulfill the quest for enlightenment through educational access.

THE INTERSECTION OF BLACK STUDIES AND EDUCATION: THE QUEST FOR CULTURAL ENLIGHTENMENT THROUGH EDUCATIONAL ACCESS

The social movements of the 1960s and 1970s strongly challenged the status quo of White dominance in every aspect of society. A series of movements triggered by the Civil Rights Movement in the U.S. led to protests by African Americans and other groups (Gates, 2002; Jean-Marie, 2006; Jean-Marie & Normore, 2008; Williamson-Lott, 2003, 2008). During that time, the Black Studies movement unfolded in historically Black colleges and universities (HBCUs), and predominantly white institutions (PWIs) throughout the U.S. by African American students with participation from many White students and faculty (Brown & Freeman, 2004; Williamson-Lott, 2003, 2008). Student protests and conferences for the institutionalization of Black Studies (Rogers, 2012) were outcries about their feelings of marginalization and challenge to higher education institutions' lack of attentiveness to their educational and cultural needs. African-Americans in the U.S. wanted their histories and cultures to be reflected in their college and university curricula (Gillborn, 1990). Through Black Studies, Blacks are placed at the center of analysis so that instances of injustice and oppression can be unearthed, unsilenced, made visible, acknowledged, and recognized, which is rooted in Afrocentricity (Asante, 1990). According to Asante (1990), Afrocentricity encourages the active agency and voice of African people in addressing social issues. Blacks in higher education institutions yearned for discourses and analysis about the interlocking social structures and systems that have marginalized their race and wanted to understand how institutions, ideologies, and policies created and perpetuate injustices (Brown & Dancy, 2009). As a result, students staged protests through various organizations and leaders who provided the platform to "push and pull the discipline of Black Studies into the academy" (Rogers, 2012, p. 21).

According to Rogers (2012), "hundreds of thousands of Black students forced the institutionalization of the discipline of Black Studies as part of a larger Black Campus Movement that diversified higher education" (p. 21). The pursuit of Black Studies was in essence a call to action on the epistemological framework of Blacks from America and the Diaspora (Bobo et al., 2004; Rojas, 2007) in which Black students can explore inevitable questions about who they are; what they think, feel and know; and what they have contributed.

Viewed as the Black Studies Movement (Bell, 2012; Marable, 2000; White, 2012), college students across universities in the United States organized themselves to draw attention to administrative officials about the inherent institutionalized racism in curricular offerings and the absence of the Black discourse in the intellectual exchange of ideas and critical thought in university classroom. They also played a significant role in the original theoretical justification for the discipline in which students developed and presented the Black Studies idea to a group of professors in 1966 (Rogers, 2012; Rojas, 2007; White, 2012).

The development of Black Studies discipline is attributed to student activists from higher education institutions throughout the U.S. For example,

Curtis Porter, University of Pittsburgh; Bertha Maxwell Roddy, University of North Carolina; Rhett Jones, Brown University; Talmadge Anderson, Washington State University; Ewart Guinier, Harvard; and Johnella Butler, Smith College were among those student activists who appeared in the literature about the Black Studies movement. They organized student protests, petitions, rallies, strikes, marches, sit-ins, and building takeovers until their demands were met, although there was some bureaucratic resistance by university officials in many institutions (Bell, 2012; Rojas, 2007; Rojas & Byrd, 2012; Williamson-Lott, 2003, 2008; White, 2012).

In sum, the Black Studies Movement can be characterized as a "collective discourse, common ground, shared strategies, and broad Black student initiative to establish Black Studies courses, and an eventual network of individuals, programs, departments, institutes, cultural and community centers, and activist outposts' (White, 2012, p. 10). Within the broader spectrum of education, the movement was a driver for racial and social uplift among Blacks by institutionalizing Black Studies depicting the richness and troublesome history of a marginalized group within American society. The activism of students and proponents of the Black Studies movement helped to develop and shape the critical analysis that was absent in mainstream literature and discourses. Rojas and Byrd (2012) make a salient claim about the contribution of Black/Ethnic Studies in the liberation of American race relations: "institutions bear the marks of the social environments that created and nurtured them.... [Black] Studies embodies a history of racial struggle, representing an intellectual vanguard opposed to Jim Crow, apartheid, and other forms of institutionalized inequality" (p. 551). In this current moment of fiscal sequestration in which questions surrounding the fate of the humanities loom large in academic discourse, scholars housed in Black Studies units across the nation must continue to speak honestly and critically about the institutions that influence the intellectual integrity and trajectory of the field (White, 2012).

THE BLACK STUDIES AND SOCIAL JUSTICE LEADERSHIP MOVEMENTS: PATHS AND PARALLELS

The Quest for Social Justice

The experience of Black people in the United States is pedagogical for all interested in leading for social justice. In 1971, Herbert Aptheker powerfully elaborates on this point:

Fundamental to the history of the United States is the struggle of the masses of its population—of every color and every ethnic and national origin—

against repression, oppression, and exploitation. Central to this record of struggle has been that waged by the Afro-American people; in so struggling, they have forged for themselves an inspiring history and they have simultaneously affected in a decisive way every aspect of the history of the United States as a whole. Every aspect of that history—whether of laborer or farmer, of student or intellectual, of the women's movement or the peace movement, whether diplomatic history or legal history or economic or political or social or ideological, whether of church or press, of cooperatives or science—everything, absolutely everything, whether looked at in some detail or examined in totality, everything that has ever appeared or ever occurred in the United states of American must be understood in terms of the relation thereto of the Black people in the United States. To the degree that that relationship is minimized-not to speak of being ignored-to that degree the historiography is false and is racist. (p. 14)

The history of Black people in the U.S. entails social, intellectual, political, economic, and physical resistance to the oppressive conditions and exploitation that permeated their lives (Aptheker, 1971; Du Bois, 1939, 1996; Franklin & Moss, 1969; Marable, 2000; Sitkoff, 1993). Consequently, tied to that history is the quest for social justice echoed in the 1955 speech of Martin Luther King, Jr., in Birmingham in which he called upon the Black community to persist in their resistance against injustices until a better world emerges: "We are impatient for justice.... When the history books are written in future generations, the historians will have to pause and say, 'There lived a great people—a black people—who injected new meaning and dignity into the veins of civilization.' This is our challenge and our overwhelming responsibility" (Sitkoff, 1993, pp. 45–46). King's resounding call for social justice was not to be taken up by Blacks only but also for supporters to continue the struggle in every aspect of society. Since King's 1955 speech, progress has been made to eradicate social inequities in American culture.

Despite progress towards a more just society in the U.S., great inequities continue to exist in many sectors of American culture. In particular, the schooling experiences of poor African American and Latino students versus White middle-class students prompt many educators and scholars to call to question the slow pace of educational attainment for marginalized groups (Brooks, 2012; Brooks & Witherspoon-Arnold, 2013; Dancy & Horsford, 2010; Jean-Marie & Mansfield, 2013). The inequities are exacerbated as our nation's schools become increasingly diverse across racial and ethnic lines (Brown & Bartee, 2009; Dancy & Horsford, 2010; Jean-Marie & Mansfield, 2013). Several scholars offer critical perspectives on the inequities that continue to persist in American schools.

Ball (2006), in her examination of the contemporary impact of the 1954 ruling of *Brown v. Board of Education,* asserts that there is much more to do to fully realize the civil rights victories of Brown because "we still have not achieved educational excellence and equity for those that Brown was meant to impact" (p. 4). Ladson-Billings and Tate (1995) maintain that "a racialized society in which discussions of race and racism continue to be muted and marginalized" (p. 47) stifles efforts toward equity and social justice. Baum (2010), in his examination of schools in Baltimore, argues that "segregation continues to limit the academic development, and social and economic opportunities of Black children particularly if they are poor, and it prevents all children from learning to work and live with others who differ by race, class, and culture" (p. ix). Brooks (2012) interrogates how race and race relations influenced the educational practice of teachers and administrators in an American urban high school. Jean-Marie and Mansfield (2013) in their work on race and racial discrimination in schools examine the need for school leaders at all levels to engage educators' inactions as well as actions considered harmful to students of color bringing more focus to achievement disparities. A common thread that is woven within these scholars' work is how social injustices are enacted and advanced in our contemporary educational system. Yet there is extraordinary belief that developing an educational agenda that embraces principles of social justice is attainable and has important implication for the field of educational leadership.

ACCENTUATING THE DESCRIPTIVE, CORRECTIVE, AND PRESCRIPTIVE APPROACHES IN THE BLACK STUDIES AND LEADERSHIP FOR SOCIAL JUSTICE MOVEMENT

Similar to what the tenets of the Black Studies movements were about, the leadership for social justice movement in the field of educational leadership is about educating students in school environments (i.e., common and higher education) that take seriously or embrace a multiracial and culturally diverse society. To provide this sort of educational environment is social justice. The parallels of the Black Studies movement with efforts on social justice in schools today are interconnected. Arguably, the social justice movement in educational leadership is an extension of the progressive movements for equality, access, and justice in the 19th and 20th century.

Both Black Studies and the current discourse on leadership for social justice confront the long history of racial injustice in society and schools and seek to eradicate it. Within Black Studies, Gates and Marable (2000) assert that the contribution of Black intellectual tradition to Black Studies sought to be descriptive, corrective, and prescriptive. These approaches are also applicable to the field of educational leadership. The *descriptive* approach of Black intellectual tradition encompasses how "scholars sought to richly describe the contexts of black life and history, examining the reality of the black experience from the point of view of black people themselves" (Gates & Marable, 2000, p. 189). As such, Black intellectuals laid the groundwork for critical examinations of the problems of race and social inequities in mainstream society and the Black community. Similarly in the discourse on leadership for social justice, application of the descriptive approach focuses on the scholarship and praxis that is evolving in the field of educational leadership. For many years, educational leadership struggled to define what leadership for social justice is. In particular, defining social justice is complex because of its abstract nature (Adams, Bell, & Griffin, 2007; Jean-Marie, Normore & Brooks, 2009; North, 2008). However, educational leadership scholars (see e.g., Cambron-McCabe & McCarthy, 2005; Capper, Theoharis & Sebastian, 2006; Dantley & Tillman, 2010; Jean-Marie et al., 2009; North, 2008; Larson & Murtadha, 2002; Marshall & Oliva, 2010; Theoharis, 2007) and special issue journals devoted to social justice in educational leadership (see, e.g., *Educational Administration Quarterly* [2004], *Journal of Educational Administration* [2007], and *Journal of School Leadership* [2007]) have begun to explicate its meaning and examine how social justice can lead to equitable schools and a just society.

Within this descriptive framework, scholars also define what social injustice is to examine its manifestations on the lives of disenfranchised people (i.e., minority students, parents and families, and poor communities) through laws, policies, and practices enacted in schools and society. Building on the descriptive nature of defining social justice and injustice within the context of educational leadership, empirical evidence (see, e.g., Brooks & Arnold, 2013; Frattura & Capper, 2007; Kose, 2007; Normore, 2008; Theoharis, 2007; Turhan, 2010; Vogel, 2011) about its manifestations in schools through practices and policies sheds understanding about the realities of marginalized groups in schools. Studies on social justice in schools seek to examine how those who are affected by it experience school. Consequently, the more descriptive the field of educational leadership is about the manifestation of social injustice, educators are compelled to engage in what Freire (2000) calls praxis (i.e., critical reflection + action) to dismantle entirely its existence in schools.

The second dimension, the *corrective approach* of the black intellectual tradition, tried to "correct the racist stereotypes and assumptions of black genetic or cultural inferiority that unfortunately still exist within much white scholarship" (Gates & Marable, 2000, p. 189). Many Black scholars through the curriculum of Black Studies in universities and institutions provide a counter-analysis and examination of the social ills that often depict the inferiority of the Black race. These scholars sought to raise the consciousness of society through multiple forms of discourse (i.e., political, social, economic, etc.) by creating spaces to engage in debates through forums and scholarships empowering individuals and communities to take actions toward a more just society. Within leadership for social justice, similar efforts in schools through reform or policies seek to eradicate the pathological stereotypes and assumptions about marginalized groups in schools. Several studies (i.e., Jean-Marie & Normore, 2010; Kose, 2007; Theoharis, 2008; Vogel, 2011) reveal how school leaders' pursuit of social justice in schools is focused on eliminating inequities in school.

Finally, the *prescriptive approach* to Black Studies was an integral part of the struggle to eradicate racism and empower Black people in which both theoretical and practical connections between scholarship and social change (Gates & Marable, 2000) were made. The emergence of the Black Studies movement was a rejection of the symbols, beliefs, and norms of the dominant society as the alternative to Blacks' inferiority status they have been labeled with since slavery. Through Black Studies, Blacks incorporated their own symbols of culture that has so long ground their bodies and spirits to survive and/or fight against injustice (Marable, 2000; Jennings, 2000; White, 2012). The curriculum in Black Studies discipline served as a conscious vanguard by its integration of a "balanced interface with progressive ideological commitment to black realties and a nonethnocentric orientation or pluralistic scholarly orientation toward black realities...these [nuances would] produce a bewildering mixture of things that can evoke pride, criticism, ambivalence, or even revulsion" (Kilson, 2000, p. 172). The prescriptive approach builds on the descriptive and corrective in that the scholarship on Black Studies was not only a celebration of heritage, self-pride, racial uplift, but it "seeks to utilize history and culture as tools through which an oppressed people can transform their lives and the entire society" (Gates & Marable, 2000, p. 189).

In the context of leadership for social justice, the prescriptive approach is where educational leadership can better integrate the theoretical and practical connection between scholarship and social change. Across the country, many preparation programs are embedding social justice in coursework and field experiences (Allen, 2006; Marshall & Oliva, 2010; Vogel, 2011); however, many school leaders do not have the adequate knowledge and training to address issues of inequity in their leadership practices (Cambron-McCabe & McCarthy, 2005; Jean-Marie et al., 2009). To be more effective, there is a need for more concerted efforts by preparation programs' curricula to explicitly address issues of social justice rather than a cursory examination or additive approach some programs adopt (i.e., a course on diversity issues or discretion of faculty to address social justice issues). Leadership preparation should model what Black Studies programs have adopted: an integration of social justice issues in the curricula that takes into account the social, political, economic, and intellectual discourse of marginalized groups.

The lessons from the legacy of the Black Studies movement have much to do with elevating the quest for social justice. The legacy of the Black Studies movement depicts how the experiences of Blacks are placed at the center of analysis so that instances of injustice and oppression can be addressed more purposefully. Black Studies sought to call attention to and confront institutionalized inequities within and beyond the university; the movement was equally concerned about social ills in society. How can public schools pursue social justice without considering what it means for the communities in which these schools/districts reside? Further, the Black Studies movement was led by marginalized groups but engaged sympathizers. The movement mobilized a diverse group and sought to build a critical mass nationally. While many preparation programs nationally are beginning to address social justice issues, many lag behind in moving this agenda forward to more adequately prepare school leaders. As a model, the institutionalization of Black Studies discipline was premised on a persistent agenda that included structural and systemic changes that compelled the diversification of higher education. As the field of educational leadership continues the fight for social justice, it has at its core the legacy of great social justice movements of the past century and a half, such as the Black Studies movement, to persist in bringing about equitable schools rather than choose to be complicit.

IMPLICATIONS FOR LEADERSHIP PREPARATION AND PRACTICE: A CURSORY LOOK AT THE FIELD

The Black Studies discipline teaches educational leaders to interrogate all education stakeholders in their identities, subject positions, and social locations. We take a similar position as Patricia Williams (1991) in her essay, "The Alchemy of Race and Rights." In the opening line of text, Williams declares that "subject position is everything" (p. 3). Black Studies stresses the importance of context, requiring analysis of when, where, why, and how Black people enter the educational setting. In addition, Black Studies promotes active engagement involving issues of identity and difference in education. We identify six practical areas to which Black Studies speaks, and for which it can have positive influence on educational leadership programs: (1) studying historical and sociocultural contexts of school and campus communities; (2) resisting cultural reproduction of educational inequality and inequity; (3) interrogating systems of oppression, privilege, and entitlement; (4) valuing experiences and perspectives of people of color; (5) monitoring and mediating cultural conflict through cross-cultural communication; and (6) identifying, preparing, and supporting culturally proficient educational leaders.

Study Historical and Sociocultural Contexts of School and Campus Communities

Education leaders must have a keen awareness and understanding of the historical and sociocultural contexts of their school and campus communities if these leaders are to be successful. They must familiarize themselves with histories of discrimination, systems of oppression, and contemporary manifestations of marginalization, which may contribute to mistrust, skepticism, and cynicism by communities and cultural groups that may have been excluded or devalued by an institution and its leaders. This information can be gained through historical research and artifacts to include newspaper reports; governmental data; school, district, and university performance reports; and informal interviews that capture the experiential knowledge of people who have been marginalized, underserved, or silenced in a particular community. Addressing the challenges of educational inequities involves knowledge of demographic shifts and the myriad cultural issues cited in this chapter that inform society and education about how groups think, know, act and react (Brooks & Miles, 2008; Dancy & Horsford, 2010; Ogbu, 1992, 2003).

Resist Cultural Reproduction of Educational Inequality and Inequity

Educational leaders must be able to discern patterns of exclusion and segregation as perpetuated through administrative policies and practices. They must analyze policies and practices with the intent of identifying those that continue to grant privilege and a sense of entitlement to one group while only offering disadvantage and limited access and opportunity to others. This work is critical in effectively recognizing and resisting the cultural reproduction of educational inequality and inequity in school organizations and throughout the education pipeline. Inequality and inequity are reproduced when education leaders fail to address diversity issues concerning decision-making, allocation of resources, and power distribution (Dancy & Horsford, 2010). Thus, education leaders must be unafraid to speak about what matters. Accordingly, Smith and Boyd-Williams (2007) argue the following about teaching post-Katrina:

> As teacher educators, we do ourselves and our students a grave disservice if we sit complacently and acquiesce to the demands of the state while ignoring the needs of the greater social whole. It is no longer acceptable, nor was it ever for us to deny or silence the validity of the voice of the marginalized on the basis of our own privilege, one born out of a guise of elevated professional educational expertise. (p. 150)

Interrogate Systems of Oppression, Privilege, and Entitlement

Gay (2007) poignantly describes racism can and does play out in the educational lives of children post-Katrina:

> Operating on the assumption that the same instructional practices are equally effective for all students is a form of academic racism. . . . No one should be surprised when it is revealed that the displaced children of Katrina performed even lower in their new schools than the old. If that does happen it will not be the fault of students, but educational systems that did not modify curriculum, content, instruction, and support services to accommodate their . . . diversity. (p. 59)

Across colleges and universities, teacher preparation programs require the study of Whiteness as it impacts teacher and learner epistemology and teacher pedagogy, and we believe this practice should be extended to the field of educational leadership. The work of scholars like Giroux (1998), Marx and Pennington (2003), Delgado and Stefancic (1997), and Leonardo (2009) provide excellent starting points for familiarizing future educational leaders to research on White privilege and Whiteness studies.

Value Experiences and Perspectives of People of Color

Leaders in educational settings must assume a similar understanding of culture as teachers. More specifically, they must understand how culture operates daily in the classroom, foster learning environments that value cultural and ethnic diversity, and understand how these environments inform student achievement. This knowledge is foundational in establishing a school or institutional culture and climate that advances student learning, engagement, and success. In the context of teaching and learning, Gay (2000) explains, "Opportunities must be provided for students from different ethnic backgrounds to have free personal and cultural expression so that their voices and experiences can be incorporated into teaching and learning processes on a regular basis" (p. 43). We agree, and believe that the experiences and perspectives of students of color should also be considered and embrace by educational leaders in their efforts to lead organizations that meaningfully educate and serve all students.

Monitor and Mediate Cultural Conflict through Cross-Cultural Communication

According to Tatum (2007), "we are confronted by the loss of civility in increasingly diverse communities" at the same time we are in desperate need of "balance, integrity, vision; a clear sense of collective responsibility and ethical leadership—in order to prepare our students for wise steward-ship of their world and active participation in a democracy" (pp. 105–106). Our commitment to preparing students educationally along the P–20 pipeline requires school, college, and university leaders who can success-fully monitor and mediate cultural conflict by modeling cross-cultural communication effectively and proficiently. Therefore, educational lead-ers and administrators must be trained and experienced to mediate in di-verse contexts and able to both navigate and negotiate opposing cultural perspectives and conflict through dialogue. These lessons can be learned and guided by the research on teachers and faculty as cultural mediators (Diamond & Moore, 1995; Gay, 2000). This work demonstrates how educa-tors must provide opportunities for students to engage in critical dialogue about conflicts among cultures and analyze inconsistencies between main-stream cultural ideals/realities and those across cultures. Just as teachers and faculty are required to do, educational administrators must assume the lead in clarifying cultural misunderstanding and fostering positive cross-cultural relationships.

Identify, Prepare, and Support Culturally Proficient Educational Leaders

One way to engage the challenges presented by a history of discrimina-tion, segregation, and oppression in U.S. education is to actively locate, hire, mentor, and promote culturally proficient leaders at every point along the P–20 educational pipeline. Schools should remember that, as organiza-tions, heterogeneity and diverse perspectives often promote the creativity necessary to engaging a higher level of critical analysis and thoughtful solu-tions to complex problems (Dancy, 2010).

REFERENCES

Adams, M., Bell, L., & Griffin. (2007). *Teaching for diversity and social justice.* New York, NY: Routledge.

Allen, L. A. (2006). The moral life of schools revisited: Preparing educational lead-ers to "build a new social order" for social justice and democratic community. *International Journal of Urban Educational Leadership, 1*(1), 1–13.

Aptheker, H. (1971). *Afro American history: The modern era.* New York, NY: Carol Pub-lishing Group.

Asante, M. K. (1998). *The Afrocentric idea.* Philadephia, PA: Temple University Press.

Ball, A. F. (Ed.). (2006). *With more deliberate speed: Achieving equity and excellence in education: Realizing the full potential of Brown v. Board of Education* (Vol. 105). Chicago, IL: NSSE.

Baum, H. S. (2010). *Brown in Baltimore: School desegregation and the limits of liberalism.* Ithaca, NY: Cornell University Press.

Bell, B. W. (2012). Passing on the radical legacy of Black Studies at the University of Massachusetts: The W. E. B. Du Bois Department of Afro-American Studies, 1968–1971. *Journal of African American Studies, 16,* 89–110.

Bloom, C. M., & Erlandson, D. A. (2003). African American women principals in urban schools: Realities, (re)construction, and resolutions. *Educational Administration Quarterly, 39,* 339–369.

Bobo, J., Hudley, C., & Michel, C. (2004). *The Black Studies reader.* New York, NY: Routledge.

Brooks, J. S. (2007). Special issue: Distributed leadership: problems, possibilities and promise. *Journal of School Leadership, 17*(4).

Brooks, J. S. (2012). *Black school white school: Racism and educational (mis)leadership.* New York, NY: Teachers College Press.

Brooks, J. S. & Arnold, N. (Eds.) (2013). *Educational leadership and racism: Preparation, pedagogy, and practice.* Charlotte, NC: Information Age.

Brooks, J. S., & Miles, M. T. (2008). From scientific management to social justice and back again? Pedagogical shifts in educational leadership, in A. H. Normore (Ed.), *Leadership for social justice: Promoting equity and excellence through inquiry and reflective practice* (pp. 99–114). Charlotte, NC: Information Age Publishing.

Brooks, J. S., & Witherspoon-Arnold, N. (Eds.). (2013). *Antiracist school leadership: Toward equity in education for America's students.* Charlotte, NC: Information Age Publishing.

Brown, M. C., & Bartee, R. (2009). *The broken cisterns of African American education: Academic performance and achievement in the post-Brown era.* Charlotte, NC: Information Age Publishing.

Brown, M. C., & Dancy, T. E. (2009). An unsteady march toward equity: The political and educational contexts of African American educational attainment. In M. C. Brown & R. D. Bartee (Eds.), *The broken cisterns of African American education: Academic performance and achievement in the post-Brown era* (pp. 17–42). Charlotte, NC: Information Age Publishing.

Brown, M. C. II, & Freeman. K. (Eds). (2004). *Black colleges: New perspectives on policy and practice.* Westport, CT: Praeger Publishers

Cambron-McCabe, N., & McCarthy, M. (2005). Educating school leaders for social justice. *Educational Policy, 19*(1), 201–222.

Capper, C. A., Theoharis, G., & Sebastian, J. (2006). Toward a framework for preparing leaders for social justice. *Journal of Educational Administration, 44*(3), 209–224.

Dancy (2010). *Managing diversity: (Re)visioning equity on college campuses.* New York, NY: Peter Lang.

Dancy, T. E. (2012). *The brother code: Manhood and masculinity among African American males in college.* Charlotte, North Carolina: Information Age Publishing.

Dancy, T. E., & Horsford, S. D. (2010). Considering the sociocultural context of school and campus communities: Toward culturally proficient leadership across the P–20 pipeline. In S. D. Horsford (Ed.), *New perspectives in educational leadership: exploring social, political, and community contexts and meaning* (pp. 153–172). New York, NY: Peter Lang.

Dantley, M. E., & Tillman, L. C. (2010). Social justice and moral transformative leadership. In C. Marshall & M. Oliva (Eds.), *Leadership for social justice: Making revolutions in education* (2nd ed., pp. 16–30). New York, NY: Allyn & Bacon.

Delgado, R., & Stefancic, J. (Eds.). (1997). *Critical white studies: Looking behind the mirror.* Philadelphia, PA: Temple University Press.

Diamond, B. J., & Moore, M. A. (1995). *Multicultural literacy: Mirroring the reality of the classroom.* White Plains, NY: Longman.

Diop, C. A. (1982). *Civilisation on Barbarie.* Paris, France: Presence Africaine.

Du Bois, W. E. B. (1939). *Black folks, then and now.* New York, NY: Holt.

Du Bois, W. E. B. (1996). *The Oxford WEB Du Bois Reader.* New York, NY: Oxford University Press.

Fenderson, J., Stewart, J., & Baumgartner, K. (2012). Expanding the history of the black studies movement: Some prefatory notes. *Journal of African American Studies, 16*(1), 1–20.

Fischer, R. A. (1971). Ghetto and gown: The birth of Black Studies. *New Perspectives on Black Studies,* 16–27.

Franklin, J. H., & Moss, A. A. (1969). *From slavery to freedom.* New York, NY: Knopf.

Frattura, E. M., & Capper, C. A. (2007). *Leading for social justice: Transforming schools for all learners.* New York, NY: Corwin.

Freidel, F. (1963). *Builders of American institutions: Readings in United States history.* Rand McNally.

Freire, P. (2000). *Pedagogy of the oppressed.* New York, NY: Continuum.

Gates, H. L. (2000). WEB Du Bois and the Encyclopedia Africana, 1909-63. *The ANNALS of the American Academy of Political and Social Science, 568*(1), 203–219.

Gates, H. L., Jr. (2002). *The African-American century: How Black Americans have shaped our country.* New York, NY: Simon and Schuster.

Gates Jr., H. L., & Marable, M. (2000). A Debate on activism in Black Studies. In M. Marable (Ed.), *Dispatches from the ebony tower: Intellectuals confront the African American experience* (pp. 186–191). New York, NY: Columbia University Press.

Gay, G. (2007). Teaching Children of Catastrophe. *Multicultural Education, 15*(2), 55–61.

Gillborn, D. (1990) *'Race', ethnicity and education: Teaching and learning in multi-ethnic schools.* London, UK: Unwin Hyman.

Giroux, H. A. (1998). Critical pedagogy as performative practice: Memories of whiteness. In C. A. Torres & T. R. Mitchell (Eds.), *Sociology of education: Emerging perspectives* (pp. 143–153). Albany: State University of New York Press.

Harris, N., Rothman, D. J., & Thernstrom, S. (Eds.) (1969). *The history of the United States: Source readings, 1600 to the present.* Austin, TX: Holt, Rinehart and Winston.

Jean-Marie, G. (2006). Welcoming the unwelcomed: A social justice imperative of African-American female leaders at Historically Black Colleges and Universities. *Educational Foundations, 20*(1–2), 83–102.

Jean-Marie, G. & Mansfield, K. (2013). Race and racial discrimination in schools: School leaders' courageous conversations. In J. Brooks & N. Arnold, (Eds.)

Educational leadership and racism: Preparation, pedagogy, and practice (pp. 19–35), Charlotte, NC: Information Age.

Jean-Marie, G., & Normore, A. H. (2008). A repository of hope for social justice: Black women leaders at Historically Black Colleges and Universities. In A. H. Normore (Ed). *Leadership for social justice: Promoting equity and excellence through inquiry and reflective practice* (pp. 1–33). Charlotte, NC: Information Age.

Jean-Marie, G., & Normore, A. H. (2010). The impact of relational leadership, social justice, and spirituality among female secondary school leaders. *International Journal of Urban Educational Leadership*, *4*(1), 22–43.

Jean-Marie, G., Normore, A. H., & Brooks, J. (2009). Leadership for social justice: Preparing 21st century school leaders for a new social order. *Journal of Research on Leadership and Education*, *4*(1), 1–31.

Jennings, J. (2000). Theorizing black studies: The Continuing Role of Community Service in the study of race and class. In M. Marable (Ed.), *Dispatches from the ebony tower: Intellectuals confront the African American experience* (pp. 177–185). New York, NY: Columbia University Press

Karenga, M. (1988). Black Studies and the problematic of paradigm: The philosophical dimension. *Journal of Black Studies*, *18*(4), 395–414.

Karenga, M. (1995). Afrocentricity and multicultural education: Concept, challenge and contribution. In B. P. Bowser (Ed.), *Toward the multicultural university* (pp. 41–61). Westport, CT: Greenwood Publishing Group.

Karenga, M. (2000). Black Studies: A critical reassessment. In M. Marable (Ed.), *Dispatches from the ebony tower: Intellectuals confront the African American experience* (pp. 162–170). New York, NY: Columbia University Press.

Kilson, M. (2000). The Washington and Du Bois leadership paradigms reconsidered. *The ANNALS of the American Academy of Political and Social Science*, *568*(1), 298–313.

King, J. (2004). Culture-centered knowledge: Black Studies, curriculum transformation, and social action. In J. A. Banks & C. A. McGee Banks (Eds.), *Handbook of research on multicultural education* (pp. 349–380). San Francisco, CA: Jossey-Bass.

Ladson-Billings, G., & Tate, W. F. (1995). Toward a critical race theory of education. *Teachers College Record*, *97*, 47–68.

Larson, C. L., & Murtadha, K. (2002). Leadership for social justice. *Yearbook of the National Society for the Study of Education*, *101*(1), 134–161.

Loder, T. L. (2005). African American women principals' reflections on social change, community othermothering, and Chicago public school reform. *Urban Education*, *40*(3), 298–320.

Marable, M. (2000). *Dispatches from the ebony tower: Intellectuals confront the African American experience*. New York, NY: Columbia University Press.

Marshall, C. (2004). Social justice challenges to educational administration. *Educational Administration Quarterly*, *40*(1).

Marshall, C., & Oliva, M. (2010). *Leadership for social justice: Making revolutions in education*. New York, NY: Allyn & Bacon.

Marx, S., & Pennington, J. (2003). Pedagogies of critical race theory: Experimentations with white preservice teachers. *International Journal of Qualitative Studies in Education*, *16*(1), 91–110.

Myrdal, G. (1994). *Black and African-American Studies: American dilemma, the Negro problem and modern democracy* (Vol. 2). Piscataway, NJ: Transaction Publishers.

Murji, K., & Solomos, J. (Eds.). (2005). *Racialization: Studies in theory and practice.* New York, NY: Oxford University Press.

Normore, A. H. (2007). Leadership for learning in the context of social justice: An international perspective. *Journal of Educational Administration, 45*(6).

Normore, A. H. (Ed). (2008). *Leadership for social justice: Promoting equity and excellence through inquiry and reflective practice.* Charlotte, NC: Information Age.

North, C. E. (2008). What is all this talk about "social justice"? Mapping the terrain of education's latest catchphrase. *Teachers College Record, 110*(6), 1182–1206.

Ogbu, J. U. (1992). Understanding cultural diversity and learning. *Educational researcher, 21*(8), 5–14.

Ogbu, J. U. (2003). *Black American students in an affluent suburb: A study of academic disengagement.* New York, NY: Routledge.

Reed, I. (Ed.). (1997). *Multi-America: Essays on cultural wars and cultural peace.* New York, NY: Viking Penguin.

Rogers, I. H. (2012). The black campus movement and the institutionalization of black studies, 1965–1970, *Journal of African American Studies, 16*(1), 21–40.

Rojas, F. (2007). *From black power to Black Studies: How a radical movement became a discipline.* Baltimore, MD: The John Hopkins University Press.

Rojas, F., & Byrd, W. C. (2012). Intellectual change in black studies: Evidence from a cohort analysis. *Journal of African American Studies, 16*(3), 550–573.

Rooks, N. M. (2006). *White money/black power: the surprising history of African American studies and the crisis of race in higher education.* Boston, MA: Beacon.

Sitkoff, H. (1993). *The struggle for Black equality: 1954–1992.* New York, NY: Hill and Wang.

Smith, P. K., & Williams-Boyd, P. (2007). For they are us: "Tools" for a post-Katrina curriculum and community. In S. P. Robinson & M. C. Brown II (Eds.), *The children hurricane Katrina left behind: Schooling context, professional preparation, and community politics* (pp. 141–151). New York, NY: Peter Lang.

Strickland, B. (1975). Black intellectuals in American social science. *Black World, 25,* 4–10.

Tatum, B. D. (2007). *Can we talk about race?: And other conversations in an era of school resegregation.* Boston, MA: Beacon Press.

Theoharis, G. (2007). Social justice educational leaders and resistance: Toward a theory of social justice leadership. *Educational Administration Quarterly, 43*(2), 221–258.

Tillman, L. (2004). Chapter 4: African American principals and the legacy of Brown. *Review of Research in Education, 28,* 101–146.

Turhan, M. (2010). Social justice leadership: implications for roles and responsibilities of school administrators. *Procedia-Social and Behavioral Sciences, 9,* 1357–1361.

Turner, J. (1969). Black Studies: A concept and a plan. *Cornell Chronicle, 1*(2), 1–8.

Vogel, L. R. (2011). Enacting social justice: Perceptions of educational leaders. *Editorial Board, 1*(2), 69–82.

West, C. (1993). *Race matters.* New York, NY: Random House Digital.

White, D. (2012). An independent approach to black studies: The Institute of the Black World (IBW) and its evaluation and support of black studies. *Journal of African American Studies, 16*(1), 70–88.

Williams, P. J. (1991). *The alchemy of race and rights.* Williams, P. J. (1991). The alchemy of race and rights. Cambridge, MA: Harvard University Press.

Williams, S. W. (1993). Black Studies: The evolution of an Afrocentric human science. *Afrocentric Scholar, 2*(1), 69–84.

Williamson-Lott, J. (2003). *Black power on campus: The University of Illinois, 1965–75.* Urbana, IL: University of Illinois Press.

Williamson-Lott, J. (2008). *Radicalizing the ebony tower: Black colleges and the Black freedom struggle in Mississippi.* New York, NY: Teachers College Press.

CHAPTER 4

WHAT SCHOOL LEADERS DO NOT KNOW ABOUT LAW WILL HURT THEM AND OTHERS

The Importance of Quality Legal Counsel and Collaborative Skills

Nancy D. Erbe
California State University–Dominguez Hills

ABSTRACT

This chapter begins with highlights of legal studies' historical perspective on social justice within the United States focusing on constitutional rights and the courts role in enforcing these rights within public schools. Leadership for social justice within legal studies in the United States is primarily conceptualized as constitutional, judicial and statutory, or technical. The American legal system has created a collective concept of social justice through years of rhetoric, dialogue, inquiry, debate, and deliberation—both judicial and legislative. Law and society literature critiques how this "justice" both incor-

Educational Leadership for Ethics and Social Justice, pages 63–74
Copyright © 2014 by Information Age Publishing
All rights of reproduction in any form reserved.

porates and seeks to influence individual and societal practice of values and ethics. This chapter continues by introducing a few key theories, concepts, and debates timely to schooling today: procedural and substantive justice, restorative versus retributive justice (discipline), and the appropriate roles of alternative dispute resolution and litigation. It recommends that all schools employ quality trustworthy legal counsel and staff and all leaders and their team (administrators, counselors, teachers, parents, students, etc.) learn the ethical and effective collaborative skills that show success with bullying and dramatically reduce violent behavior.

A young girl lies seriously injured in a British hospital and captures headlines around the world. The reason? She courageously insisted on her and other girls' right to an education. One of my students at California State University Dominquez Hills was similarly treated—thrown out of her family home and forced to live on the streets because she determined to proceed with obtaining her education. While most Americans may assume that education is readily available to all interested in the United States (hereafter "U.S."), contemporary access in the U.S. did not occur without a fight—a legal fight. The U.S. may be relatively unique in its educational history (Riskin & Westbrook, 1997). A legal case, *Brown versus Board of Education*, was filed and used to confront the segregation of Black and White American schools and demand government respect for the U.S. Constitution, which requires equal protection for all U.S. citizens. Not only was the lawsuit brought and won, but judicial oversight over a period of time ensured compliance (Riskin & Westbrook, 1997). This is not meant to imply that the struggle against segregation is over. This brief history is offered only to introduce the critical role law has played and continues to play in U.S. schools.

The law—constitutional, statutory, and judicial—plays an essential activist and regulatory role in U.S. public schools: prohibiting corporal punishment and legislating special education as a few prominent examples. Because U.S. law is constructed through a continuous process of interpretation, reinterpretation, and argument, a challenge compounded by the complexity of allowing different jurisdictions (city, county, state, federal) to construct different laws, the process of adequately acquainting oneself with the law relevant to a particular set of facts can be daunting. Law schools provide three years of rigorous studies simply to prepare professionals to begin this task.

Various scholars of law and society argue that law's most important role does not require such technical expertise (Ewick & Silbey, 1998). Instead, collectively created law attempts to influence the broader collective with the aspiration and hope that the majority will choose to comply and even adopt its underlying principles and values (Ewick & Silbey, 1998). Whether or not this actually occurs is a shifting area of study and discussion within the social sciences. Their findings, however, matter little when a school leader is faced with the exception: a set of circumstances that may result in school liability if not handled in accord with all relevant laws and the interpretation (precedent) that will be used by decision makers in the courts within that school's jurisdiction(s) (Fine, 2008).

As introduced in the abstract above, now that this chapter has briefly presented a historical perspective on legal studies and U.S. public schools, as well as the perspective of law and society scholars, it will recommend that school leadership employ quality legal counsel to effectively navigate the U.S. legal system with supporting rationale. It then briefly introduces several contemporary legal debates impacting U.S. schools. Last, but arguably most important, it concludes with the strong recommendation that all school leaders and community members study and commit to mastering the collaborative skills that are proving themselves with bullying, reduction of violent behavior and other tough and critical challenge faced by U.S. schools today.

CRITICAL IMPORTANCE OF PARTNERING WITH QUALITY AND TRUSTWORTHY LEGAL COUNSEL

A school's lawyer has so much influence and power that s/he can destroy or potently inhibit a school's success and effectiveness (Fine, 2008). On the other hand, selecting the right lawyer and law firm as counsel and advocate can transform a school's climate and guide it towards a soaring future. In short, the school district or board's choice of lawyers will make an enormous difference in a school. The author writes from her experience as a school lawyer for public schools as well as years consulting with and teaching a wide range and variety of school leaders. Her courses have included Dispute Resolution and Education. The U.S. presidency demonstrates that this is not simply a matter of hiring a lawyer who attended an Ivy League or other school rated highly in popular polls. Former President Bush graduated from Yale, while President Obama graduated from Harvard. Yet their leadership legacies, intelligence, and decision making differ enormously.

Likewise, given the aggressive marketing campaigns that occur within law, schools cannot rely solely on reputation and even political connections. While Washington, DC is renowned for its wealthy lobbyists, and years ago, a school may have benefited from hiring the daughter of a local judge, in current times, such behavior results in ethics complaints filed against conflicts of interests and generates expensive and contentious lawsuits. School leaders are advised to assess their lawyers' leadership qualities for themselves, not once, but every time they seek and receive legal advice. The best of school lawyers truly care about the schools they represent, are highly intelligent and up to date in school and related law, and are also schooled in the collaborative leadership skills and reflective practice described later in this chapter.

Some schools still attempt to function with no, too little or inadequate proactive, or preventative, legal counsel. The author has seen terrified, paranoid schools result. The leadership in these schools predictably cautions their members to do less and less, with long lists of "do nots," in the deluded hope of avoiding lawsuits. Ironically, and too often tragically, these schools fail to adequately provide services like special education that are mandated and prescribed by law. They also fail to intervene with bullying and other behaviors that can result in lawsuits. Some, with unionized employees, fail to adequately document performance issues. All lead to expensive lawsuits. Schools must have adequate and wise legal counsel to avoid lawsuits. Avoiding lawyers, wishful thinking, and inaction will inevitably backfire. On the other hand, employing a lawyer who does not understand her or his impact on a school system and is not educated in collaborative alternatives to litigation and, ideally, collaborative leadership, may also lead to a contentious, adversarial, and punitive school climate that incites and escalates destructive and expensive conflict.

While U.S. lawyers are highly influential in critically important ways and often take on key leadership roles, particularly political, very few have received any leadership education. This is slowly changing as law schools like Ohio State offer leadership classes and law firms recognize the need to give their lawyers such education at the Center for Creative Leadership, as one example. A more common trend in legal education that helps fill this gap and is particularly beneficial to organizations with many stakeholders, or constituencies, like schools, is legal education in collaborative alternatives to litigation: interest-based ("win–win") negotiation and mediation as the most popular processes taught. Ideally, a lawyer has sought and received extensive two-year graduate education in these processes beyond the normal law school's one or two courses or the standard forty-hour training. Alternatively, a lawyer has been mentored in mastering these processes through practice and feedback. Such lawyers are prepared to help schools develop effective dispute resolution and prevention systems through effectively engaging stakeholders (students, parents, teachers, leaders, community members, etc.) early on in relationships and often. Ideally, constructive problem-solving, open and civil communication, and otherwise working together become the school norms at all levels and in every interaction (Erbe, 2011).

If a school cannot find a lawyer equipped with collaborative conflict resolution skills, it can also ask its employees to invest in such education and skill mastery, particularly those involved with special education, student discipline, and other arenas where the school has received complaints or experienced problems (Friend & Cook, 2010). The schools least likely to face lawsuits are those that ask and require all teachers, administrators, and others supervising and interacting with students to have fundamental conflict resolution (integrative negotiation and facilitative mediation) skills. The skills need to be strong enough so that these employees are skilled in assertively intervening when they observe bullying while simultaneously being warm and welcoming to communication and problem-solving with all concerned within their schools. This includes parents (Friend & Cook, 2010).

CONTEMPORARY DEBATES IN LEGAL STUDIES

As a lawyer who has represented U.S. public schools and taught school leadership for the last twenty years, I advise all school leaders to learn as much as they can about school law and its implications and possibilities throughout their careers. Just as lawyers devote themselves to continuing legal education, administrators doing the same are prepared for true legal partnership (Stefkovich, 2006). The adage "two minds are better than one" has real meaning and impact in legal decision making. Dissent is valued, tough questioning plays an important role, and analysis of real-world consequences is complex and far-reaching. A few key modern debates within legal studies and permeating public school conflict resolution are introduced here.

Procedural Versus Substantive Justice

Most current school leaders will be familiar with this distinction between procedural and substantive justice because special education and disciplinary hearings invoke the procedural due process requirements. The average American, in contrast, is more familiar with substantive justice. In lay terms, substantive simply means that the "substance" or letter of all law relevant to the facts of a particular case must be respected. Procedural justice, however, focuses on and adds process requirements. Given the regular conduct of quasi-legal or administrative hearings within U.S. schools, leaders must be adequately educated and guided in both substantive and procedural justice (Fine, 2008). The substance of all relevant law must be respected while also ensuring that all legal proceedings provide due process: adequate opportunity for all concerned to be heard, the opportunity to know and respond to evidence presented against oneself, and so forth (Ewick & Silbey, 1998). While procedural justice requirements may be the same or very similar case to case, depending on the facts of a particular case, different substantive laws and their case law interpretation may need to be considered. Quality legal counsel is necessary for both and particularly important with determining the substantive law relevant case by case (Fine, 2008).

Restorative Versus Retributive Justice/Discipline

Contemporary schools and broader societal legal systems around the world are exploring and testing disciplinary and criminal alternatives to punishment, or retributive justice. The traditional school disciplinary and societal criminal justice systems are often sufficient introduction to retributive justice, particularly given the popularity of retribution, law enforcement, and court proceedings in U.S. media (television and film) and various parts of the world. Thus, this section will focus on introducing its emerging alternative—restorative justice. For those readers relatively unfamiliar with the U.S. criminal justice system, a brief introduction is provided here with reference to help them learn more (Fine, 2008). It is a state-controlled or authority-based system, and crime is viewed as against the state (Fine, 2008) rather than individual persons. Underlying assumptions include that fairness requires the same or equivalent punishment for same or similar crimes and that punishment (like suspension or expulsion) deters repeat crime (Fine, 2008).

While there are many and powerful proponents of punishment as a means of controlling (deterring) crime and other unwanted behavior, several studies show that punishment can actually model, teach, and, ironically, reward violent behavior (through gross neglect of human need and attention to unwanted behavior) (Erbe, 2003). Yet this is not the primary reason for restorative justice's emergence as an alternative to traditional justice. Victims of crime, angry that they were often excluded from legal criminal proceedings, have rallied to demand inclusion and consideration (Van Ness & Heetderks, 2010). Restorative victim–offender mediation offers them the opportunity to meet the person(s) who has harmed them, describe how they have been harmed and otherwise impacted, and ask questions of the offender. Community members harmed, such as family members of a victim or offender or students in a school who have witnessed bullying or other violence, are also welcome to participate in victim offender mediation. Normally, victim–offender mediation occurs when the victim requests it and the offender admits accountability for the alleged crime. The process proceeds with all concerned negotiating and agreeing to the offender's repair of harm (Erbe, 2003).

The results of victim–offender mediation have been impressive with first-time juvenile offenders. Research shows that recidivism, or repeat offending, is reduced by as much as 26% (Nugent, Williams, & Umbreit, 2003). When juvenile offenders who have participated in restorative justice do re-offend, research shows that the subsequent offense is less serious than their first offense (Umbreit, Coates & Vos, 2004). Umbreit, Coates and Vos posit that the reason is the increased empathy that first-time offenders develop as a result of participating in victim–offender mediation.

Schools have become interested in restorative rather than the traditional punitive discipline for obvious reasons (Giroux, 2011). Any school leader knows the risks of losing students entirely after suspension and expulsion, since those punished are often those struggling with education, and increasingly special education students who need more, not less, mentoring, structure, and responsiveness to needs (Osborne & Russo, 2011). While nonviolence policies theoretically serve a purpose in their attempt to protect school communities, they rarely serve to reduce and prevent violence in practice—not unless they are partnered with intensive restorative discipline or another other community-based conflict resolution program (Mackey & Stefkovich, 2010). While these programs do not replace necessary mental health resources, they are important components of the most effective and healthy school leadership, as all serve to permeate and shape a positive proactive problem-solving school culture.

Appropriate Roles of Alternative Dispute Resolution and Litigation

Alternative dispute resolution encompasses mediation (special education and other), administrative hearings, and many other alternatives to litigation that are less formal than litigation (Nolan-Haley, 2011). These alternatives have dramatically grown in use in legal systems within and outside the U.S. since the 1970s in response to court cases overwhelming systems and taking longer for resolution. Academic critique explores the limits of lawsuits as well as their costs (Riskin & Westbrook, 1997). Many schools know these costs intimately and painfully: the damage in reputation as well as enormous outlays in money and school time to legal teams. Equally important is the damage to relationships within and outside the school—damage that makes school leadership more difficult with every lawsuit fought, including lawsuits won.

Mediation as an alternative to litigation and quasi-legal proceedings, or administrative hearings, was formally introduced to and mandated for U.S. schools with special education legislation (Friend & Cook, 2010). School leaders aspiring to minimize costs as much as possible while building a positive (and effective) school climate and community are well advised to become closely acquainted with the facilitative mediation process and masterful with its skills. Alternatives to litigated conflict should be seriously researched, considered, and attempted any time a school would benefit from preserving and strengthening relationships and reputation and minimizing cost (financial, time, etc.). Litigation is only appropriate when it is necessary to stop, expose, and remedy injustice/wrong or create important precedent for the future. To ensure the best possible experience with alternative conflict processes, school leaders must hire masterful mediators and other alternative dispute resolution professionals using similar processes to those described earlier in hiring lawyers. Even more caution and care needs to be exercised with alternative practitioners. Unlike lawyers, who are licensed and can be censured for unethical practice, most U.S. states do not license alternative practitioners. Thus, for example, anyone can promote himself or herself as a mediator. Many lawyers and retired judges do, assuming that their legal and judicial experience is enough to provide alternatives to litigation. They do not realize the collaborative skill mastery needed for stellar alternative dispute resolution (Erbe, 2003).

Collaborative Skills/Processes Reducing School Bullying and Violent Behavior

The collaborative skills introduced above are proving themselves with the school challenge of bullying when practiced consistently and skillfully by school leadership, teachers, and staff—in short, school adults (Erbe, 2011). When practiced together with the student body and mental health resources, dramatic and exemplary reductions in violent student behavior occur (Erbe, 2011).

While introducing and describing these collaborative skills in their entirety requires more than one chapter, the reference list contains several resources for school leadership interested in learning more about these skills for themselves and their schools. I teach in an undergraduate and graduate program that focuses on this skill development and includes curriculum on reducing school violence. For the last pages of this chapter, I will introduce and describe the skills that have shown to be effective in tackling common school leadership challenges (Erbe, 2011). The first is collective negotiation-discussion and buy-in regarding process parameters: school and classroom. Such "no bullying" norms demonstrated success in Norway's schools, as one example, in reducing and even eliminating school bullying (Erbe, 2003). In one international study, these rules reduced bullying behavior by fifty percent or more in schools around the world, including those in Norway, England, Germany, and the United States. This same study described the keys to this success as positive, warm, engaged adult role model leaders consistently asserting and enforcing rules and non-hostile consequences (Erbe, 2003).

Similarly dramatic results in reduction of violent behavior occurred in my experience when I designed a treatment program for repeat violent offenders, ages 10–18, that integrated all aspects of facilitative mediation, including ground rules like those introduced above (Erbe, 2011). This project began with a full-day retreat in which youth offenders and all adults (staff, counselors, teachers, social workers, etc.) comprehensively identified and detailed problematic behavior and discussed, negotiated, and agreed to collective rules and the consequences for breaching the rules. At the end of the day, all were united in their understanding and approach to violent and other problematic behavior. In the days after the retreat, daily documented problem behavior reduced to less than fifty percent of what was documented before the retreat. As essential to this approach as negotiated "ground rules" and consequences, was, as in the study described above, their consistent assertion by positive concerned engaged adult role models—in short, school leadership. Rand researchers, the Los Angeles County Human Relations Commission, and I have proposed the need for longitudinal study of such models.

I recommend a similar approach to building nonviolent classrooms and schools. Of course, teachers and school leaders must be prepared to be the positive, concerned, engaged role models that are needed for this approach to succeed. A good place to start with developing critical capacity is what mediation calls impartiality, or learning to treat all concerned with equivalence and fairness. This must be done to the satisfaction of all observing a particular process. I have previously published reflective questions with *Teaching Tolerance,* a project of Southern Poverty Law Center—"a place for educators to find thought provoking news, conversation and support for those who care about equal opportunity and respect for differences in schools" (http://www.tolerance.org/). My questions are intended to help all teachers and school leaders scrutinize their approach and see themselves as their students and others in their school community see them (Erbe, 2011). Important questions to ask include: Do students perceive me as treating all equally? Welcoming and encouraging everyone's participation? Suspending judgment? Carefully listening for understanding?

Reframing is another mediation skill that can serve school leaders. Mediation literature refers to reframing as detoxifying or laundering language (Erbe, 2003). Related is what negotiation and mediation literature refers to as generous "tit for tat," or forgiveness math (Erbe, 2011). Rather than react "tit for tat" with hostile language or behavior, the responder (school leader) is coached not to react in kind and to model higher ground through extending an olive branch, or opportunity to cooperate for mutual gain. With hostile or nasty language, the listener leader is taught how to listen for deep understanding of the human need being expressed. Reframing is stating what has been heard to emphasize the human need expressed in positive, productive language. Naturally, in the heat and fire of hostile conflict, especially personal attack, skillful listening and paraphrasing take much practice. A school leader who is beginning to learn such skills must be encouraged. Small efforts can reap great results. Any progress in collaborative conflict and communication skill development will bear fruit (Erbe, 2011). Appreciative mentoring and the research documenting its effectiveness in encouraging the best of students is one important example (Erbe, 2011). Research showing that a percentage of gifted students are able to embrace schooling and find the resilience to survive and thrive despite abuse and neglect in their homes is remarkable. School leaders who warmly greet and acknowledge students, who show interest in their wellbeing, and who are available to listen and problem-solve can make enormous difference in students' lives even while struggling to learn and master collaborative and other leadership skills.

Many schools are also championing conflict resolution and peer mediation programs for students (Bodine, Crawford, & Schrumpf, 2002) like the no violence curriculum co-authored by Erbe and funded by the U.S. Department of Justice (Erbe, Singleton, & Williams, 1996). At their best, they are quite popular with students and helpful to school conflict resolution and culture. These student conflict resolution programs are not a substitute, however, for school adults exercising the leadership and skills introduced in this chapter (Giroux, 2011). Santee High School in Los Angeles is a case study of the best of student conflict resolution combined with requisite school leadership (Erbe, 2011). Upon opening in 2006, it experienced a violent eruption that lasted two days and resulted in 34 arrests. Principal Carbino took immediate, comprehensive, and integrated action that worked. He then analyzed his success, attributing funding to hire generous mental health counseling as his most important step. He also consulted with neighboring businesses and communities as well as parents, staff, and students—not just once but repeatedly—eventually negotiating a school safe zone. Consequently, the students formed an overseeing and student-run Peace Council for their school. Violence became virtually nonexistent.

I have taught students from about 80 different countries and many diverse ethnic groups. One student did a fascinating and insightful training project where he observed lack of empathy between staff working with youth from their same and his own ethnic group. In my experience as a lawyer representing public schools, I have observed that the adults working within schools can likewise be each other's worst enemy—fighting each other rather than working together in service to their students. If a school leader is challenged by this type of adult and staff contention, the first steps towards building a culture of peace within the school must begin with the adults in conflict. An approach similar to what has been described as dramatically reducing student bullying and violent behavior can also be effective with adults. The school leader might be well advised to hire professional and masterful mediators to assist with this tough transformational process. Investing in long-term staff skill training and coaching has been recommended earlier in the chapter and is critical with entrenched, systemic conflict.

I have been intimately involved in such change process. The most troubling characteristic I have observed in school after school is school leadership's denial of tensions that are patently evident to an outside observer. School leaders repeatedly act as public relations mascots for their schools rather than leaders who are actively aware of and prepared to address the tensions within and between youth and adults. Having taught some of the community harmed by the horrific Columbine school tragedy in Colorado, I fear that too many school leaders are simply ignoring signs, putting reputation and appearances before human wellbeing and needs, and otherwise avoiding the leadership that their schools critically need. Fortunately, conflict resolution skill training can build the confidence that optimally results in leaders capable of greater honesty when faced with troubling and challenging signs (Erbe, 2003).

CONCLUSION

School leaders in the U.S. must be educated in legal studies relevant to schools and prepare to partner with quality trustworthy lawyers who are up-to-date experts in ever-changing school law and devoted to the best interests of the school(s) they represent. One sign of such expertise today is friendly familiarity with the many alternatives to litigation, particularly the masterful mediation that will save on legal costs, preserve school reputation, and, most importantly, strengthen the school's myriad relationships. School leadership is well advised to further educate itself in how victim–offender mediation is proving effective with restorative school discipline and how the collaborative skills that constitute effective mediation are also useful in eradicating school bullying and reducing; even eliminating, violent behavior

REFERENCES

Bodine, R., Crawford, D., & Schrumpf, F. (2002). *Creating the peaceable school.* Champaign, IL: Research Press.

Erbe, N. (2003). *Holding these truths: Empowerment and recognition in action (Interactive Case Study Curriculum for Multicultural Dispute Resolution).* Berkeley, CA: Berkeley Public Policy Press.

Erbe, N. (2011). *Negotiation alchemy: Global skills inspiring and transforming diverging worlds.* Berkeley, CA: Berkeley Public Policy Press.

Erbe, N., Singleton, L., & Williams, L. (1996). *Initiating "no violence" education for students and teachers.* Boulder, CO: Safeguard Law-Related Education Program.

Ewick, P., & Silbey, S. (1998). *The common place of law.* Chicago, IL: University of Chicago Press.

Fine, T. (2008). *American legal systems: a resource and reference guide.* Dayton, OH: Lexis-Nexus.

Friend, M., & Cook, L. (2010). *Interactions: Collaboration skills for school professionals.* Boston, MA: Pearson Education, Inc.

Giroux, H. (2011). *On critical pedagogy.* New York, NY: Bloomsbury Academic.

Mackey, H., & Stefkovich, J. (2010). Zero-tolerance policies and administrative decisionmaking: The case for restorative justice based school discipline reform. In A. Normore (Ed.), *Global perspectives on educational leadership reform:*

the development and preparation of leaders of learning and learners of leadership (pp. 243–262). Bingley, West Yorkshire, UK: Emerald Group Publishing.

Nolan-Haley, J. (2011). *Alternative dispute resolution in a nutshell.* St. Paul, MN: West Publishing.

Nugent, W., Williams, R,., & Umbreit, M. (2003). Participating in victim-offender mediation and the prevalence and severity of subsequent delinquent behavior: A meta-analysis. *Utah Law Review, 1,* 137–165.

Osborne, A., & Russo, C. (2011). Discrimination under section 504 and the Americans with disabilities act. In A. Normore (Ed.), *Leadership in education, corrections, and law enforcement: a commitment to ethics, equity and excellence* (pp. 209–228). Bingley, West Yorkshire, UK: Emerald Group Publishing.

Riskin, L., & Westbrook, J. (1997). *Dispute resolution and lawyers.* St. Paul, MN: West Publishing.

Stefkovich, J. (2006). *Best interests of the student.* London: Routledge.

Umbreit, M., Coates, R., & Vos, B. (2004). The impact of victim offender mediation: Two decades of research. In P. Kratchoski (Ed.) *Correctional counseling and treatment* (pp. 86–99). Long Grove, IL: Waveland Press.

Van Ness, D., & Heetderks, K. (2010). *Restoring justice.* New Providence, NJ: Matthew Bender.

CHAPTER 5

BENDING TOWARD JUSTICE?

What Public Policy Can Tell Us about Leadership for Social Justice

Genevieve Siegel-Hawley

ABSTRACT

In a society experiencing rapid demographic transformation and rising inequality, schools play a fundamental role in fostering social and racial justice, economic mobility, and healthy democratic participation. Since *Brown v. Board of Education*, public policy—defined generally as government laws, actions, regulations, or funding priorities—has dramatically influenced the pursuit of equity and access within the U.S. educational system. This chapter explores the arc of education policy in the aftermath of *Brown* and illuminates key tensions that have shaped its evolution. Understanding how this macrolevel history should influence contemporary policy efforts to ensure equity in schools is a critical component of leading for social justice. The chapter closes with recommendations for school leadership preparation and practice.

Educational Leadership for Ethics and Social Justice, pages 75–92
Copyright © 2014 by Information Age Publishing
All rights of reproduction in any form reserved.

GROWING DIVERSITY, INCREASING STRATIFICATION—
AND WHY IT MATTERS

On May 17, 2012, the 58th anniversary of the landmark *Brown v. Board of Education* ruling, newspapers across the country reported on a major demographic milestone. For the first time in the history of the United States, White infants accounted for just under half of the newly born population. A number of states and major metropolitan areas, including California, Texas, Hawaii, New Mexico, and Washington, DC, had already passed this marker (Morello & Mellnick, 2012; Tavernise, 2012). Indeed, in the nearly sixty years since the landmark *Brown* decision, the U.S. has grown rapidly more diverse.

The nation's school enrollment also reflects the tremendous shift towards a society with no clear racial majority. Figures indicate that White students account for just 52% of first graders in the U.S. (Orfield, Kucsera & Siegel-Hawley, 2012). Enrollment statistics vary significantly by region, as the Midwest and Northeast will likely continue to report substantial White majorities for some time, while the South and the West report much more significant changes. In the West, for example, less than two-fifths of first-graders are White (Orfield et al., 2012).

At the same time, school segregation levels remain very high for Black and Latino students (Frankenberg & Orfield, 2012; Heilig & Holme, 2013; Orfield et al., 2012; Reardon, Grewal, Kalogrides, & Greenberg, 2012). Roughly two out of every five Black and Latino students attend intensely segregated schools (where Whites make up 0–10% of the enrollment) across the nation, and 14% and 15% of Latino and Black students, respectively, attend "apartheid" schools (Orfield et al., 2012), where Whites account for 1% or less of the enrollment. Similar figures are much more severe in the country's largest metropolitan areas (Orfield et al., 2012). Racially isolated schools also continue to closely overlap with schools of concentrated poverty. Indeed, nine times out of ten, schools that are intensely segregated by race also serve very high proportions of students qualifying for free and reduced priced lunch (Orfield & Lee, 2005). Black and Latino students are more than three times as likely Whites to be in high poverty schools and twelve times as likely to be in schools where nearly all students are low-income (Orfield & Lee, 2005).

A growing body of research documents increasing stratification in our broader society. Over the past three decades, growth in the U.S. economy has not coincided with upward social mobility for all segments of the population. Instead, wealth and advantage has become increasingly concentrated in the upper strata of society (Duncan & Murname, 2011). And at a time when postsecondary education has become ever more critical to success, the educational attainment gap between wealthy and poor students has widened

(Baily & Dynarski, 2011). Educational opportunity and achievement gaps also abound (Flores, 2007; Ladson-Billings, 2006; Reardon, 2011).

Increasing stratification amid the growing diversity of the nation's school enrollment has serious implications for student trajectories. More than six decades' worth of social science research shows clear benefits for students of all races attending integrated schools, as well as serious harms for those enrolling in racially and economically isolated ones (Linn & Welner, 2007; Orfield, Frankenberg, & Garces, 2008; Mickelson, Bottia, & Lambert, 2013). With few exceptions, schools segregated by both race and poverty are linked to fewer experienced teachers, higher levels of teacher and staff turnover, less challenging and engaging curricula, and lower graduation rates than other settings (Clotfelter, Ladd & Vigdor, 2006; Palardy, 2013; Rumberger & Palardy, 2005). Well-designed and integrated schools, on the other hand, are associated with better educational outcomes, reduced levels of stereotyping and prejudice, more friendships across racial lines, strong social networks, and, for black students, higher earning potential and health benefits later in life (Braddock, 2009; Johnson, 2011). Moreover, integrated K–12 settings tend to have perpetuating effects, prompting students to seek out more integrated colleges, neighborhoods, and workplaces later in life (Wells & Crain, 1994).

Many of the benefits described above speak to a broad reading of the goals of public schooling in the U.S. Though policy efforts in recent decades have highlighted the academic outcomes of students, often measured narrowly by test scores (Darling Hammond, 2010), crucial social and civic functions of education have been widely recognized in the past (Rothstein, Jacobsen, & Wilder, 2008). Fundamentally, in a nation still struggling mightily to make good on the promise of *Brown*, how future policies respond to the urgent need for more just and equitable educational systems is of paramount concern. Understanding our past efforts to address deeply rooted inequalities—as well as the significant shifts that have occurred in recent decades—is a first step in moving forward.

ARC OF EDUCATION POLICY SINCE BROWN

The 1954 *Brown* decision outlawing state-sponsored segregation in American public schools helped ignite the modern Civil Rights era (McAlpine, Tidwell & Jackson, 1988). It also ushered in sweeping new social and educational policies that emphasized redistributive justice and equity (Bok, 1992). President Lyndon Johnson's Great Society and War on Poverty, which included programs like Project Head Start, in addition to the Civil Rights Act (1964), the Voting Rights Act (1965), the creation of the Equal Opportunity Employment Commission (1965), the Elementary and Secondary

Education Act (1965), the Fair Housing Act (1968) and the Medicare and Medicaid Amendments to the Social Security Act (1965), all grew out of the same era.

The underlying principles guiding many of the education-related policies in the 1960s emphasized schools as instruments of social mobility and opportunity (Kantor & Lowe, 2013). The idea was not new. An 1848 report by the great Horace Mann, the Secretary of the State Board of Education in Massachusetts, famously reads: "Education then, beyond all other devices of human origin, is a great equalizer of the conditions of men,—the balance wheel of the social machinery" (p. 1). What was novel, however, was the federal government's willingness to embrace a broad array of programs specifically designed to promote equity and access to quality schooling (Orfield, 1999). Prior to the Great Society and War on Poverty, the New Deal helped cement the idea that the U.S. government could and should be responsible for ensuring the wellbeing of its citizens. Yet the plethora of New Deal programs did not emphasize education in a fundamental way, focusing instead on jobs and income (Kantor & Lowe, 2013). By contrast, the Johnson administration's policy initiatives zeroed in on providing preschool education for low-income children and families, extra funding for schools with high concentrations of disadvantaged students, as well as an expansion of post-secondary scholarships and loans—all of which demonstrated a commitment to opening up and equalizing the K–16 educational pipeline. And since many of the programs emphasized the need for extra resources or opportunities for traditionally underserved groups, they upheld a central tenet of justice: that goods be distributed equally, unless an unequal distribution would benefit the disadvantaged (Rawls, 1971).

The Struggle for Racial Justice and School Desegregation Efforts

It is profoundly important to understand that the initiatives linked to the Great Society and War on Poverty were developed alongside the effort to dismantle de jure segregation in 17 southern and border states. Indeed, the struggle for racial justice overlapped with and influenced policies designed to equalize social and educational conditions more generally. In terms of school desegregation, several crucial mechanisms, and one key legal decision, helped overcome the decade-long "massive resistance" to *Brown* (Clotfelter, 2004). Title VI of the Civil Rights Act of 1964 allows the government to withdraw federal funding if a public entity is found to be discriminating on the basis of race. Government officials persuaded numerous recalcitrant school districts across the south to quickly desegregate by threatening to halt the flow of federal dollars to their school systems (Orfield, 1969). In

1968, the U.S. Supreme Court also stepped in clarify what a desegregated school system actually looked like, introducing a set of guidelines for eliminating dual educational programs (*Green v. New Kent County*, 1968). The combination of legislative and judicial force, accompanied by strategic executive efforts, helped the South quickly become the most integrated region of the country for Black students (Le, 2010; Orfield, 1978).

Concerted federal action to put school desegregation into effect was only sustained for a short period of time before being radically curtailed. Three years after handing down an important decision allowing school districts to use transportation to break the link between segregated schools and housing, a reconfigured Supreme Court exempted most suburbs from school desegregation obligations (Irons, 2002; *Milliken v. Bradley*, 1974). As noted civil rights scholar Gary Orfield has remarked, "Urban school desegregation became the only substantial effort to break the self-perpetuating nature of metropolitan segregation in the 20th century and this policy has been fiercely resisted from the outset and critically limited within three years of the first favorable Supreme Court decision in 1971" (2010, p. 3). Saving the suburbs, along with a return to "neighborhood schools," was a key element of Nixon's second election platform, and many of the executive actions and policies enacted under his tenure reflected that commitment (Lassiter, 2007; Ryan, 2010). Yet despite these significant setbacks, many of the gains made during the period of most active enforcement of the law were preserved well into the 1980s (Orfield & Eaton, 1996).

Student assignment policies emphasizing desegregation helped ensure that many schools roughly reflected overall district racial demographics. But policies supporting second-generation segregation, or the "racially correlated allocation of educational opportunities within schools" (Mickelson, 2001, p. 5), typically accomplished through tracking, began to take root (Oakes, 2010). As the nation wrestled with overturning centuries-long structures of oppression and discrimination, one modest piece of legislation, the Emergency School Aid Act (ESAA) of 1972, offered federal funds to newly desegregated districts supporting the development of inclusive curricula, the building of community support for desegregation, and the training of faculty for diversity (Hodges, 2011; Orfield, 1978). Notably, one of the ESAA funding guidelines required districts to show evidence that they had eliminated second-generation segregation issues (Hodges, 2011). Yet within-school inequities endured, in part because government enforcement of desegregation failed to wholeheartedly sustain the urgent need for training on best practices for teaching and leading in newly diverse schools (Banks & Banks, 2004; Orfield, 2009). Nor did government officials initiate or maintain comprehensive work to eliminate harmful patterns of second-generation segregation, even as federal data began to systematically document its existence (U.S. Department of Education, 1968–2009).

Widening Educational Access for More Historically Excluded Groups in the 1970s

The push to expand access to equal educational opportunities for historically marginalized students in many ways continued through the late 1960s and the 1970s (Minow, 2010). The federal government passed the Bilingual Education Act (1968), the Individuals with Disabilities Education Act (1974), and the Americans with Disabilities Act (1975). Each helped establish influential federal and legal mandates related to the education of language minority students and students with disabilities. Gender inequities were also addressed through Title IX, which outlawed discrimination on the basis of sex in any program receiving federal funding. In conjunction with federal efforts recognizing education as a human and civil right available to all groups, support for multicultural education also grew (Bank & Banks, 2004; Grant & Sleeter, 2011). Such efforts largely remained under the purview of schools, however, with little to no formal government support.

Shift from Equity and Access to Standards and Accountability

In 1983, the publication of a searing government report entitled *A Nation at Risk* helped dramatically alter the federal approach to education policies. Using Cold War imagery and alarmist language, the report sounded a call for higher educational standards and achievement in the face of what it presented as evidence of American decline. *A Nation at Risk* became a touchstone for an era of educational policy that continues today (Mehta, 2013). Reforms that flowed from the report included standards and accountability, high-stakes testing, and the explosion of school choice options like charter schools (Petrovich & Wells, 2005; Ravitch, 2010).

The push for higher standards and more accountability culminated in the bipartisan No Child Left Behind Act (NCLB) of 2001, which dramatically escalated the federal role in education. The act required that all groups of students reach proficiency in key subjects by the year 2014 (see Normore & Brooks, 2012). As that deadline rapidly approaches, stalled efforts to reauthorize NCLB (which has reverted back to its original moniker, the Elementary and Secondary Education Act) in a divided Congress has prompted the Obama administration to issue waivers to states meeting certain criteria. Like the administration's other major educational initiative, Race to the Top, receipt of waivers and federal dollars has been attached to states' willingness to adopt the policies supported by the U.S. Department of Education (Ayers & Owen, 2012; Normore & Brooks, 2012). Those policies, which emphasize accountability, teacher performance and evaluation, charter schools, and school turnarounds, have largely been a continuation of the education platforms of the previous three administrations (Carter & Welner, 2013).

Two Eras of Education Policy: Key Distinctions and Tensions

In contrast to the ideological underpinnings of the preceding era, the new reforms have been fueled by a desire to prepare future workers to compete in a global economy and demonstrate faith in market-based solutions to educational problems. As the terms of the debate shifted, a new paradigm emerged, one that held schools largely responsible for eliminating broad societal inequalities. While the push for equity and access during the 1960s and '70s placed a good deal of emphasis on leveling the educational playing field for all students, the period was also characterized by important policies and laws designed to counteract discrimination in jobs and housing and to strengthen the social safety net (though efforts in the latter direction were not as wide-ranging as those that characterized the New Deal) (Kantor & Lowe, 2013). Since the advent of the Reagan administration, however, weakened enforcement of civil rights laws and dramatic cuts in welfare, housing, job training and public spending in general have coincided with sharply rising inequality (Duncan & Murname, 2011; Orfield & Ashikanze, 1999). But given the prevailing educational paradigm, many Americans today expect improved academic achievement—largely measured by test results—to solve an economic and social crisis that reaches far beyond the confines of the schoolyard.

The two dominant education policy frameworks of the past half-century stem from very different analyses of the root causes of inequitable educational outcomes in the United States. One diagnosis viewed historical discrimination, segregation, and intergenerational poverty as fundamental issues, while the other focused on low expectations for students, poor educational management, burdensome bureaucracies and teachers' unions, and inadequate public/private sector competition to stimulate school improvement. It stands to reason, then, that the two have prescribed widely varying policy solutions to the problem. The ongoing tension between these approaches is crystallized in the current debate pitting those who favor a "bigger, broader, bolder" approach to education reform against those who support the accountability and competition principles guiding NCLB and market-based reform (Broader, bolder approach, 2009; Noguera, 2011).

The Bold Approach highlights comprehensive, wraparound services that seek to alleviate the role that socioeconomic status plays in educational opportunity and achievement outcomes. One of the more widely cited examples is the Harlem Children's Zone, which offers low-income families "cradle to career" support like Baby College (training for expecting and new parents), preschool, and K–12 settings (Tough, 2008). As important as these efforts are, though, they fail to take into account the important influence that the context and/or composition of school enrollment has on student achievement (Palardy, 2013). The Bigger, Broader, Bolder Approach thus illuminates an important tension in policy efforts: whether reform should be focused on improving educational conditions in disadvantaged schools and communities (in place) or providing students with an opportunity to relocate to alternative setting (mobility) (Hughes, 2002).

Other tensions are embedded within the two policy eras, including an emphasis on the individual versus collective good (Hoschild & Scrovenick, 2003) and the political question of whether education should primarily come under the purview of the federal, state, or local government (Mehta, 2013). What has typically not been questioned is public support for a strong government role in education (Hocschild & Scrovenick, 2003; Tyack & Cuban, 1995). Disputes regarding the most effective level—whether it is federal, state, or local—of government involvement remain, but nearly all Americans view public education as essential social policy and worth backing with high levels of spending (Hoschild & Scrovenick, 2003). Given that education has been at the center of our social welfare efforts since Johnson's Great Society, it is perhaps not surprising that our citizenry feels this way. Yet despite general consensus regarding the importance of government support, the arc of education policy outlined here underscores the considerable and heated debates around best approaches to reform.

OUTCOMES LINKED TO TWO ERAS
OF EDUCATION POLICY

To evaluate the impact of the two very different streams of policy that have dominated our educational system in the aftermath of *Brown*, a summary overview of related outcomes is in order. The National Assessment of Educational Progress (NAEP) affords a longitudinal, national look at student achievement since the 1970s (in contrast to the varied tests employed at the state level). Mapping the historical sweep of policy interventions discussed above onto the trend lines, some patterns begin to emerge. First, NAEP data covering what was arguably the height of NCLB implementation, between the years 2004 and 2008, did not show a significant narrowing of the racial achievement gap (Dillon, 2009; Lee, 2007). Updated data from 2012 indicate that stubborn Black–White gaps remained, with little to no progress in closing them among 13- and 17-year-olds since 2008 (National Center for Education Statistics, 2013). Second, while the achievement gap between

White students and Black and Latino students has gradually lessened over time, it closed most dramatically during the time period associated with federal efforts to expand access and equity in education and in other areas of society. Indeed, in a groundbreaking 2008 book on the achievement gap, *Steady Gains and Stalled Progress* (Magnuson & Waldfogel, 2008), scholars cited a host of factors contributing to its persistence over the past few decades. Chief among these were rising economic and social inequality in the 1980s and 1990s, which cyclically affected parent education levels (known to be very influential in predicting a child's academic success), along with waning commitment to reform policies associated with the Civil Rights movement (Magnuson & Waldfogel, 2008).

More recently, a compilation of cutting-edge research has highlighted the growing influence of economic inequality on educational achievement and outcomes. Prominent scholars convened across disciplines to examine contemporary trends in income inequality, rapidly shifting labor markets, and educational equity and access. Studies associated with this project found that the rising inequality associated with the current policy era is linked to stark income-based gaps in child development, early skills, schools, educational attainment, expectations, family resources, neighborhood contexts, and job opportunities (Duncan & Murnane, 2011). Inequities in each of these dimensions have clear implications for the life chances of children in poverty.

In the face of widely varying policy prescriptions for educational opportunity and achievement gaps, alongside mounting evidence that the approaches of the previous era did more to narrow those gaps, renewed attention to the lessons from the 1960s and 1970s is crucial. Importantly, changing demographic, political, and legal forces in many schools and districts offer leaders for social justice a chance to revisit ideas from the earlier era in an effort to address persistent challenges related to educational inequality. Lacking strong leadership and guidance in this direction from the federal government, it becomes increasingly important for educational leaders at lower levels—in districts and in schools—to understand how they can promote greater equity and access within their own spheres of influence.

HOW EDUCATIONAL LEADERSHIP FOR SOCIAL JUSTICE CAN INFLUENCE EQUITY AND ACCESS

The following section discusses efforts to promote social justice within districts and schools. Leaders in each of these arenas exercise considerable authority over the structure and delivery of schooling, and these dimensions in turn impact students' access to equitable opportunities. Indeed, educational leaders armed with knowledge of the impact of past and present policy efforts, together with a firm grounding in the principles of social justice, have the capacity to exert a great deal of influence on educational processes in their local communities (Marshall & Young, 2006).

District-Level Efforts

At the district level, the leadership of Montgomery County, Maryland's former superintendent, along with the actions of his administration, provides a strong example of efforts to reduce inequities under the current educational paradigm.

Confronted with stark learning gaps and a divided district with clearly demarcated zones of high and low opportunity, Montgomery's superintendent emphasized "twin imperatives"—moral and economic—for the school system (Childress, Doyle& Thomas, 2009). His straightforward and open style of communication helped make the case that doing what was best for *all* children was not only just and right but critically important to the county's economic future (Childress et al., 2009). With strong, guiding principles, the district initiated a series of data-driven policies designed to promote equity and access. These included extensive teacher development and support, extra per-pupil funding for schools located in the low-opportunity area of the county, accompanied by full-day kindergartens and reduced class sizes, as well as more equitable guidelines for entrance into advanced placement and honors courses (Childress et al., 2009).

Interestingly, in terms of student outcomes, the example of Montgomery County showcases the aforementioned tension between policy efforts designed to reach students "in place" versus those geared towards giving students the ability to move to higher-opportunity environments. Most of the superintendent's new educational initiatives focused on improving conditions for students in racially and linguistically isolated, higher poverty areas of the district. However, a nationally recognized, inclusionary housing policy in Montgomery County, which sets aside a portion of any new development for low-income families, offers a pathway for mobility to low-poverty schools. Recent research comparing the two approaches found that low-income students benefiting from the housing policy (e.g., enrolling in low poverty schools) performed better on state math, and to a lesser extent, reading, tests than students enrolling in the schools receiving extra per-pupil funding (Schwartz, 2010). Such findings underscore the additional need for district-level social justice leadership around issues influencing the racial and economic makeup of schools, policies like student assignment and redrawing school attendance boundaries.

Underlying circumstances in Montgomery County are not altogether unlike those in other large, suburban districts throughout the country (see, e.g., Frankenberg & Orfield, 2012). The policies that have taken root there, however, are groundbreaking and worthy of careful consideration. If district leaders around the country choose to follow suit, principals and teachers must be willing partners in and advocates for efforts to lead for social justice.

School-Level Efforts

At the level of the individual school, a number of lessons from the earlier educational policy paradigm can help promote more equitable educational and social outcomes for all students. Many stem from an influential theory introduced by Harvard psychologist Gordon Allport in 1954. Allport's "intergroup contact theory" outlined the institutional conditions necessary to reduce prejudice between different groups. He hypothesized that institutions must provide strong leadership visibly supportive of diversity, ensure that all group members are treated equally, and facilitate cooperation and shared goals among members of different groups (Allport, 1954). In the six decades since the theory was introduced, research from around the world has demonstrated again and again that those conditions are, in fact, linked to reduced prejudice and improved intergroup relationships (Pettigrew, 2008; Pettigrew & Tropp, 2006).

Ethical Leadership

As school enrollments in many districts rapidly undergo change, the importance of strong, ethical leadership around issues of equity and diversity becomes ever more imperative. Extensive research documents the importance of leadership that models responsive and appropriate behavior in diverse settings (Hawley, 2007a; Pettigrew & Tropp, 2006; Starratt, 2004). Bringing together all members of the school community, including teachers, staff, students and parents, to identify barriers to the success of the school is an important first step (Hawley, 2007b). Once equitable school organizational structures are in place, administrators are largely responsible for implementation and oversight. Such structures might involve policies for assigning students to mixed ability classrooms (i.e., detracking), student discipline, handling perceived discrimination and interracial conflicts, implementing professional development focused on diversity, and taking action to reinforce the idea that working and learning with a diverse group of people is valuable and important (Banks, Cookson, Gay, Hawley, & Irvine, 2001; Skyrla, McKenzie, & Schuerich, 2008). When executing each of these policies, administrators and educators should be aware of the impact of verbal and nonverbal communication related to issues of diversity (Perry, 2008), taking steps to model evenhanded concern for all parties.

Teacher Leadership

Another key equity policy relates to the assignment of teachers. In many schools, the most experienced teachers instruct higher-level courses, leaving newer instructors to teach classes with lower-achieving students (Kalgorides, Loeb, & Beteille, 2012). The reverse should be true if school leaders are committed to social justice. Institutionalizing "distributed leadership for social justice"—or the idea that all teachers and staff, along with school leaders, engage in and are responsible for efforts to increase educational access and opportunity (Brooks, Jean-Marie, Normore, & Hodgins, 2007) can help ensure widespread buy-in around the reassignment of teachers, among other equity-oriented policies.

Inclusive School Structures

Inclusive school structures also extend to the classroom. Teachers obviously play a central role in developing students' academic and social skills. They, like administrators, must serve as role models attuned to the benefits of diversity (Hawley, 2007a). To that end, better training for teachers working in racially and economically diverse classrooms is a widely acknowledged necessity (Au, 2009; Ladson-Billings, 1994; Pollock, 2008). The training can help raise awareness about institutional and personal biases and lay the foundation for continuously seeking out information and resources related to diversity.

Culturally Responsive Leadership

Leadership and instruction that uses the daily experiences of students to bridge the gap between prior knowledge and new content is often cited as an effective strategy in diverse schools and classrooms (Horsford, 2010; Moll, 1992; Sailor, 2002). Ensuring that instructional materials and curriculum reflect the contributions of a wide range of groups is also important (Grant & Sleeter, 2011). And, in keeping with Allport's theory, placing students in flexible, heterogeneous, and cooperative learning groups can help improve academic and social outcomes (Slavin, 1995; Cooper & Slavin, 2001).

In short, acknowledging and taking actions to further the idea that diversity, equity, access, and excellence are interrelated and vital must become a fundamental premise of leading and teaching for social justice. Constant efforts to communicate about and evaluate the effectiveness of practices that impact equitable student outcomes are essential for growth and improvement. Fundamentally, educational leaders in school and districts play a key role in interpreting and implementing higher-level initiatives, and they should strive to do so in a manner that builds upon what social science tells us about the two dominant eras of education policy in the past half-century.

RECOMMENDATIONS FOR LEADERSHIP PREPARATION

The rapid pace of demographic transition and deepening patterns of segregation and inequality, along with a policy framework that largely fails to identify these factors as critical to student outcomes, is indicative of the challenges and possibilities confronting the next generation of school leaders. Many of the key conditions for ensuring social justice within schools and districts relate to a clear understanding of ongoing inequities in society at large. Leaders need a solid grounding in overarching history and policy efforts associated with schools and other social institutions in order to best identify systematic inequalities in their own contexts.

As such, educational leadership preparation for social justice should foster deep knowledge of the societal contexts within which schools are embedded, together with explicit connections to leaders' professional and personal experiences. Multidisciplinary coursework that promotes an understanding of the historical, political, economic, legal, social, and demographic contexts surrounding schools, in addition to classes aimed at preparing leaders for the instructional and day-to-day management of schools, is absolutely crucial. Within this framework, teaching strategies (e.g., written reflections, intercultural storytelling) that help prospective leaders link their own life experiences to the new information they are encountering is essential to fostering shifts in beliefs and practices (Oliva & Anderson, 2006; Tanaka, 2007). Finally, a fundamental commitment to social justice should be a common thread running through a school leadership program's faculty research interests, curriculum, and teaching and should also drive a commitment to fostering both a diverse student body and faculty (Oliva & Anderson, 2006).

As renowned educational scholar William Ayers has noted, "We live in a time when the assault on disadvantaged communities is particularly harsh and at the same time gallingly obfuscated" (2006, p. 87). Schools and those who work within them play a critical role in helping to make societies more just. It stands to reason, then, that educational leaders and teachers should be at the forefront of a push to revisit the lessons of a former era in order to broaden the focus of our current policy framework. The educational and life trajectories of future generations—and the rising racial majority—depend upon our collective ability to undertake far more serious and widespread efforts to combat deeply rooted inequalities.

REFERENCES

Allport. G. (1954). *The nature of prejudice.* Reading, MA: Addison-Wesley.

Au, W. (2009). *Rethinking multicultural education: Teaching for racial and cultural justice.* Milwaukee, WI: Rethinking Schools.

Ayers, W. (2006). Trudge toward freedom: Education research in the public interest. In G. Ladson-Billings & W. Tate (Eds.), *Education Research in the public interest* (pp. 81–97). New York, NY: Teachers College Press.

Ayers, J., & Owens, I. (2012). *No Child Left Behind waivers: Promising ideas from second round applications.* Washington, DC: Center for American Progress.

Baily, M., & Dynarski, S. (2011). Inequality in postsecondary education. In G. Duncan & R. Murname (Eds). *Whither opportunity? Rising inequality, schools and children's life chances* (pp. 117–132). New York, NY: Russell Sage Foundation.

Banks, J., & Banks, C. (2004). *Handbook of research on multicultural education* (2nd ed.). San Francisco, CA: Jossey-Bass.

Banks, J. A., Cookson, P., Gay, G., Hawley, W. D., & Irvine, J. J. (2001). *Diversity within unity:Essential principles for teaching and learning in a multicultural society.* Seattle, WA: University of Washington Center for Multicultural Education.

Bok, M. (1992). *Civil rights and the social programs of the 1960s: The social justice functions of social policy.* Westport, CT: Praeger.

Broader, Bolder Approach to Education Task Force. (2009). Mission statement. Retrieved from http://www.epi.org/files/2011/bold_approach_full_statement-3.pdf

Braddock, J. (2009). Looking back: The effects of court-ordered desegregation. In C. Smrekar, C., & E. Goldring (Eds.). *From the courtroom to the classroom: The shifting landscape of school desegregation* (pp. 3–18). Cambridge, MA: Harvard Education Press.

Brooks, J., Jean-Marie, G., Normore, A., & Hodgins, D. (2007). Distributed leadership for social justice: Influence and equity in an urban high school. *Journal of School Leadership, 17*(4), 378–408.

Carter, P., & Welner, K. (Eds). (2013). *Closing the opportunity gap: What America must do to give every child an even chance.* New York, NY: Oxford University Press.

Childress, S., Doyle, D., & Thomas, D. (2009). *Leading for equity: The pursuit of excellence in Montgomery County Public Schools.* Cambridge, MA: Harvard Education Press.

Clotfelter, C. (2004). *After Brown: The rise and retreat of school desegregation.* Princeton, NJ: Princeton University Press.

Clotfelter, C., Ladd, H., & Vigdor, J. (2006). Who teaches whom? Race and the distribution of novice teachers. *Economics of Education Review, 24*(4), 377–392.

Cooper, R., & Slavin, R. (2001). Cooperative learning programs and multicultural education: Improving intergroup relations. In F. Salili & R. Hoosain (Eds.), *Multicultural education: Issues, policies, and practices* (pp. 15–33). Charlotte, NC: Information Age.

Darling Hammond, L. (2010). *The flat world and education: How America's commitment to equity will determine our future.* New York, NY: Teachers College Press.

Dillon, S. (2009, April 28). 'No Child Law' is not closing racial gap. *New York Times.* Retrieved from http://www.nytimes.com/2009/04/29/education/29scores.html?_r=0

Duncan, G., & Murname, R. (2011). *Whither opportunity? Rising inequality, schools and children's life chances.* New York, NY: Russell Sage Foundation.

Flores, A. (2007). Examining disparities in mathematics education: Achievement gap or opportunity gap? *The High School Journal, 91*(1), 29–42.

Frankenberg, E., & Orfield, G. (Eds.). (2012). *The resegregation of suburban schools: A hidden crisis in American education.* Cambridge, MA: Harvard Education Press.

Grant, C., & Sleeter, C. (2011). *Doing multicultural education for achievement and equity* (2nd ed.). New York, NY: Routledge.

Green v. County School Board of New Kent County, 391 U.S. 430 (1968).

Hawley, W. (2007a). Designing schools that use student diversity to enhance learning of all students. In E. Frankenberg & G. Orfield (Eds.), *Lessons in integration: Realizing the promise of racial diversity in American schools* (pp. 31–56). Charlottesville, VA: University of Virginia Press.

Hawley, W. with Rollie, D. (Eds). (2007b). *The keys to effective schools: Educational reform as continuous improvement.* Thousand Oaks, CA: Corwin Press.

Heilig, J., & Holme, J. (2013). Nearly 50 years post-Jim Crow: Persisting and expansive school segregation for African American, Latina/o, and ELL Students in Texas. *Education and Urban Society, 45*(5), 609–632.

Hodges, E. (2011, April). *The Emergency School Aid Act, 1970–1981: The inducement as a policy tool for school desegregation.* Paper presented at American Education Research Association. Vancouver, British Columbia.

Horsford, S. (Ed.). (2010). *New perspectives in educational leadership: Exploring social, political, and community contexts and meaning.* New York, NY: Peter Lang.

Hoschild, J., & Scrovenick, N. (2003). *The American dream and public schools.* New York, NY: Oxford University Press.

Hughes, M. (2002). A mobility strategy for improving opportunity. *Housing Policy Debate, 6*(1), 271–297.

Irons, P. (2002). *Jim Crow's children: The broken promise of the Brown decision.* New York, NY: Penguin Books.

Johnson, R. C. (2011). *Long-run Impacts of school desegregation and school quality on adult attainments.* NBER working paper #16664. Cambridge, MA: National Bureau of Economic Research.

Kalgorides, D., Loeb, S., & Beteille, T. (2012). Systematic sorting: Teacher characteristics and class assignments. *Sociology of Education, 86*(2), 103–123.

Kantor, H., & Lowe, R. (2013). Educationalizing the welfare state and privatizing education: The evolution of social policy since the New Deal. In P. Carter & K. Welner (Eds.), *Closing the opportunity gap: What America must do to give every child an even chance* (pp. 25–39). New York, NY: Oxford University Press.

Ladson-Billings, G. (1994). *The dreamkeepers: Successful teachers of African American children.* San Francisco, CA: Jossey-Bass Publishers.

Ladson-Billings, G. (2006). From the achievement gap to the education debt: Understanding achievement in U.S. schools. *Education Researcher, 35*(7), 3–12.

Lassiter, M. (2007). *The silent majority: Suburban politics in the Sunbelt South.* Princeton, NJ: Princeton University Press.

Le, C. (2010). Racially integrated education and the role of the federal government. *North Carolina Law Review, 88*, 725–786.

Lee, J. (2007). Can reducing school segregation close the achievement gap? In E. Frankenberg & G. Orfield (Eds.) *Lessons in integration: Realizing the promise of racial diversity in American schools* (pp. 74–100). Charlottesville: University of Virginia Press.

Linn, R., & Welner, K. (Eds.). (2007). *Race-conscious policies for assigning students to schools: Social science research and the Supreme Court cases.* Washington, DC: National Academy of Education.

Magnuson, K., & Waldfogel, J. (2008). *Steady gains and stalled progress: Inequality and the black–white test score gap.* New York, NY: Russell Sage Foundation.

Mann, H. (1848). *Twelfth annual report to the Massachusetts State Board of Education.* Boston, MA.

Marshall, C., & Young, M. (2006). The wider societal challenge: An afterword. In C. Marshall & M. Oliva (Eds.), *Leadership for social justice: Making revolutions in education* (pp. 307–315). Boston, MA: Pearson.

McAlpine, R., Tidwell, B., & Jackson, M. (1988). Civil rights and social justice: From progress to regress. In *Black Americans and public policy* (pp. 1–24). Washington, DC: The National Urban League.

Mehta, J. (2013). How paradigms create politics: The transformation of American educational policy, 1980–2001. *American Education Research Journal.* Retrieved from http://aer.sagepub.com/content/50/2/285.abstract

Mickelson, R. (2001). Subverting *Swann*: First- and second-generation segregation in the Charlotte-Mecklenburg schools. *American Educational Research Journal, 38*(2), 215–252.

Mickelson, R., Bottia, M., & Lambert, R. (2013). A meta-regression analysis of the effects of school and classroom composition on mathematics outcomes. *Review of Educational Research, 83,* 121–158.

Milliken v. Bradley, 418 U.S. 717 (1974).

Minow, M. (2010). *In* Brown's *wake: Legacies of America's educational landmark.* New York, NY: Oxford University Press.

Moll L. (1992). Bilingual classroom studies and community analysis: Some recent trends. *Educational Researcher, 2*(2), 20–24.

Morello, C. & Mellnick, T. (2012 May 17). Census: Minority babies are now the majority in United States. *Washington Post.* Retrieved from http://articles.washingtonpost.com/2012-05-17/local/35458407_1_minority-babies-census-bureau-demographers-whites

National Center for Education Statistics. (2013). *The nation's report card: Trends in academic progress 2012* (NCES 2013–456). Washington, DC: National Center for Education Statistics, Institute of Education Sciences, U.S. Department of Education.

Noguera, P. (2011). A broader and bolder approach uses education to break the cycle of poverty. *Phi Delta Kappan, 93*(3), 8–14.

Normore, A. H., & Brooks, J. S. (2012). Instructional leadership in the era of No Child Left Behind. In L. Volante (Ed.), *School leadership in the context of standards-based reform: International perspectives* (pp. 41–67) New York, NY: Springer.

Oakes, J. (2010). *Keeping track: How schools structure inequality* (2nd ed.). New Haven, CT: Yale University Press.

Oliva, M., & Anderson, G. (2006). Dilemmas and lessons: The continuing leadership challenge for social justice. In C. Marshall & M. Oliva (Eds.), *Leadership for social justice: Making revolutions in education* (pp. 279–306). Boston, MA: Pearson.

Orfield, G. (1969). *The reconstruction of southern education: The schools and the 1964 Civil Rights Act.* New York, NY: Wiley/Interscience.

Orfield, G. (1978). *Must we bus? Segregated schools and national policy.* Washington, DC: Brookings Institution Press.

Orfield, G. (1999). Policy and equity: A third of a century of educational reforms in the United States. *Prospects Quarterly Review of Comparative Education, 29*(4), 579–594.

Orfield, G. (2009). *Reviving the goal of an integrated society: A 21st century challenge.* Los Angeles, CA: UCLA Civil Rights Project/Proyecto Derechos Civiles.

Orfield, G. (2010). A life in civil rights. *Political Science and Politics, 43*(4), 661–670.

Orfield, G., & Ashikanze, C. (1999). *The closing door: Conservative policy and black opportunity.* Chicago, IL: The University of Chicago Press.

Orfield, G., & Eaton, S. (1996). *Dismantling desegregation: The quiet reversal of* Brown v. Board of Education. New York, NY: The New Press.

Orfield, G., & Lee, C. (2005). *Why segregation matters: Poverty and inequality.* Cambridge, MA: Harvard Civil Rights Project.

Orfield, G., Frankenberg, E., & Garces, L. M. (2008). Statement of American social scientists of research on school desegregation to the U.S. Supreme Court in *Parents v. Seattle School District and Meredith v. Jefferson County. The Urban Review, 40*(1), 96–136.

Orfield, G., Kucsera, J., & Siegel-Hawley, G. (2012). *E pluribus . . . separation: Deepening double segregation for more students.* Los Angeles, CA: UCLA Civil Rights Project/ Proyecto Derechos Civiles.

Palardy, G. (2013). High school socioeconomic segregation and student attainment. *American Educational Research Journal.* Retrieved from http://aer.sagepub.com/content/early/2013/03/25/0002831213481240.abstract

Perry, P. (2008). Creating safe spaces in predominately white classrooms. In M. Pollock (Ed.), *Everyday anti-racism: Getting real about race in schools* (pp. 226–229). New York, NY: The New Press.

Petrovich, J., & Wells, A. (Eds.). (2005). *Bringing equity back: Research from a new era in American educational policy.* New York, NY: Teachers College Press.

Pettigrew, T. (2008). Future directions for intergroup contact theory and research. *International Journal of Intercultural Relations, 32*(3), 187–199.

Pettigrew, T., & Tropp, L. (2006). A meta-analytic test of intergroup contact theory. *Journal of Personality and Social Psychology, 90*(5), 751.

Pollock, M. (2008). *Everyday anti-racism: Getting real about race in schools.* New York, NY: The New Press.

Ravitch, D. (2010). *The death and life of the great American school system.* New York, NY: Basic Books.

Rawls, J. (1971). *A theory of justice.* Cambridge, MA: The Belknap Press of Harvard University Press.

Reardon, S. (2011). The widening academic achievement gap between the rich and the poor: New evidence and possible explanations. In G. Duncan & R. Murname (Eds.), *Whither opportunity? Rising inequality, schools and children's life chances* (pp. 91–116). New York, NY: Russell Sage Foundation.

Reardon, S., Grewal, E., Kalogrides, D., & Greenberg, E. (2012). *Brown* fades: The end of court-ordered school desegregation and the resegregation of American public schools. *Journal of Policy Analysis and Management 31*(4), 876–904.

Rothstein, R., Jacobsen, R., & Wilder, T. (2008). *Grading education: Getting accountability right.* New York, NY: Teachers College Press.

Rumberger, R., & Palardy, G. (2005). Test scores, dropout rates and transfer rates as alternative indicators of school performance. *American Education Research Journal 41*, 3–42.

Ryan, J. (2010). *Five miles away, a world apart: One city, two schools and the story of educational opportunity in modern America.* New York, NY: Oxford University Press.

Sailor, W. (Ed.). (2002). *Whole school success and inclusive education: Building partnerships for learning, achievement and accountability.* New York, NY: Teachers College Press.

Schwartz, H. (2010). *Housing policy is school policy: Economically integrative housing promotes academic success in Montgomery County, MD.* Washington, DC: The Century Foundation.

Skyrla, L., McKenzie, K., & Schuerich, J. (2008). *Using equity audits to create equitable and excellent schools.* Thousand Oaks, CA: Corwin Press.

Slavin, R. (1995). *Cooperative learning: Theory, research, and practice* (2nd ed.). Boston, MA: Allyn & Bacon.

Starratt, R. (2004). *Ethical leadership.* San Francisco, CA: Jossey-Bass.

Tanaka, G. (2007). *The intercultural campus: Transcending culture and power in higher education.* New York, NY: Peter Lang.

Tavernise, S. (2012, May 17). Whites account for under half of births in U.S. New York Times. Retrieved from http://www.nytimes.com/2012/05/17/us/whites-account-for-under-half-of-births-in-us.html?pagewanted=all

Tough, P. (2008). *Whatever it takes: Geoffrey Canada's quest to change Harlem and America.* New York, NY: Houghton Mifflin.

Tyack, D., & Cuban, L. (1995). *Tinkering toward utopia: A century of public school reform.* Cambridge, MA: Harvard Press.

U.S. Department of Education. (1968–2009). Civil rights data collection. Retrieved from http://ocrdata.ed.gov/

Wells, A. S., & Crain R. L. (1994). Perpetuation theory and the long-term effects of school desegregation. *Review of Educational Research, 6,* 531–555.

CHAPTER 6

IN PURSUIT
OF SOCIAL JUSTICE

The Influence of Anthropology
in Facilitating Models of Participation,
Agency, and Equity in Education

Diane Rodriguez-Kiino and George J. Petersen

ABSTRACT

The central purpose of this chapter is to illustrate the critical role that anthropology has played in supporting social justice frameworks in education that seek to increase student participation, build and develop human agency, and ensure equitable resource distribution. The chapter will examine chief theories, constructs, and arguments in anthropology that have contributed to and extended the understanding of social justice in school and society. Further, in an era of ongoing vast societal shifts, it is imperative to synthesize and understand how school leaders serve as cultural reproducers, transmitting knowledge, mores, and values to students and learners. A final distinctive contribution of this chapter includes a collection of strategies rooted in anthropology to bolster the development of educational leaders in pursuit of social justice in K–12 schooling.

Educational Leadership for Ethics and Social Justice, pages 93–112

In Paulo Freire's (1973) germinal work *Education for Critical Consciousness*, he argues that a duality exists in human society: engaging in life as a *subject* or *object*. *Subjects* are individuals who pursue meaning and purpose in life, and make cultural contributions to society. They are cognizant of their reality, chart their own course, and respond attentively and critically to their environment. Hence, subjects are empowered to take action. Subjects, Freire contends, are integrated persons who construct and co-construct history and culture. In contrast, *objects* are those who have learned to adapt to their circumstances as a result of social oppression. Freire explains, "If man is incapable of changing reality, he adjusts himself instead" (1973, p. 5). In a sense, these individuals have retreated from or acquiesced to the prevailing hierarchical forces. Out of self-preservation, they conform to, rather than deviate from, the norm (Freire, 1973). Objects are less change agents and cultural producers than they are compliant receptacles of information.

Central to Freire's theory is the belief that education is fundamental to the creation of subjects and objects. Thus, three related questions guide the introduction to this chapter on anthropology and social justice. First, what are the *pedagogical conditions* that undergird the development of subjects and objects? Second, how are these learning environments *framed and influenced*? Third, how does one *understand* the important conditions necessary to maximize the development of learners as subjects?

In thinking about the first question, the creation of objects in United States K–12 education is an alarming reality underpinning educational inequality and opportunity gaps to achievement—grave realities that especially impact historically underrepresented students. In the following passage, for example, Geneva Gay (2000) paints a dreadful picture of what it means when low-income urban learners have teachers who disregard student culture:

> Students of color, especially those who are poor and live in urban areas, get less total instructional attention; are called on less frequently; are encouraged to develop intellectual thinking less often; are criticized more and praised less; receive fewer direct responses to their questions and comments; and are reprimanded more often and disciplined more severely. (p. 63)

While not all historically underrepresented poor students endure substandard teaching and learning, this harrowing context, for some, is a reality. And in these particular school environments students are less likely to be co-constructors and authors of their history, as they are afforded minimal genuine opportunities to use their voice for change, have their actions and accomplishments applauded, and exercise real-time decision-making and analytic skills. These opportunity gaps undermine core educational principles of social justice: notably, participation, agency, and equity. Gay (2000) underscores the ramifications of these learning environments, which reproduce objects, instead of subjects. She states, "If educators continue to be ignorant of, ignore, impugn, and silence the cultural orientations, values, and performance styles of ethnically different students, they will persist in imposing cultural hegemony, personal degradation, educational inequity, and academic underachievement upon them" (p. 25).

Contrarily, when K–12 educators and school communities commit to social justice practices that integrate culturally inclusive, fair, and equitable environments, students are more often supported as subjects, or authentic and empowered beings. This speaks directly to the second question posed earlier related to approaches that frame and influence learning. Social justice pedagogical frameworks can serve as vehicles in advancing the convergence of empowerment and authenticity whereby students participate and engage in a life that honors their true selves (Splitter, 2009).

Social justice approaches provide educational communities with the knowledge and skills to emphasize transformative teaching and learning environments (Adams, Blumenfeld, Casteneda, Hackman, Peters, & Zuniga, 2010). Yet, before examining social justice, it is important to recognize how one would problematize *social injustice* in school, thus addressing question three—how do we understand what is or is not transformative teaching and learning? Ethnographic research, grounded in cultural comparative anthropology, is one method of inquiry to "understand sociocultural problems in communities or institutions...and to bring about positive change" (LeCompte & Schensul, 1999, p. 6). Ethnographers are first and foremost responsible for interpreting culture, which Wolcott (1985, p. 191) claims can be found in "what people *do*, what they *say* (and *say they do*), or some uneasy tension between what they *really do* and what they *say they ought to do*" (emphasis in original). Employing an ethnographic lens in schools allows educational anthropologists and other researchers to conduct an in-depth examination of school culture and the relationships that exist among key constituency groups. The purpose of this chapter is to describe the impact of anthropology as a social science discipline on social justice frameworks in school and society. Specifically, we will examine the underpinnings of applied ethnographic methodology as a tool for advancing justice in the classroom.

SOCIAL JUSTICE IN CONTEXT

Social justice pedagogical frameworks in school and the broader society facilitate and support education for critical consciousness and the development of subjects, in contrast to objects. That is, social justice education provides the structure—both theoretically and practically—to empower students to live as integrated and authentic actors, constructing history and culture for themselves and their communities. Because social justice conceptual frameworks, classroom contexts, and relationships vary significantly across United States schools, there is no strict social justice formula to nurture integrated, critically conscious learners. That said, social justice frameworks abound and are fundamental to contextualize and grasp within the context of teaching and learning. The following notable examples position social justice within a broader educational framework. These particular approaches undergird the purpose of this chapter to describe the influence of anthropology in the pursuit of social justice in United States K–12 schooling.

In *Teaching for Diversity and Social Justice*, Bell (1997) argues that social justice education is both a "process and a goal":

> The goal of social justice education is full and equal participation of all groups in a society that is mutually shaped to meet their needs. . . . The process for attaining the goal of social justice we believe should also be democratic and participatory, inclusive and affirming of human agency and human capacities for working collaboratively to create change. (pp. 3–4)

From this vantage point, Bell emphasizes two related points intersecting social justice and school communities. First, *social justice for all* translates to student agency and active participation in classroom settings. Second, students in social justice learning communities are also participants in the construction and design of fair and equitable environments. Thus, learners are stakeholders who have the power to produce and influence change.

Marshall and Oliva (as cited in Normore & Blanco, 2008) highlight the role of change-makers who strive to theorize and eradicate the uneven distribution of power in schools. They maintain "that social justice theorists and activists focus inquiry on how institutional norms, theories and practices in schools and society lead to social, political, economic, and educational inequities" (2008, p. 224). Normore and Blanco argue that social justice advocates seek to dismantle these very power structures, which they assert are rooted in "gender, social class, race, ethnicity, religion, disability, sexual orientation, language, and other systems of oppression" (2008, p. 224).

Finally, in Carlisle, Jackson, and George's (2006) study on the multiple meanings of social justice principles in low-income, urban classrooms, the authors developed a five-pronged framework aimed at supporting the future consideration, replication, scalability, and evaluation of social justice pedagogical frameworks. In order to proclaim social justice education, the following five criteria must be in place:

- *Inclusion and equity*: The school promotes inclusion and equity within the school setting and larger community by addressing all forms of social oppression.

- *High expectations*: The school provides a diverse and challenging learning environment that supports student development, holds all students to high expectations, and empowers students of all social identities.
- *Reciprocal community relationships*: The school recognizes its role as both a resource to and beneficiary of the community.
- *System-wide approach*: The mission, resource allocation structures, policies and procedures, and physical environment exemplify its commitment to creating and sustaining a socially just environment between and among various constituency groups and in all areas of the system.
- *Direct social justice education and intervention*: The school's faculty, staff, and administration are committed to "liberatory education," advocate for social justice, and directly confront manifestations of social oppression (p. 57).

In the Carlisle et al. (2006) model, students are central to equity-minded policies and practices. However, the faculty and staff are directly responsible for wielding their power in such a way that they meet discrimination and oppression head-on. Taken together, social justice models in United States K–12 schools and society provide a pedagogical framework for understanding, accepting, and affirming cultural differences, core to equality and academic achievement. What is more, the models aim to resist oppressive systems that undermine effective teaching and learning contexts. Social justice education frameworks are inclusive, consciousness-raising efforts that build on the cultural strengths of individuals and collective groups to empower historically subordinated learners and enact critical change. With these themes in mind, it is important to chronicle the influence of anthropology as a social science discipline in facilitating social justice principles.

This chapter examines the role of anthropology, and more narrowly, educational anthropology, in researching and advancing participation, agency, and equity in schools and society. We will review historical anthropological milestones, chief theories, constructs, and arguments that have contributed to and extended the understanding of social justice education. We will synthesize how teachers serve as cultural reproducers, transmitting knowledge, mores, and values to learners. Guided by educational anthropological tenets, we conclude with a set of recommendations that impact the professional development of educational leaders in pursuit of social justice. The complex history of educational anthropology, as an academic discipline and society of scholars, begins this section.

HISTORY OF EDUCATIONAL ANTHROPOLOGY

While distinguishing the role of anthropology in furthering agency, equity, and participation in school, it is important to first acknowledge the discipline's (1) central premise, (2) academic subfields, and (3) research methodology. Anthropology is "the comparative study of human societies and cultures" (Nanda & Warms, 2002, p. 1). Imperative to this discussion, then, is the definition of culture, explained by Goodenough as "the concepts, beliefs, and principles of action and organization" of a particular population (as cited in Wolcott, 1985, p. 192). For the purpose of this chapter on social justice education, culture is defined in the context of culturally responsive teaching and learning, whereby it is "a dynamic system of social values, cognitive codes, behavioral standards, worldviews, and beliefs used to give order and meaning to our own lives as well as the lives of others" (Gay, 2000, p. 8).

Five main tenets of anthropology guide its examination and perception of human culture: applied anthropology, archaeology, biological anthropology, cultural anthropology, and linguistic anthropology. Anthropologists have a proclivity to understand and respect local culture—from the earliest primitive societies to Generation Z, the 21st century, and beyond (Fetterman, 1998). This understanding is rooted in qualitative research known as ethnography, which is "the art and science of describing a group or culture" (Fetterman, 1998, p. 1). Ethnographic methods will be fleshed out extensively in relation to social justice models in education, but it is important to note that ethnographers spend countless hours in the field, documenting the culture of a selected group.

Educational anthropology is considered a subdivision of the wider discipline, largely melding theory and practice from applied, cultural, and linguistic anthropology (Levinson & González, 2008). Scholars have disputed the main objectives of educational anthropology throughout its history. These contested terrains include but are not limited to philosophical purpose and research methods. More specifically, the division has struggled with answering the following questions: *What is the role of educational anthropology? For what purpose do educational anthropologists conduct research?* The following section seeks to overlay these central concerns with the discipline's historical evolution in the context of social justice.

The Role of Educational Anthropology

In 1987 founding educational anthropologist George Spindler pointed to the paramount responsibility of the discipline: to examine cultural transmission, or the process of teaching "young people how to think, act, and feel appropriately" (Spindler, 1997, p. 276). Educational anthropologists have long assumed that both schools and society educate and socialize youth. However, they have also maintained that schools in particular reproduce vast forms of inequity by indoctrinating learners to acquiesce to hegemonic cultural norms. Levinson and Holland (1996, p. 1) stress this point: "Ironically, schooled knowledges and disciplines may, while offering certain freedoms and opportunities, at the same time further draw students into dominant projects of nationalism and capitalist labor formation, or bind them even more tightly to class, gender, and race inequality."

The link to social justice is very clear—*educational anthropologists theorize that academic structures can and do sustain dominant forms of inequity, impeding social justice for all.* While this chapter is limited to understanding schooling as a source of cultural reproduction, educational anthropologists do emphasize that academic systems work in tandem with and against other institutional structures (e.g., religion, family, media, etc.).

Extending Spindler's (1997) line of reasoning and this anthropological supposition, Levinson and González (2008) situate cultural transmission within a pedagogical framework. They assert that educational anthropology is the study of "teaching and learning—that is, of acquiring, transmitting, and producing cultural knowledge for interpreting and acting upon the world. Anthropologists of education wish to understand how teaching and learning are organized socially and culturally" (Levinson & González, 2008, p. 2). More directly, Erickson notes that educational anthropologists study the "unintended consequences of instruction" (2011, p. 27). Nader and Sursock (as cited in Brooks, 2008) affirm the idea that educational anthropologists seek to discover the ways in which social justice and inequity morph according to cultural context and the impact that hierarchical classification systems have on the manifestation of social justice and inequity.

As a whole, these perspectives on culture suggest that researchers in the field document, distill, and explicate the problems of inequity and social injustice in United States K–12 schools. The question then becomes, what does one *do* with this information?

Conducting Research in Educational Anthropology

In her 2009 outgoing presidential address to the Council on Anthropology and Education (CAE), a subdivision of the American Anthropological Association, González emphasizes the discipline's primary aim to study school culture. She cautions, though, that to merely document the cultural transmission process is insufficient. Rather, ethnographic researchers must act in transformative ways for the advancement of social justice. González declared, "our work is not simply to describe, but to transform, not only to analyze, but to alter the neoliberal logics that attribute educational blame, responsibility, and value" (2010, p. 123). Yet to date, purist anthropologists disagree with González's perspective endorsing applied research or research for collective action. For example, Wolcott (1985) suggests that ethnographic researchers must be conscientious of the limitations of the research endeavor. He argues, "The ethnographic goal of understanding another way of life is not sufficient for reform-oriented educators who expect 'understanding' to be linked with efforts at improvement" (1985, p. 200). Wolcott (2011) further reminds readers that traditional anthropological research is value-neutral, positivist, and descriptive. While applied research for the improvement of society is always admirable, Wolcott contends that those benevolently executing applied research are doing so voluntarily, and are not necessarily advancing traditionalist anthropological inquiry:

> What sets these applied or "practicing" anthropologists apart are their direct and immediate efforts to make their work as anthropologists applicable to everyday problems and needs. These scholars are not as concerned about whether their efforts are anthropological, or whether they are contributing to the discipline, as whether they can muster the available anthropological resources that might be of help in resolving human problems. (2011, p. 107)

These perspectives notwithstanding, problematizing social injustice in school demands action-oriented, applied research, as the creation of objects in the context of teaching and learning perpetuates inequality and academic underachievement. In her address, González provocatively questions who would examine social injustice in school from a cultural perspective, if not educational anthropologists. Though researchers in other disciplines come to mind (e.g., cultural sociologists, etc.), González stresses that educational anthropologists are morally compelled to draw the connection between culture, equity, and learning outcomes. Reviewing the evolution of educational anthropology brings to light the discipline's expressed consideration of social justice.

Early 1900s Through Mid-20th Century

The link between anthropology and education dates back to the late 19th century (Eddy, 1997). However, circa 1920, educational anthropology reached a turning point as a result of shifts in academia related to increased research funding, a push for interdisciplinary partnerships, and the addition of anthropology departments in higher education (Eddy, 1997). Originally, anthropology as a field largely concentrated on international ethnographic fieldwork that examined developing societies abroad in an effort to draw distinctions between domestic cultural values and those under research investigation. Ultimately, the study of foreign culture, particularly during childhood, began to inform educational practice in the United States, and from this enlightened perspective, cultural diversity in school emerged as a salient theme throughout the early twentieth century.

The Stanford Conference on Education and Anthropology in 1954 marked a significant milestone in the burgeoning partnership between anthropology and education. Coordinated by Spindler, the conference centered on future interdisciplinary alliances and paved the way to formally recognize educational anthropology as a legitimate field of study with practical research application (Eddy, 1997). Conference themes as summarized by Spindler included the following: "The search for a philosophical as well as a theoretical articulation of education and anthropology; the necessity for sociocultural contextualization of the educative process; the relation of education to 'culturally phrased' phases of the life cycle; the nature of intercultural understanding and learning" (cited in Eddy, 1997, p. 13). Though social justice had not yet been popularized in United States K–12 education, Spindler's call for increased awareness of the relationship between culture and knowledge acquisition helps set the stage for ethnographic research to have as a central focus social justice pedagogy.

Civil Rights Movement to Current

The Civil Rights movement represented a watershed point in the development of educational anthropology and ethnographic research methods. It was during this period that the United States government expressed greater interest in employing qualitative research to inform federal education policy for disenfranchised populations. Ethnographic research, for example, played an important role in the 1954 *Brown v. Board of Education of Topeka* Supreme Court case (Eddy, 1997). Levinson and González (2008) confirm this paradigm shift and propose that an increasingly pluralistic society required a deeper examination of school culture. They posit, "In the United States, the civil rights movements, racial desegregation, and the growth of ethnic diversity through 'new immigration' of the 1960s brought forth the need to conceptualize the relationship between ethnic minorities and their schools" (Levinson & González, 2008, p. 3). It was this social unrest in pursuit of empowerment and authenticity that furthered the multidirectional relationship between social justice and educational anthropology, prompting researchers to investigate (a) how the purposeful design of education systems serves to perpetuate inequity in United States societies and (b) the counter-response of families and community stakeholders (Levinson & González, 2008). Likewise, critical theorists were similarly contemplating issues of inequity in schools and eager to push the boundaries of purist educational ethnography, perceived by these scholars as "too atheoretical and neutral" (Anderson, 1989, p. 249). Critical ethnography thus became the intersection of critical theory and ethnography, concentrating on themes such as "the role of schools in the social and cultural reproduction of social classes, gender roles, and racial and ethnic prejudices" (Anderson, 1989, p. 251).

In the mid 20th century, qualitative inquiry to examine human agency extended conversations central to the Civil Rights movement. As a result, qualitative research garnered increased support, influencing the practice of ethnography in schools and the cooperation between education and anthropology. For example, in 1963, the federal government funded an initiative to commission educational anthropologists to develop teacher training materials for urban educators (Eddy, 1997). These professional development resources and activities were based on numerous hours of ethnographic data collection, to include interviews and direct observations. Concurrently, George Spindler and his wife Louise were involved in a variety of publication efforts that bolstered the application and notoriety of educational anthropology and ethnographic research, namely *Education and Culture: Anthropological Approaches* in 1963 (Eddy, 1997).

These political, investigative, and literary breakthroughs and the continued expansion of anthropology as a field marked the threshold of a new era of educational anthropology. The field experienced increased visibility, formal acceptance in higher education schools of education, academic conferences, fellowships, and peer-reviewed research publications (Eddy, 1997). These and other achievements spawned the development of the Council on Anthropology and Education (CAE), the chief professional society for theorists and practitioners in the specialization. And as noted earlier, CAE continues to support educational anthropologists in their work as professional advocates of social justice, combating social inequality in school. The professional society's formal stance against inequity in learning communities reflects the discipline's ardent support of social justice pedagogical frameworks. For example, the current CAE mission statement underscores its commitment to social justice via applied research and also places significant emphasis on creating a community of interdisciplinary ethnographic researchers aiming to eradicate oppression or social injustice:

> The mission of the Council on Anthropology and Education is to advance anti-oppressive, socially equitable, and racially just solutions to educational problems through research using anthropological perspectives, theories, methods, and findings.

> The Council advocates for: (1) Research that is responsive to oppressed groups. (2) Research that promotes practices that bring anthropologists, scholars from other disciplines, and educators together to promote racial and

social justice in all settings where learning takes place. (Council on Anthropology and Education, n.d., para 1)

Again, in this context, the focus on applied ethnographic research as a cornerstone for equity and equality in United States K–12 classrooms is clear. With this in mind, we now turn to a review of ethnography as a primary method of inquiry.

ETHNOGRAPHY

Grounded in the construct of culture, anthropologists of education implement ethnographic research methods to observe and record the process by which learners acquire knowledge, information, values, and beliefs in school and society (Spindler, 1997). Said another way, "The purpose of ethnographic research is to describe and interpret cultural behavior" (Wolcott, 1985, p. 190). With this principle at the fore, this section contains several underlying assumptions. First, as one of the five traditional methods of qualitative inquiry, ethnographic research is, most broadly, the study of culture (Creswell, 2012). However, this chapter focuses strictly on ethnographic research in schools. Second, in its purest form, ethnographic research is positivistic and value-neutral, requiring the researcher to remain entirely objective. This chapter on the role of ethnography in advancing social justice principles underscores applied research methods. That is, this section highlights ethnography as a problem-centered form of activism, whereby the researcher's personal history and fieldwork experiences are assumed to facilitate his or her perspectives of the cultural transmission process.

Although ethnography is the study of culture, the intersection of school culture and applied research suggests a more nuanced understanding of ethnographic research methods. LeCompte and Schensul (1999), for example, define applied research as "concerned with understanding sociocultural problems and using these understandings to bring about change in communities, institutions, and groups" (p. 6). In the case of this chapter, the connection between social justice, school culture, and applied research presupposes that injustice or oppression is the problem under review.

As a form of qualitative inquiry, how might ethnographic research methods be particularly appropriate in a classroom setting? LeCompte and Schensul (1999) offer the following seven general traits of ethnographic research:

- It is carried out in a natural setting, not in a laboratory.
- It involves intimate, face-to-face interaction with participants.
- It presents an accurate reflection of participants' perspectives and behaviors.

- It uses inductive, interactive, and recursive data collection and analytic strategies to build local cultural theories.
- It uses multiple data sources, including both quantitative and qualitative data.
- It frames all human behavior and belief within a sociopolitical and historical context.
- It uses the concept of culture as a lens through which to interpret results (p. 9).

While these traits characterize broader ethnographic practices, each criterion can be applied more narrowly to doing ethnography in a school classroom, as corroborated by Wolcott (1975) and Spindler and Spindler (1997a). Wolcott, for example, identifies the conceptual structures with which to possibly organize an ethnographic report of school culture (we say possibly here, as every culture is uniquely different and there are no formalized reporting templates in ethnography). Wolcott's time-tested ideas include "economic organization, ethos or worldview...political organization...social organization...cultural stability and change, and cultural transmission/enculturation" (p. 123). Spindler and Spindler's (1997a) analysis of what it takes to produce "good ethnography" also parallels LeCompte and Schensul's (1999) seven characteristics. Yet they additionally advise ethnographic researchers to clarify their role as emic (insider) or etic (outsider) participant observers in the reporting process (1997a). On a related note, Spindler and Spindler caution that researchers must be very transparent about the role or position they occupy in a particular investigative setting.

Erickson (1973) juxtaposes original ethnographic understandings of fieldwork in native villages with those present in school ethnography. Drawing from renowned anthropologist Bronislaw Malinowski's broad characterization of fieldwork, Erickson describes the native village as "a total community in which members hold ascribed statuses, are bound together by reciprocal rights and obligations, exchange goods, and in which knowledge is traditional and slowly changing" (1973, p. 11). In sharp contrast, Erickson portrays school communities in the following manner: "a partial community whose members (ideally) hold achieved statuses, in which rights and obligations are not reciprocal, in which the goods and services exchanged differ markedly in kind, and in which knowledge is non-traditional and rapidly changing" (1973, p. 11). This early scholarship on the application of ethnography in schools points to several distinctions in the context of social justice. First, members of a school community do not inherit their roles at birth. Rather, administrators, staff members, teachers, and students alike earn their positions and equivalent rank within a socially stratified organization. School communities are thus comprised of both subjects and objects, or those empowered to enact change and those who remain deferential to the dominant culture, respectively.

Second, members of school communities do not have equal access to cultural and academic capital. Consistent with Bourdieu's (1983) supposition that societies privilege some while disadvantaging others, certain subgroups within school communities are reliant upon those with clout and positionality to create, share, and/or impart academic resources, constructive feedback, funding, high expectations, knowledge, skills, and technology. There is a widely held underlying assumption related to social arrangements and power distribution in United States schools that *students learn from teachers*, and not contrariwise (Freire, 1973, 2009; Kincheloe & McLaren, 2002; McLaren, 2009). Further, what students do indeed learn is generally "technical or practical knowledge," as opposed to "emancipatory learning," which helps learners conceptualize "how social relationships are distorted and manipulated by relations of power and privilege" (McLaren, 2009, p. 64). Third, with the onset of technology and 21st-century learning standards, knowledge is changing rapidly. A disparity thereby exists between those who have access to knowledge and those who do not. Quite simply, subordinated school populations have fewer opportunities to access democratic classroom environments, where students create and redistribute knowledge (hooks, 2009; Freire, 2009). Thus, for over a century, ethnographic researchers have depicted social inequities in the classroom and developed a lexicon specific to oppressive learning conditions. This repertoire of constructs and ideas is congruent with the body of knowledge on social justice education.

CHIEF CONSTRUCTS

Through their research and practice, educational ethnographers have played a salient role in revealing the complexities of culture and learning in United States K–12 classrooms. Ethnographers have expounded upon chief constructs analogous to and overlapping with literature in the area of social justice education. In the context of this chapter, these conceptual frameworks include cultural transmission, cultural acquisition, cultural production, cultural discontinuity, the cultural deficit model, and culturally responsive teaching. We operationalize these terms here to provide a richer perspective of ethnographic inquiry in schools.

Cultural transmission theory is central to the anthropology of education and the process of conducting ethnographic research worldwide. Broadly, the term means "the passing on of basic cultural knowledge and values across generations" (Levinson & González, n.d., p. 6). However, given the educational anthropological assumption that schools reproduce structural inequality in American society (Levinson & Holland, 1996), the transmission of culture on school campuses has significant social justice implications. In the excerpt below, Spindler and Spindler (1997b) contextualize cultural transmission in school, reminding readers that the sphere of influence within a formal pedagogical setting is far-reaching and is comprised of several stakeholders:

> Education is seen as cultural transmission and the major instrument of cultural survival, but the learning of culture, the school, and the social structure, the exercise of power, the effect of culturally based values on teacher perceptions, the informal transmission of values, the roles of the school administrator and teacher, and American culture as a specific context for schooling were all considered relevant. (p. 58)

In this excerpt, Spindler and Spindler argue that certain authority figures—teachers and administrators alike—uphold a personal belief system and have the capacity to wield power over students. Subsequently, students are positioned as objects, or the recipients of culture. McLaren reinforces this notion by bifurcating culture into two subgroups: dominant (those who transmit culture) and subordinate (those who receive culture):

> Dominant culture refers to social practices and representations that affirm the central values, interests, and concerns of the social class in control of the material and symbolic wealth of society. Groups who live out social relations in subordination to the dominant culture are part of the subordinate culture. (2009, pp. 65–66)

McLaren's example intimates an equally important concept connected to cultural transmission literature: notably, hegemony, or the influence or control over oppressed populations (Darder, Baltadano, & Torres, 2009). In school settings, Levinson and Holland (1996) argue for a culture that is "a continual process of creating meaning in social and material contexts" (p. 13) rather than a set of ideas that is rigid and predetermined. In this context, constituency groups, like students, teachers, and administrators, produce, mold, and transmit culture.

While cultural transmission focuses on the dissemination or diffusion of culture, *cultural acquisition* is its antipodal construct. Cultural acquisition is the process by which learners gain new knowledge in a cultural context (Levinson & González, 2008). Thus, important to this conversation are the nuanced understandings of how students acquire new language, customs, and belief systems and what perspectives they might bring to the learning process. Extrapolating from Gans' (2007) research on immigrant communities, we understand the cultural acquisition process to include acculturation and assimilation. Those who acculturate, Gans argues, assume a new identity willingly, and with or without acceptance from the dominant group. He provides two hallmark examples related to immigrants living in the United States: "when parents push their children to do well in school or status-seekers [who] learn the lifestyles of those whose status they seek to achieve" (2007, p. 153). Assimilation, on the other hand, requires acceptance by the dominant society, which may arbitrarily limit access to newcomers. In both acculturation and assimilation, subordinate group members minimize personal traits and characteristics to appear more like the dominant group (Gans, 2007). Gans' work cautions that acquiring a new cultural persona does not guarantee increased opportunities for success.

Cultural production is the cross-fertilization of cultural transmission and acquisition. Levinson and González (2008) define it as "in the process of acquiring transmitted knowledge, individuals or subcultures can modify or extend the knowledge in effect organizing the knowledge for themselves while producing and adding new knowledge to the common stock" (p. 7). Thus, within a school, those populations who can access, amend, produce, and organize knowledge to their advantage maintain both cultural and political capital compared to those who cannot, reflecting the subject and object duality. Levinson and Holland (1996) draw attention to students and other constituents who serve as both recipients and creators of culture, by stating, "For while the educated person is culturally produced in definite sites, the educated person also culturally produces cultural forms" (p. 14).

Discovering *discontinuities* in United States K–12 schooling is a signature trait of ethnographic research in the classroom. Ethnographers have been recognized for spotlighting the incongruence between what is practiced at home and what is learned in school. Via ethnography in schools and society, researchers can "identify differences between [students'] respective communication patterns, linguistic codes, and kinesic and cognitive styles" (Levinson & Holland, 1996, p. 8). A 2010 policy brief for the United States Department of Education sponsored by the CAE undergirds this theme and contends the following: "Young children and their parents are still struggling when school doesn't connect to the experiences they have in their families and communities. Young children do not benefit from overly standardized curriculum, especially when they are exclusively rewarded for behaving and thinking in one particular way" (Adair, 2010, p. 2).

These themes are tangential to a conceptual framework known in educational anthropology as the *cultural deficit model*, whereby "ethnic minority students tended to do more poorly in school because their cultures of origin used different espistemologies, styles of communication, and participant structures to educate children at home" (Levinson & González, 2008, p. 8). This model places the blame squarely on the learner, attributing academic underachievement to student culture and low socioeconomic status.

Instead, Gay (2000) and Villegas (as cited in Bartolome, 2009) insist school educators look inward and enact culturally responsive approaches that hold schools accountable for improving academic achievement. Arguing that the deficit model is detrimental to student success, Villegas recommends culturally responsive instruction, "to create instructional situations where teachers use teaching approaches and strategies that recognize and build on culturally different ways of learning, behaving, and using language in the classroom" (in Bartolome, 2009, p. 346) Thus, the focus of culturally responsive teaching is on student assets and their important contributions to the production of knowledge, rather than what students do not know. As Gay claims, "Far too many educators attribute school failure to what students of color don't have and can't do" (2000, p. 23).

Though not an exhaustive list of what educational anthropologists discover in fieldwork, operationalizing these particular constructs is important in demonstrating the nexus between anthropology, K–12 schools, ethnographic methods, and social justice. However, these theoretical underpinnings must align with practical experiences largely crafted and implemented by professional development and graduate education programs for teachers and educational leaders. The following section on strategies and recommendations offers three proposals that integrate traditional educational anthropological tenets in professional development and graduate education models.

STRATEGIES AND RECOMMENDATIONS

Rooted in educational anthropology, we provide the following suggestions to bolster the development of educational leaders in pursuit of social justice in K–12 schooling:

Professional development and graduate education for teachers and administrators: Normore and Blanco (2008) remind readers that the discourse of social justice, leadership, and teaching are inextricably linked. In educating teachers and school leaders to foster and create socially just environments, it is imperative to prepare them to promote learning communities focused on student agency and active participation. Such engagement includes venues where all members of the educational community participate in the construction and design of a fair and equitable milieu. These complex levels of leadership and understanding are rooted in key domains of professional development and graduate education and include: (1) clearly articulated program goals that include valuing difference, (2) culturally responsive curricula, (3) pre-professional experiences related to inclusivity, and (4) research pursuits in the community. Within these four areas of professional development and graduate education, the themes of democracy, equity, care, and compassion can be interwoven with outcome measures and accountability systems. Thus, it behooves graduate schools of education and other professional development entities to create the space for enlightenment, to include deliberate discussions of organizational issues of power, gender, social class, race, religious traditions, disability, sexual orientation, language, and other embedded systems of oppression that have for years marginalized individuals and entire groups of people. Further, it must be made explicit that though educational leaders often benefit from these power structures and are reticent to dismantle them, they serve as advocates for social justice when they seek to dismantle these very power structures.

Ethnographic research grounded in school and society: Educational ethnographers have played a salient role in revealing the complexities of culture and learning in United States K–12 education. Moreover, their methods and observations have illustrated ideas and hypotheses that correspond with extant research and literature in the area of social justice education. Ethnography, which offers a problem-centered form of activism, has brought into sharper focus multifaceted issues such as power, clout, positionality, academic capital and access, and how these issues influence educators, school culture, and more importantly the voice and roles of students and families who have been historically marginalized. In seeking more equitable and just school communities, it is imperative to recognize the proven social inequities in school organizations. Applying ethnographic principles of research in professional development and graduate education programs advances a quest to more fully understand issues of access, culture, power, and leadership in school. Further, understanding this method of inquiry positions educational leaders to influence the creation and sustainability of an organizational ethic of inclusivity and justice, bridging the chasm of those who have access to knowledge and those who do not and empowering educational leaders to enact change and to dismantle power structures.

Fieldwork that explores the multiple identities of all constituency groups (e.g., students, parents, teachers, and administrators): In a world where schools face constant political shifts and ever-diminishing economic support, preparing educators for this often turbulent environment obligates professional development and graduate education programs to create field experiences that view K–12 educational environments from a larger systems perspective. With this in mind, graduate learners should have the opportunity to participate in ethical and self-reflective pre-professional practices in authentic school settings. Ideally, this type of fieldwork provides exposure to diversity and the opportunity to implement advanced educational theories of multicultural program development, policy, and administration. Further, fieldwork experiences should require graduate learners to solve complex academic, social, and resource issues, as undoubtedly these struggles link directly to inclusivity and systemic inequities. This hands-on engagement should provide graduate learners with the opportunity to demonstrate a commitment to opposing organizational systems that have historically oppressed and marginalized individuals and groups. Developing a genuine interpersonal awareness of how one's beliefs, values, and past experiences affect attitudes toward "others" should be central to the fieldwork experience. This deeper self-reflection acknowledges that K–12 school educators are integrated into a community of "others" while they are obligated to plan and implement activities where "others" are expected to learn and are given multiple opportunities to demonstrate their learning. Thus, it is of paramount importance that fieldwork experiences encompass opportunities to work closely with diverse peoples, cultures, and languages, enabling graduate learners to work for change and work against fundamental inequities in the K–12 educational system.

For decades, educational anthropology has contributed to the body of knowledge on social justice education. Educational anthropologists' long-standing and ardent pursuit to uncover covert forms of discrimination and prejudice has advanced social justice pedagogical frameworks, both theoretically and practically. As recounted in this chapter, the relationship between social justice and educational anthropology is inextricable and compels educators and school leaders to serve as microethnographers, examining the cultural underpinnings of their schools and communities. With the goal of creating more equitable environments for all learners, the strategies and recommendations above detail how professional development and graduate education programs can teach graduate learners how to adopt an anthropological lens in an effort to advance and enact social justice principals in K–12 classrooms.

REFERENCES

Adair, J. K. (2010). *Ethnographic knowledge for early childhood*. Retrieved from http://www.aaanet.org/sections/cae/wp-content/uploads/2011/10/Ethnography__ECE_Brief_Final_Adair2.pdf

Adams, M., Blumenfeld, W., Casteneda, C., Hackman, H., Peters, M., & Zuniga, X. (2010). *Readings for Diversity and Social Justice*. New York, NY: Routledge.

Anderson, G. (1989). Critical ethnography in education: Origins, current status, and new directions. *Review of Educational Research, 59*(3), 249–270.

Bartolome, L. I. (2009). Beyond a methods fetish: Toward a humanizing pedagogy. In A. Darder, M. P. Baltodano, & R. Torres (Eds.), *The critical pedagogy reader* (pp. 338–355). New York, NY: Routledge.

Bell, L. (1997). Theoretical foundations for social justice education. In M. Adams, L. Bell, & P. Griffin (Eds.), *Teaching for diversity and social justice: A sourcebook* (pp. 3–15). New York, NY: Routledge.

Bourdieu, P. (1983). Forms of capital. In J. Richardson (Ed.), *Handbook of theory and research for the sociology of education* (pp. 241–258). New York, NY: Greenwood.

Brooks, J. (2008). Introduction. In I. Bogotch, F. Beachum, J. Blount, J. Brooks, & F. English (Eds.), *Radicalizing educational leadership: Dimensions of social justice* (pp. 1–15). Rotterdam, The Netherlands: Sense Publishers.

Carlisle, L. R., Jackson, B. W., & George, A. (2006). Principles of social justice education: The social justice education in schools project. *Equity & Excellence in Education, 39,* 55–64.

Council on Anthropology and Education. (n.d.). *CAE Mission.* Retrieved from http://www.aaanet.org/sections/cae/sample-page/cae-mission/

Creswell, J. (2012). *Qualitative inquiry and research design: Choosing among five approaches.* Thousand Oaks, CA: Sage Publications.

Darder, A. Baltodano, M.P., & Torres, R. (2009). Critical pedagogy: An introduction. In A. Darder, M. P. Baltodano, & R. Torres (Eds.), *The critical pedagogy reader,* (pp. 1–26). New York, NY: Routledge.

Eddy, E. M. (1997). Theory, research, and application in educational anthropology. In G. D. Spindler (Ed.), *Education and cultural process: Anthropological approaches* (3rd ed., pp. 4–25). Prospect Heights, IL: Waveland Press, Inc.

Erickson, F. (1973, July). What makes school ethnographic? *Council on Anthropology and Education Newsletter, 4,* pp. 10–19.

Erickson, F. (2011). *Culture.* In B. A. Levinson & M. Pollack (Eds.), *A companion to the anthropology of education* (pp. 25–33). Hoboken, NJ: Blackwell Publishing Ltd.

Fetterman, D. M. (1998). *Ethnography: Step by step* (2nd ed.). Thousand Oaks, CA: Sage.

Freire, P. (1973). *Education for critical consciousness.* New York, NY: Continuum.

Freire, P. (2009). From pedagogy of the oppressed. In A. Darder, M. P. Baltodano, & R. Torres (Eds.), *The critical pedagogy reader,* (pp. 52–60). New York, NY: Routledge.

Gans, H. J. (2007). Acculturation, assimilation and mobility. *Ethnic and Racial Studies, 30*(1), 152–164.

Gay, G. (2000). *Culturally responsive teaching: Theory, research, and practice.* New York, NY: Teacher's College Columbia University.

hooks, b. (2009). Confronting class in the classroom. In A. Darder, M. P. Baltodano, & R. Torres (Eds.), *The critical pedagogy reader* (pp. 135–141). New York, NY: Routledge.

Kincheloe, J. L., & McLaren, P. (2002). Rethinking critical theory and qualitative research. In Y. Zou & E. T. Trueba (Eds.), *Ethnography and schools: Qualitative approaches to the study of education* (pp. 87–138). Lanham, MD: Rowman & Littlefield.

LeCompte, M. D., & Schensul, J. J. (1999). *Designing and conducting ethnographic research.* Lanham, MD: Rowman & Littlefield.

Levinson, B. A., & Holland, D. C. (1996). The cultural production of the educated person: An introduction. In B. A. Levinson, D. E. Foley, & D. C. Holland (Eds.), *The cultural production of the educated person: Critical ethnographies of schooling and local practice* (pp. 1–53). Albany, NY: State University of New York Press.

Levinson, B., & González, N. (2008). Anthropology of education in a global age. Translated into French for A.V. Zanten (Ed.), *Dictionnaire de Pedagogie* (pp. 12–16). Paris: Presses Universitaires de Francais.

McLaren, P. (2009). Critical pedagogy: A look at the major concepts. In A. Darder, M. P. Baltodano, & R. Torres (Eds.), *The critical pedagogy reader* (pp. 61–83). New York, NY: Routledge.

Nanda, S., & Warms, R. L. (2002). *Cultural anthropology* (7th ed.). Belmont, CA: Thomson Learning.

Normore, A. H., & Blanco, R. (2008). Leadership for social justice and morality: Collaborative partnerships, school linked services and the plight of the poor. In A. H. Normore (Ed.), *Leadership for social justice: Promoting equity and excellence through inquiry and reflective practice* (pp. 215–252). Charlotte, NC: Information Age Publishers.

Spindler, G. D. (1963). *Education and culture: Anthropological approaches.* New York, NY: Holt, Rinehart and Winston.

Spindler, G. D. (1997). The transmission of culture. In G. D. Spindler (Ed.), *Education and cultural process: Anthropological approaches* (3rd ed., pp. 275–309). Prospect Heights, IL: Waveland Press.

Spindler, G. D., & Spindler, L. (1997a). Ethnography: An anthropological view. In G. D. Spindler (Ed.), *Education and cultural process: Anthropological approaches* (3rd ed., pp. 50–55). Prospect Heights, IL: Waveland Press.

Spindler, G. D., & Spindler, L. (1997b). Cultural process and ethnography: An anthropological perspective. In G. D. Spindler (Ed.), *Education and cultural process: Anthropological approaches* (3rd ed., pp. 56–74). Prospect Heights, IL: Waveland Press.

Splitter, L. J. (2009). Authenticity and constructivism in education. *Studies in philosophy and education, 28*(2), 135–151.

Wolcott, H. F. (1975). Criteria for an ethnographic approach to research in schools. *Human Organization, 34*(2), 111–127.

Wolcott, H. F. (1985). On ethnographic intent. *Educational Administration Quarterly, 21*(3), 187–203.

Wolcott, H. F. (2011). If there's going to be an anthropology of education . . . In B. A. Levinson & M. Pollack (Eds.), *A companion to the anthropology of education* (pp. 97–111). Hoboken, NJ: Blackwell Publishing Ltd.

CHAPTER 7

CHANGING VIEWS OF ECONOMICS OF INEQUALITY AND IMPLICATIONS FOR LEADERSHIP AND LEARNING

Lynn Ilon and JuYoung Lee
Seoul National University

ABSTRACT

The adoption of knowledge economics as a lens from which to view learning has substantially changed the way that learning is defined. The manner in which inequality is viewed is one of the shifts from neoclassical economics to knowledge economics. This shift influences the view of learning. The role of inequality can be reexamined when viewed through the lens of knowledge economics because, among other unique characteristics of knowledge as an economic unit, it produces value in a manner substantially different from material or service goods. This chapter begins by reviewing the dominant theory of economics and its view of equality. It then contrasts this view with the new view of knowledge economics. This contrast is examined in light of learning and equality. These changes occur because of specific characteristics of knowledge as an economic unit, so some of these characteristics are then described. The reexamination of these issues stems from many aspects, but the

Educational Leadership for Ethics and Social Justice, pages 113–133
Copyright © 2014 by Information Age Publishing
113

root of the reexamination is the characteristics of knowledge as an economic unit. Although this seemingly mundane, theoretical, and sometimes arcane assessment has been underway for many years (Warsh, 2007), this chapter will discuss how the results are often surprising, robust, and substantially consequential for the interplay of education, educational leadership, ethics, and social justice.

The new view of knowledge economics began as a thought that societies advanced when large, new ideas came into play for that society. When ocean-going sailing ships could move around the world and trade (or plunder), whole nations grew in wealth. When the green revolution found ways of getting more produce out of a hectare of land, Asia began to move out of poverty toward industrialization. When antibiotics were discovered, some large-scale diseases began to be controlled. When people first began to discover how to plant crops, they were freed to begin to build civilizations. This notion, that it is the power of *ideas* that explained how societies and civilization leaped forward, began a rethink of how economics worked. Ultimately, it is challenging the very fundamentals of long-held neoclassical economics and is a classic epistemological battle within a profession (Kuhn, 1970; Mirowski, 2009; Warsh, 2007). But, primarily, it has caused economics to ask how knowledge and ideas work as economic units. This, necessarily, has caused researchers to ask the question of what knowledge is in an age of digitization—when actual facts are so abundant and easily accessible that the notion that they must be memorized is substantially questioned (Sawyer, 2006a; Weinberger, 2011). So, attention has turned from knowledge defined as facts to knowledge defined as "flow" learning (Sawyer, 2006a).

But this flow, this learning, is not taking place in the usual learning venues. It is taking place in a whole new digitized learning environment (Chatti, Jarke, & Frosch-Wilke, 2007; Weinberger, 2011). As ideas are passed around the world—across borders, shared and combined—the view that this economic unit (knowledge, ideas, innovations), which is creating vast value for societies and individuals, can easily be owned, controlled, and sold is under considerable scrutiny (Nieves & Osorio, 2013). The heretofore basis for understanding the distribution of goods and even services—when most goods and services were exclusive, easily owned, and controlled—now gives way to new thinking when ideas are shared, combined, and globally distributed (Edwards et al., 2013). Underlying this rethinking is a very specific economics that leads, in a clear fashion, to rethinking the idea of equity, ethics, and its relationship to education. In so doing, the very definitions of education and equity need to be rethought along with their linkages.

This chapter will attempt to build a framework of understanding of these emerging views. Important in understanding how these views are changing the nature of education is contrasting them with the prevailing views of education and social justice (closely connected with the field of ethics) from an economics view, so the chapter begins there. It then proceeds to outline new literatures and theoretical links that are emerging given the basis of knowledge economics. The chapter then uses three examples to show how not only the links between education and social justice are changing, but the very definitions of education are changing with it. Finally, the chapter ends with an examination of the new parameters of equality and equity in education, the implications for educational leaders, and the questions that are arising.

TRADITIONAL VIEWS OF EDUCATION AND ECONOMICS

Until Romer (1993) introduced his thinking about the economics of ideas to the World Bank in 1992, the theoretical relationship between education and economics had been rather straightforward since the rise of human capital theory. This is largely attributed to Theodore Shultz's address to the American Economic Association in 1960 (Schultz, 1961).

The theory of human capital derives from an underlying notion that societies attempt to maximize their collective wellbeing. Each individual, given a particular set of resources, attempts (rationally) to maximize his or her happiness. Given an ability to freely trade and to use their labor, individuals will use these resources to maximize their happiness over a lifetime. When each person within the society does this, then the society has reached its maximized point of happiness—known as maximum social welfare[1] (Fitzpatrick, 2001; Johannsson, 1991).

Human capital theory posits that individuals can increase their resource base by investing in education—thereby being more productive, increasing their wealth and income, and thus increasing their lifetime happiness. In so doing, individuals increase their welfare while the societies' total sum of overall welfare is also increased. The more individuals are educated, the higher overall social welfare (Bowman, 1996; Rosen, 1989). Although the entire society benefits from at least some education for all individuals, the society does not benefit from investing in an unrestricted stream of education for all. Because education results in *both* private and public benefits, the society must find a balance between investing public funds in education and requiring advanced levels of education be paid for by the individuals who will benefit from the increased income.

Psacharopolous (1981) attempted to show that it was the lower levels of education that most benefited society for investment in education. That is, society benefited from the increased productive gains when it educated its people in elementary school and, to a lesser extent, in high school. Later research has shown that higher education may well have positive return to society (Baum, Ma, & Payea, 2010), but, whatever the balance between public funding and private funding of education, the economic goal is clear—maximize overall societal wealth and income. If this maximization goal means educating the best and brightest with better and higher levels of education, then so be it. Redistribution of educational resources can then be done, but this redistribution is not germane to the goal of maximization. Therefore, no notion of equity or equality is part of the equation. Education is a means toward maximization.

Few have questioned this from a purely economic point of view. Birdsall, Ross, and Sabot (1995) take a close look at Asian economies, however, and show that reduced poverty, reduced income inequality, and high-quality basic education stimulated growth. Ilon (2011) shows that, in the case of Korea, over a 50-year period, education inequality was reduced (to one of the lowest levels throughout the world) while the economy grew simultaneously. But this effect is difficult to establish across a broad range of countries because the most educated countries are also the countries where economic growth is the most stable—that is, changes in educational equality may not be associated with much change in economic growth (Thomas, Wang, & Fan, 2001).

It is interesting to note that the rethinking of equity issues in the field of economics centers on the very fundamental notion of education—the acquisition, construction, sharing, and building of knowledge. In examining how knowledge is learned, built, and created, the very construction of schooling had to be reexamined. But schooling was not where this reexamination began. Rather, the examination began with the construct of knowledge. About the time of the substantial emergence of knowledge economics, there began a fundamental rethink about whether income inequality really did have a negative effect on economic growth as had long been assumed by many economists (Forbes, 2000). The theory of knowledge economics (now known as "new growth theory") was behind some of this reexamination (Aghion, Caroli, & García-Peñalosa, 1999). The economics field had begun to accept the notion that the analysis of knowledge as an economic unit is changing the field of economics. But it is these fundamentally different characteristics (than either goods or services) that are causing the difficultly in being integrated it into the mainstream of economics. Partly this was due to the challenge of empirical testing. Mirowski (2009) explains, "Everyone seems to believe that knowledge is the key to economic success, and yet our most-developed schools of economic thought are mired in the most frightful muddles when it comes to modeling knowledge in an economic setting" (p. 144). One major challenge has been substantial rethinking of welfare theory—including how equality and equity affect a society's overall happiness. In knowledge economics, equity is highly linked to learning.

NEW VIEWS OF EDUCATION AND ECONOMICS

Although the initial literature on knowledge economics appeared as an economic theory (Romer, 1993),[2] considerable work has been added in a number of fields. In the field of economics, much of the focus has been around the notion that ideas have vastly different economic characteristics than good or services. Because ideas (music, innovations, solutions to problems, collective discourse, information) can be digitized, they can be spread around the world with little or no cost and affect millions of lives without anyone having to buy or sell anything. Everyone can share the idea, create the idea, and build on the idea without taking anything away from anyone else (unlike sharing an apple, for example, or a haircut). And ideas are difficult to own and control. All of these characteristics make the economics of knowledge difficult, if not impossible, to fit into the theories and formulas of existing neoclassical economics, so, in effect, a new economics is being invented.

It is relatively easy to see how an idea like Smartphone technology has begun to change the world, but this "idea" merges old industrial economics with new knowledge economics. Smartphones, after all, are physical products (embedded with substantial knowledge) that can be bought and sold. A Smartphone cannot be shared, and its ownership is possible to be controlled, bought, and sold. A better way to understand knowledge economics is to examine a pure idea and its impact on society. In 1978, the medical journal *Lancet* published an editorial talking about the impact of a simple medical finding—that the additional of salt and sugar to water allowed the intestine to absorb liquid much faster than water itself (Lancet, 1978). This simple idea, possibly backed by substantial medical research, has led to the annual reduction in the mortality rate of children dying from acute diarrhea from 5 million to 1.3 million (World Health Organization, 2002). Most of this reduction has no market transactions—the idea is applied within poor households or local clinics. The idea has spread throughout the world, has vast global social welfare benefits, and has nearly all the characteristics of knowledge economics.

Although the example of how the knowledge of rehydration substantially changed society's wellbeing at first appears to have nothing to do with education, in fact, it has vast implications. It shows how new ideas and knowledge can be created, spread, and shared and impact society without having to go through formal schooling venues. Unlike the former theory of human capital, which assumed that only through schooling could knowledge have productive consequences that improved society, the new theory shows that even the most seemingly mundane knowledge can be rapidly spread, distributed through social networks rather than through formal schooling, have vast social welfare consequences, and impact society not through markets (incomes and productivity) but directly through changing human lives.

The consequences are that the focus on education is changing from schooling to lifelong learning (Giovannini, Hall, Morrone, & Giulia, 2009; OECD, 2004). Education is no longer measured in schooling terms, but in learning terms (Field, 2006; Ouane, 2011). Further, learning is being redefined as moving away from skills and knowledge acquisition to creativity and innovation (Johnson & Andersen, 2012; Sawyer, 2006b). Learning 2.0 is beginning to redefine the way people learn, from teacher-driven to dynamic student-driven learning (Cochrane, 2011; Depover & Schneider, 2012).

Romer's first notion of the kinds of idea that put whole societies on the path to rapid growth may have fit a familiar notion of "technological change" (1991). But the exploration of the characteristics of knowledge, knowledge's ability to be digitized, and the spread of IT systems throughout the world has raised Romer's original concept to a very different plane. Knowledge, in the form of facts, skills, and information, is now easy and cheap to access for much of the world and increasingly so for increasingly more people each year. This same technology now makes it possible, even rewarding, for people to combine their thinking, ideas, creativity, and possibilities in a unique, human way to build collective ideas that evolve, change, and adapt. Humans can now build whole systems of knowledge on a collective basis, and that knowledge builds on itself dynamically. Participants are rewarded with increased knowledge and access to better networks of knowledge at the same time that they help create new knowledge.

In such a world, it is difficult to maintain old views of welfare economics. The once firmly held notion that distribution of resources either did not matter or could not matter (Arrow, 1963) was giving way to a new view based on the idea that a valuable resource could be widely distributed without a market. This non-market good could also impact millions of lives simultaneously, could be "owned" by everyone or anyone, and could come from any sector—not just through industry.

The same technology that gives knowledge and power to change the lives of people who have lived on the margins previously has also created a network of linkages that ties rich and poor ever closer together. Transportation, finance, communication, learning, social network, and globalization of industries create vast linkages resulting in interdependencies that the world had not previously experienced. Whereas, before technology, the world could reasonably be divided between countries of rich or poor, East or West, North or South, Christian, Buddhist, or Muslim, now the world has links and connections that melt these borders.

The field of security studies began to redefine itself as the study of some of these interdependencies with a strategic view (Lynn-Jones & Miller, 1995; Woods, 2005). Others focused on the global costs of neglecting particularly poor countries known as fragile states (Rice, 2006). In either view, there is a cost to neglecting these interdependencies and inequalities between countries. The interdependencies include such things as migration, global disease, political and social unrest, environmental degradation, and famine. The solutions to these global challenges are often viewed in terms of social justice. Managing and mitigating human needs such as poverty and basic needs stabilizes the world. In all cases, education and access to learning are seen as the means of this mitigation. All the early works in these two closely linked literatures occurred before the Arab Spring, which taught the world the power of social networks and collective learning to challenge entire government and spread across borders. The fact that the early literature focused on the threat of global inequalities and the need to mitigate them demonstrates that equality, ethics, equity, and knowledge were taking on an entirely different relationship even at the beginning of knowledge economics.

Again, although the existence of these so-called "weak states" and their links to wealthier countries seems a far cry from the topic at hand—social justice and education leadership—that distance is only illusionary. This is because the traditional views of education have been so closely tied to schooling and schooling so closely tied to production (DeYoung, 1989). But, through the lens of knowledge economics, one can see a new link of education through social networks, lifelong learning, and a global system of knowledge distribution. In this view, the social wellbeing of societies is linked to each other through health, environment, political, and social networks. The stability of such global systems is highly linked to education—whether education is defined as formal schooling systems or informal knowledge systems (Eizenstat, Porter, & Weinstein, 2005; Rotberg, 2002).

Much of this early theoretical work, coming from the fields of economics, development studies and technology may seem far afield from the traditional view of education, which has generally had some familiar characteristics. In this view, education is generally thought to be nationally planned, expertise driven, contained within institutions, and circumscribed by curriculum, learning objectives, and competencies. In this view, educational leaders are the planners and managers. But it is the very contrast of this global system—digitized, dynamic, collective, socially networked, and spread through non-markets—that is not only reshaping our definitions of education but is establishing the parameters of social justice and learning. In this new world, leadership involves helping to direct policies such that the natural flow on learning and information becomes accessible to the widest number of people (Foray & Lundvall, 1996). To understand just how this works, it is necessary to understand how knowledge works on its own.

CHARACTERISTICS OF KNOWLEDGE

Historically, knowledge has been produced, transmitted, and transferred by highly educated people (elites) and sent, largely one way, from the top to the bottom. This possession of knowledge was often exclusive knowledge. As education was a way of transmitting knowledge from the top to the bottom, traditional educational systems have been viewed as a way to maintain elite power (Apple, 1993; Van Doren, 1992). Although the elites often acquired more knowledge (or more valuable knowledge) than ordinary people, some knowledge has traditionally shifted to non-elites through the schooling system.

This is changing. There is now a revolution in the economic paradigm combined with technological innovation. Anyone in the world can produce, transmit, and transfer knowledge. It flows though learning and a social network and accumulates with collective practices and adaptive ways (Lundvall & Johnson, 1994; Vicari & Troilo, 2000) . Learning is becoming less elitist.

Although systems of knowledge that exclude users due to ownership, membership, or money still exist and will continue to exist, the characteristics of knowledge in this digital, networked age create the conditions for a fundamental shift. This can be seen by understanding how knowledge creates a valuable contribution to society, which contrasts with the creation and ownership of physical products (Foray & Lundvall, 1996).

First, knowledge is *not excludable*. It can be used by many people at the same time, and it is mobile, whereas physical goods can only be used by one person (or group) at a time and move slowly as a physical unit. Because knowledge has this characteristic, it tends to leak and diffuse among people. Thus, it is hard to control its use, ownership, and distribution.

Second, it is *not easily owned*. Knowledge, in this digitized world, has limited value if it is hidden. Knowledge moves toward freedom and wide distribution. Although one can establish intellectual property rights, sometimes it makes more sense to distribute new ideas broadly, because that distribution has power in itself.

Third, it is *cumulative*. It keeps adding to the existing body of knowledge. Fourth, it is *not depletable*. Thus, new knowledge builds on old knowledge and accumulates. In so doing, it always increases in supply. The creation of knowledge causes people to want more knowledge—unlike physical goods, where it is assumed that wide possession of something (lots of people are eating apples, for example) causes the demand to shrink (people want a different fruit eventually). Thus, different from natural resources, knowledge can create its own supply and demand.

Fifth, it is *cheap to replicate* because it has increasing returns of scale. Physical products have diminishing returns of scale. The use of physical products, like oil, causes the price of oil to rise (because supply is limited).

Thus, each unit of oil costs a bit more to produce (increasing returns to scale). Knowledge may have very high costs to produce in the beginning, but is cheap to replicate. Once an idea goes on the internet (or is digitized in some other format), anyone can access it for very little money.

Sixth, it is *networked and transferable.* Depending on advanced technology, knowledge can be spread through the internet and social networks. Physical goods must be sold through a market, owned and have controlled distribution. But knowledge grows naturally through networks (Barabasi, 2005).

Finally, it can be *substituted for physical goods.* Although it cannot replace all of physical goods, knowledge can replace the need for some of them. For example, Skype can replace a physical business trip to save costs. In the previous example, the invention of new coding to transmit the internet will save substantial investment in more equipment (routers), electricity, and the cost of building and installing cables throughout the world.

Whereas, in the traditional view of knowledge, schools passed on knowledge so that individuals could be more productive *through the marketplace,* these new characteristics of knowledge show that knowledge has its own independent rules of exchange, creation, and value generation that can be independent of schools and capital markets. Thus, the traditional view that education = schools is no longer held. Education is now viewed as the exchange of ideas, the building of new knowledge, and the acquiring of skills and information in a variety of ways according to context and needs of individuals, societies, communities, and networks. Educational leaders are not necessarily only school leaders, but also policymakers who manage learning systems rather than direct schools (Senge, 2010).

EXAMPLES OF THE NEW ECONOMICS AND NEW EQUALITY

Many of these characteristics point to a very different environment in which learning and knowledge creation contribute to the welfare of individuals and their societies. In the economics built around industrial societies, quantitative accumulation was the goal of a society. In a knowledge society, sustainability is the goal (Giovannini et al., 2009). In an industrial society, distribution of resources only mattered once accumulation was maximized, but in a knowledge society, distribution is the very means by which ideas are created—it is the essence of social welfare. In an industrial society, facts, data, and skills were emphasized for industrial gain. In a knowledge society, flow of information among people is emphasized because accumulated knowledge and collective knowledge adds to the total wellbeing of society (Free Word Academy, n.d.; Romer, 1991; Sen, 1995; Von Krough, Nonaka, & Nishiguchi, 2000).

These characteristics are all linked to equality. Either the characteristic *contributes to* a more equal society, or the characteristic is a *function of* a more equal society. The following are three examples to show how these characteristics work. In each case, the definition of education must be viewed as learning (rather than, necessarily, formal education), and the flow of learning must be viewed as a network (rather than an institution). In so doing, the environment for social justice is reframed.

Medical Breakthrough Using Crowd Sourcing

The first example shows the interplay of expertise and collective knowledge. In 2011, gamers playing an online protein-folding game (Foldit, n.d.) helped to determine the structure of an enzyme that needed to be understood in order to further the fight against HIV and AIDS. After more than a decade of trying by scientists, engineers, and automated computer programs, the structure of the HIV protein was finally "folded" (Olivarez-Giles, 2011). The folding patterns were not obvious and had eluded these experts. But gamers in the University of Washington stepped in and created an online game and made it public. In so doing, they challenged the online gaming community to work collectively to find the precise folding patterns (Freeman, 2011). Gamers did not have to know anything about the science or the protein. They just needed to view the structure (of the molecule) and intuit, step-by-step, which moves might lead to a particular final structural form. One group, known as "Eternal Motion Machine," reportedly logged 50 million moves (Foldit, n.d.).

Under the former theory of how education worked with economics, the value of people's labor was assumed to approximate the rate they were paid (human capital theory). This rate was also assumed to approximate their relative contribution to society. Using this valuation scheme, the expert's labor, over decades, was worth perhaps millions of dollars, while the gamers' labor would have been worth nothing.

But in the emerging view of knowledge economics, the goal of a sustainable society (recognizing that we are all linked together) would value the gamers' contribution as very high. Without the ability to build knowledge collectively as gamers had done, this scientific solution would not have been possible. Of course, the scientists made a substantial contribution as well. Their work conceived of the problem, and the scientists must now use the results to design a medical intervention.

The principle lesson in this example is that networks of learning are allowing social value to be created by groups of people collectively. Their contribution is inherently valued as their contribution to a better society—not how much they were paid to do the job. Although the gamers may well have "exchanged" their thinking power and time for a chance to learn (new challenge, group dynamic, learn how this new technique can work), they were drawn to the challenge, in large part, because the outcome was so significant for the wellbeing of the larger society.

In the schooling view of education, individuals are generally thought to be taught "expert" knowledge that will reap reward in terms of future income and productivity. In contrast, this example shows that collectives of people, often working outside of their regular work hours, often defining this "work" as "fun," created millions of dollars' worth of value without compensation. Rather, they were not compensated by money—but they were compensated through new networks, through new understandings of how to create knowledge, and through the satisfaction of learning how to create value for their society. Educational leaders will need to begin to think of learning outside of the schooling paradigm. Increasingly, their students, neighbors, church members, civic organization colleagues, and distant social network linked friends will be creating knowledge within these social networks, drawing from these social networks and creating value for society within these social networks. How is educational leadership thinking of knowledge through social networks?

New Technology and Sustainability

The second idea is an example of how ideas can change the use of resources simply by introducing a new idea. In so doing, as knowledge increasingly plays a larger role in the wellbeing of societies, it also shows how knowledge economics helps us understand how societies more sustainable through knowledge creation.

Australia's Centre for Ultrahigh Bandwidth Devices for Optical Systems (CUDOS) recently developed data a new way to encode data that increases the efficiency of existing fiber optic cable networks. The new encoding scheme squeezes information into "spaces" that had been left empty using existing fiber optic encoding (Monash University, 2013). The new data capacity is so much larger that it is alleged that all of the world's internet traffic could be transmitted via a single fiber. Professor Lowry, part of the research team, says, "Rather than laying hundreds of new parallel optical fibers to boost network capacity, we can make more efficient use of the existing network by tweaking the way data is transmitted over long distances" (Quick, 2013). Although the internet became available first in the wealthiest neighborhoods in the wealthiest countries, its falling prices and increased access has meant that even remote places now have increasing access to the internet:

> On a global scale, Africa has recorded some of the strongest telecom growth rates over 2005-2010, as falling prices and greater competition have allowed a greater proportion of the continent's populace access to networks and services. Sub-Saharan Africa alone saw a rise of 428.7% in Internet users over 2005–2010, by far the largest regional increase. (Europmonitor International, 2011)

In this example, the economic impact is purely from a new idea. The idea, and only the idea, plays a role in reducing resource costs (less electricity) and saving investments in equipment. In so doing, the ability to create ideas and spread them digitally[3] allows for the possibility that the creation of new ideas reduces resource usage. Ideas and the learning that goes into them helps create a more sustainable society.

Internet and Free Societies

The internet, itself, serves as a third example. It shows how learning takes place to free people. It works in a networked way, using principles of social network theory (Anklam, 2009; Barabasi, 2005), such that its power and influence spreads through natural paths of influence. Such systems do not like to be owned and controlled. Unlike physical goods or even services where ownership and control are much easier to establish, digitized knowledge is much harder to hold on to, to assure it cannot be spread and to control.

The internet has become much more than a system of information flow. It has become a system that is changing the nature of societies and the interface of citizens and their governments. Reflecting on his trips to North Korea and Burma, Eric Schmidt of Google remarked:

> [Autocratic regimes] can't completely shut [the internet] off because the Internet is too important for their business and their other goals. So a little bit of Internet in there will bring some openness and some ideas to every single country.... Countries that have the Internet already are not going to turn it off. And so the power of freedom, the power of ideas will spread, and it will change those societies in very dramatic ways.... All they have to do is turn it on a little bit and they can't turn it back. Once the ideas are in, you cannot kick them out of the country. (National Public Radio, 2013)

This is closely allied with a major redefinition of economic development emerging from the work of Amyrta Sen whose Nobel Prize-winning work helped redefine social welfare from welfare "maximization" to human welfare (Sen, 1995). His redefinition "means that more people vote, literacy rates rise, average years of schooling go up, and life expectancy increases. The goal of economic development thus becomes expanding individual choices or opportunities and providing more positive freedoms to people" (Robeyns,

2005, p. 98). His work has been a base for the new knowledge economics along with several other Nobel Prize winners (Giovannini et al., 2009).

NEW THINKING ABOUT THE ROLE OF LEARNING AND INEQUALITY

In neoclassical economics, inequality was not an issue for economic theory to address. Neoclassical economics contends that the best society is one where the overall wealth and income of the society is maximized—regardless of distribution (Johannsson, 1991).[4]

The possibilities of new access, creation, and ownership of knowledge have caused new thinking about the role of learning and inequality. Below are descriptions of three major paradigm shifts that have caused the re-thinking of inequality and social justice in economics and, by extension, to learning and education.

First, the paradigm in economics related to education has changed from human capital (production) to providing access to learning (learning economy[5]). Encompassing advances in information technology, flexible specialization, changes in the process of innovation, and new assessment of how societies are driven by knowledge, the field has emerged since the 1990s (Lundvall & Johnson, 1994). Knowledge is likely to be an outcome and output of learning—"interactive learning." Interactive learning produces and uses new knowledge in an organization or group.

Because access to facts and information is increasingly cheap and accessible for many people throughout the world, the trend is to move away from traditional education where access to facts, skills, and information comes from a particular source (textbook or teacher's instruction). Because such access is driven by physical and labor resources (classrooms, texts, infrastructure, teachers), it is expensive. Access is limited to group access (generally schools) around a rigid schedule and often in a hierarchically fragmented manner (built around specific places at a certain time). But the new economics of knowledge shows that knowledge can be relatively cheaply accessed and dispersed. Because facts, skills, and information are widely and cheaply available, it frees resources (time, money, labor) to focus on high-order learning—innovation, creativity, and knowledge creation (Cunningham, 2007; Sawyer, 2006a; Von Krough et al., 2000).

The second paradigm shift emphasizes strengthening people's capabilities. Amaryta Sen theorized that this type of focus allows people and groups to come up with new ideas, especially in their own context (Robeyns, 2005; Sen, 1995). According to Sen's capability-centered approach, societal well-being depends upon empowering a person's capability to pursue his or her objectives. "A capability set represents a person's opportunities to achieve well-being. We may also say that is represents a person's freedom, with 'freedom' being understood in the positive rather than the negative sense—that is, in terms of 'freedom to...', rather than 'freedom from...'" (Sugden, 1993, p. 1951).

It is the acquisition of these capabilities that defines the wellbeing of a society. Implicitly, people who have little or no access to these capabilities handicap the society. Thus, justice enters directly into this equation. Giving people the right to access their capabilities promotes social wellbeing as well as increasing the society's social justice. Sen's definition of equality provided the theoretical framework to the UN Human Development (Ashford & Hall, 2011). According to the UN Human Development, *equality* is the "process of enlarging people's choices" (UNDP, 1990, p. 10).

The final paradigm shift joins Sen's thinking about societies with the notion that knowledge is a *created* resource that societies can foster. New ideas, innovations, and ways of adapting are central to a society's ability to build successful and sustainable lives. In order to foster these new ideas and innovations, societies must provide access to increasing levels of learning as a means of pursuing societal wellbeing. Concurrently, access to learning provides people with the ability to use and build new knowledge. It is in the society's best interest to assure a strong access to learning for everyone. In this instance, relatively equitable distribution of resources (e.g., networks of learning and education) has direct effects on the society's wellbeing.

Whereas ideas and innovations can come from anywhere, including poorly educated communities, many ideas and innovations will result from people who are educated and can easily use global networks of knowledge. There are, however, some issues related to the equitable provision of higher education. Today's access to higher education comes with high costs and is often only easily accessible to wealthier people in the society (Alon, 2009; Unterhalter & Carpentier, 2010).

An alternative is emerging with innovative technologies and ideas (Barr & Tagg, 1995; Berge, 2000). Through these new technologies, each individual can produce, transmit, and transfer knowledge via innovative technologies. Examples can be found in learning 2.0, MOOCs (Johnstone, 2005), Khan Academy (Thompson, 2011), Coursera (Lewin, 2012), and the Global Knowledge Institute (GKI, 2012). They provide free or low-cost higher education and follow the nature of knowledge. The "learning ecology" is likely to be created in an open-source environment (Barron, 2006). More people can learn without any barriers of cost, time, and place. This same technology provides the means whereby these same learners can produce and distribute new knowledge.

CONCLUSION

The paradigm of knowledge economics patterns the process of change from industrial economy to knowledge economy. The old view, which has interpreted the role of education in economics as unswayed by social justice, cannot explain the growing importance of equality and social justice in this era of knowledge economy. Because the new view of social welfare involves the ability (or capability) of individuals to create, innovate, develop and share new ideas, the focus is no longer on industrial productivity. Rather, individuals and groups contribute to social well-being in many ways through these new ideas—work, civic life, social organizations, social networks, political participation, and family life.

This is not to say that human capital, funneled through industry, becomes irrelevant. Individuals and society will always benefit from education and learning (i.e., knowledge flow) and certainly build human capital. It can be important for every individual as a knowledge creator to access higher education or higher levels of learning. But the prevailing economic paradigm cannot encompass human capital that contributes to society apart from employment (or the value of one's labor). As the example (above) of the gamers who solved a critical medical problem without being paid for their labor shows, the ability to be creative has value beyond the cost of labor. Under these conditions, the ability of society to create broad access to learning is a positive input to that society. The long-held neoclassical view that society benefits only from wealth/income accumulation does not fit this scenario.

This has profound implication for educational leadership. Since the growth of industrial production and the subsequent massification of schooling, educational leadership has been viewed as a profession that either manages or guides schools or school policies in large part. But, as learning is redefined in this new era, people are likely to take control of their own learning experiences, expectations, and goals. Whereas nations and communities once had an economic stake in assuring that everyone (or nearly everyone) had enough education to be part of the economic production machine, the learning system that is evolving requires that leadership change its focus from directly government schooling to setting the guidelines for greater access to opportunities to learn. Leadership is not so much the leadership of schools or systems as much as it is the insight to provide the parameters that provide for an equitable learning system and globally linked access.

There are important limitations in what we have presented. First, we have largely dwelled on inequality with respect to the field of economics. We did not deal with the notions of inequality generally used in the education literature. This literature usually derives from the fields of sociology and political science.

Unlike neoclassical economists, sociologists and political scientists argue that inequality substantially affects the overall wellbeing of a society. Rawls (1971) insisted that justice (equity) is based on a social contract of fairness that is important for a healthy society. For many who study education, an individual country may focus on maximizing growth, but there are very real political and social costs to inequality. This obvious fact may underlie the rebirth of Keynesian economic policy after several global financial crises (Krugman, 2009).

Another limitation of what has been addressed in this chapter is that that new view is still unformed as a full theory. It has no mathematical model, so any notion of wellbeing in the society cannot be clearly measured. Because many of the new concepts directly contradict the prevailing view of economics, many scholars remain skeptical that a new theory is emerging—even as they acknowledge that knowledge is a driving force in modern economies (Mirowski, 2009; Temple, 1999). Despite the mathematical limitations and the still unformed full theory of knowledge economics, there is a growing acceptance of the ideas because they explain so much of the new phenomenon of social wellbeing, equality, and spread of knowledge that is visible today (Warsh, 2007).

Consequently, the entire area of social justice and inequality in economics and education needs considerably more investigation. Human capital needs to be reexamined in light of the new theory and its implications for equality and social justice. Although the theory of human capital and the theory of knowledge economics are incompatible, the *notions* of knowledge and human capital remain viable today (as they are, in fact, viable in each theory). Google is a good example. It is one of leading companies in the knowledge-based industry and operates, substantially, along the precepts of knowledge economics. Yet Google employs considerable human capital.

This chapter has outlined two converging trends. First, the emergence and growing prominence of a theory of knowledge economics questions whether the field of economics can rightly disregard inequality. Second, trends emerging and analyzed through the lens of the economics of knowledge have shifted thinking on how learning is spread, built, disseminated, and shared. As both these emerging views depend heavily on the widespread use of learning, they set the stage from considerable reexamination of the role of equality in social wellbeing. It is interesting to note that both trends center on the importance of learning in knowledge creation, dissemination, and societal wellbeing. So, in this new era, learning, equality, and social justice are substantially tied together.

NOTES

1. It is important to note that the term "welfare" is being used in this chapter as it is commonly understood in economics. That is, it refers to wellbeing (or happiness or utility as economists tend to call them)—either the wellbeing of an individual or the wellbeing of an entire society. Thus, most economists believe that the goal of a society is to maximize its wellbeing.
2. Although the emergence of the theory is attributed to Romer (1993), his work is based on the earlier work of Solow (1957).
3. Physical manifestations of ideas such as musical LP records, books, hand-painted artwork do not have the same quality. Since they are not in digital form, their ownership, access, and costs of production are more in keeping with industrial economics. It is the digital form that reduces distribution costs, encourages rapid spread, and is cheap or free to duplicate.
4. Although it may seem obvious that a more equal society is a better society, neo-classical economics rejects this idea. In order for a society to be more equal, someone (rich) has to give up something to someone else (poor, likely). In this transfer, however, it cannot be clear that the person giving up something lost less in value (happiness) than the receiver gained in value (happiness). This is because we cannot compare the relative value each person placed on this transfer. Society's net gain or loss is, thus, unknown. So, redistribution (a more equal society) has unknown consequences for the society (Arrow, 1963).
5. As the theory of knowledge economics evolves, the name used for the theory is also evolving. When introduced, the theory was called endogenous technological change (Romer, 1991). Many policy organizations refer to the theory as knowledge economics (Schleicher, 2006; "Society for Knowledge Economics," n.d.). Later, a more common name was new growth theory (Cortight, 2001). Lundvall and Johnson (1994) coined the term "learning economy," which seems to be used quite commonly now.

REFERENCES

Aghion, P., Caroli, E., & García-Peñalosa, C. (1999). Inequality and Economic Growth: The Perspective of the New Growth Theories. *Journal of Economic Literature, 37*(4), 1615–1660.

Alon, S. (2009). The Evolution of Class Inequality in Higher Education Competition, Exclusion, and Adaptation. *American Sociological Review, 74*(5), 731–755.

Anklam, P. (2009). Ten years of net work. *The Learning Organization, 16*(6), 415–426.

Apple, M. (1993). The politics of official knowledge: Does a national curriculum make sense? *Discourse, 14*(1), 1–16.

Arrow, K. (1963). *Social choice and individual values.* New York, NY: Wiley.

Ashford, N., & Hall, R. (2011). *Technology, globalization, and sustainable development: transforming the industrial state.* New Haven, CT: Yale University Press.

Barabasi, A. L. (2005). Science of networks: From society to the web. In K. Nyiri (Ed.), *A sense of place: The global and the local in mobile communication* (pp. 415–429). Vienna, Austria: Passagen.

Barr, R., & Tagg, J. (1995). From teaching to learning—A new paradigm for undergraduate education. *Change: The Magazine of Higher Learning, 27*(6), 12–26.

Barron, B. (2006). Interest and self-sustained learning as catalysts of development: A learning ecology perspective. *Human Development, 49*(4), 193–224.

Baum, S., Ma, J., & Payea, K. (2010). *Education pays, 2010: The benefits of higher education for individuals and society. Trends in Higher Education Series.* New York, NY: College Board Advocacy & Policy Center.

Berge, Z. (2000). Why not reengineer traditional higher education? In L. A. Petrides (Ed.), *Case studies on information technology in higher education: Implications for policy and practice* (pp. 209–216). Hershey, PA: Idea Group Publishing.

Birdsall, N., Ross, D., & Sabot, R. (1995). Inequality and growth reconsidered: Lessons from East Asia. *The World Bank Economic Review, 9*(3), 477–508.

Bowman, M. J. (1996). The human investment revolution in economic thought. *Sociology of Education, 38*(2), 111–137.

Chatti, M. A., Jarke, M., & Frosch-Wilke, D. (2007). The future of e-learning: A shift to knowledge networking and social software. *International Journal of Knowledge and Learning, 3*(4), 404–420.

Cochrane, T. D. (2011). Beyond the yellow brick road: Mobile Web 2.0 informing a new institutional e-learning strategy. *Journal of Asynchronous Learning Networks, 15*(4), 60–68.

Cortight, J. (2001). *New growth theory, technology and learning: A practitioner's guide (No. 4).* Washington, D.C.: U.S. Economic Development Administration

Cunningham, S. (2007). The creative economy: Patterning the future. *Dialogue: Academy of the Social Sciences in Australia, 26*(1), 15–23.

Depover, C., & Schneider, D. (2012, June). Opportunities and requirements for socio-constructivist learning in Web 2.0. In *World Conference on Educational Multimedia, Hypermedia and Telecommunications* 2012(1), 1861–1869.

DeYoung, A. J. (1989). *Economics and American education: A historical and critical overview of the impact of economic theories on schooling in the United States.* New York, NY: Addison-Wesley Longman.

Edwards, P. N., Jackson, S. J., Chalmers, M. K., Bowker, G. C., Borgman, C. L., Ribes, D., ... Calvert, S. (2013). *Knowledge infrastructures: Intellectual frameworks and research challenges* (Working Paper). Retrieved from http://deepblue.lib.umich.edu

Eizenstat, S. E., Porter, J. E., & Weinstein, J. M. (2005). Rebuilding weak states. *Foreign Affairs, 84*, 134.

Europmonitor International. (2011, October 10). Regional focus: Africa experiencing fastest growth in internet users worldwide. *Europmonitor International.* Retrieved from http://blog.euromonitor.com/2011/10/regional-focus-africa-experiencing-fastest-growth-in-internet-users-worldwide.html

Field, J. (2006). The learning economy. In J. Field (Ed.), *Lifelong learning and the new educational order* (pp. 69–100). Stroke on Trent, UK: Trentham Books.

Fitzpatrick, T. (2001). *Welfare theory: An introduction.* New York, NY: Palgrave.

Foldit. (n.d.). Foldit. *Solve Puzzles for Science.* Retrieved from http://fold.it/portal/

Foray, D., & Lundvall, B.-A. (1996). The knowledge-based economy: from the economics of knowledge to the learning economy. In D. Foray & B.-A. Lundvall

(Eds.), *Employment and growth in the knowledge-based economy* (pp. 11–32). Paris, France: OECD.

Forbes, K. J. (2000). A Reassessment of the relationship between inequality and growth. *The American Economic Review, 90*(4), 869–887.

Free Word Academy. (n.d.). New growth theory: Creativity. *Global Leader.* Retrieved from http://www.freeworldacademy.com/globalleader/ecodev.htm

Freeman, D. (2011, September 20). Gamers solve HIV puzzle that stymied scientists. *CBS News.* Retrieved from http://www.cbsnews.com/8301-504763_162-20108763-10391704.html

Giovannini, E., Hall, J., Morrone, A., & Giulia, R. (2009). *A framework to measure the progress of societies.* OECD Working Paper. Paris, France: OECD. Retrieved from http://www.oecd.org

GKI. (2012). Global Knowledge Alliance. Retrieved from http://www.gkalinks.org

Ilon, L. (2011). Can education equality trickle-down to economic growth? The case of Korea. *Asia Pacific Education Review, 12*(4), 653–663.

Johannsson, P. O. (1991). *An introduction to modern welfare economics.* Cambridge, UK: Cambridge University Press.

Johnson, B., & Andersen, A. D. (2012). *Learning, Innovation and inclusive development: New perspective on economic development strategy and development aid.* Aalborg, Denmark: Aalborg University Press. Retrieved from http://vbn.aau.dk

Johnstone, S. M. (2005). Open educational resources serve the world. *Educause Quarterly, 28*(3), 15.

Krugman, P. (2009, February 9). How did economists get it so wrong? *New York Times.* Retrieved from http://www.nytimes.com/2009/09/06/magazine/06Economic-t.html?pagewanted=all&_r=0

Kuhn, T. (1970). *The structure of the scientific revolution.* Chicago, IL: University of Chicago Press.

Lancet. (1978). Water with sugar and salt. *Lancet, 2,* 300–301.

Lewin, T. (2012, July 17). Universities reshaping education on the web. *New York Times.* Retrieved from http://www.nytimes.com/2012/07/17/education/consortium-of-colleges-takes-online-education-to-new-level.html?pagewanted=all

Lundvall, B. A., & Johnson, B. (1994). The learning economy. *Industry and Innovation, 1*(2), 23–42.

Lynn-Jones, S., & Miller S. (Eds.). (1995). *Global dangers: Changing dimensions of international security.* Cambridge, MA: MIT Press.

Mirowski, P. (2009). Why there is (as yet) no such thing as an economics of knowledge. In H. Kincaid & D. Ross (Eds.), *The Oxford handbook of philosophy and economics* (pp. 99–156). Oxford, UK: Oxford University Press.

Monash University. (2013, March 25). Improving the flow of the fibre optic freeway. *Phys.org.* Retrieved from http://phys.org/news

National Public Radio. (2013, April 23). Google execs Say "the power of information is underrated": *All Tech Considered.* NPR.org. Retrieved from http://www.npr.org/blogs/alltechconsidered/2013/04/23/178620215/google-execs-say-the-power-of-information-is-underrated

Nieves, J., & Osorio, J. (2013). The role of social networks in knowledge creation. *Knowledge Management Research & Practice, 11*(1), 62–77.

OECD. (2004, February). *Lifelong learning.* Paris, France: Author.

Olivarez-Giles, N. (2011, September 19). Foldit gamers help unlock possible AIDS-fighting protein. *LA Times*. Retrieved from http://latimesblogs.latimes.

Ouane, A. (2011). Evolution of and perspectives on lifelong learning. In J. Yang (Ed.), *Conceptual evolution and policy developments in lifelong learning conceptual evolution and policy developments in lifelong learning* (pp. 24–39). Paris, France: UNESCO. Retrieved from http://literacyportal.net

Psacharopoulos, G. (1981). Returns to education: An updated international comparison. *Comparative Education, 17*(3), 321–341.

Quick, D. (2013, April 7). Closing the gap to improve the capacity of existing fiber optic networks. *Gizmag*. Retrieved from http://www.gizmag.com/cudos-fiber-optic-network-capacity/26969/

Rawls, J. (1971). *A theory of social justice*. Cambridge, MA: Harvard University Press.

Rice, S. (August 2, 2006). *Global poverty, weak states and insecurity*. Presented at the The Brookings Blum Roundtable: Session I; Poverty, Insecurity and Conflict, Washington, D.C.: Brookings Blum Roundtable. Retrieved from http://www.brookings.edu/~/media/research/files/papers/2006/8/globaleconomics%20rice/08globaleconomics_rice.pdf

Robeyns, I. (2005). The capability approach: a theoretical survey. *Journal of Human Development, 6*(1), 93–117.

Romer, P. (1991). *Endogenous technological change* (Working Paper No. 3210). National Bureau of Economic Research. Retrieved from http://www.nber.org

Romer, P. (1993). Two strategies for economic development: using ideas and producing ideas. In L. Summers & S. Shekhar (Eds.), *Proceedings of the World Bank annual conference on development economics 1992* (pp. 63–92). Washington, D.C.: World Bank. Retrieved from http://documents.worldbank.org/curated/en/1993/03/699081/proceedings-world-bank-annual-conference-development-economics-1992

Rosen, S. (1989). Human Capital. In *Social Economics* (pp. 136–1555). New York: W.W. Norton.

Rotberg, R. I. (2002). The new nature of nation–state failure. *The Washington Quarterly, 5*(3), 83–96.

Sawyer, K. (2006a). The new science of learning. In K. Sawyer (Ed.), *Cambridge handbook of the learning sciences* (pp. 1–16). New York, NY: Cambridge University Press.

Sawyer, K. (2006b). Educating for innovation. *Thinking Skills and Creativity, 1*(1), 41–48.

Schleicher, A. (2006). *The economics of knowledge: Why education is key for Europe's success*. Lisbon Council. Retrieved from http://www.lisboncouncil.net//index.php?option=com_downloads&id=85

Schultz, T. (1961). Investment in human capital. *The American Economic Review, 51*(1), 1–17.

Sen, A. (1995). Rationality and social choice. *American Economic Review, 85*(1), 1–24.

Senge, P. M. (2010). *The fifth discipline: The art & practice of the learning organization*. New York, NY: Crown.

Society for Knowledge Economics. (n.d.). *The world has changed, are you ready to change with it?* Retrieved from http://www.ske.org.au/

Solow, R. (1957). Technical change and the aggregate production function. *Review of Economics and, 39*(3), 312–320.

Sugden, R. (1993). Welfare, resources, and capabilities: A review of inequality re-examined by Amartya Sen. *Journal of Economic Literature, 31*(4), 1947–1962.

Temple, J. (1999). The new growth evidence. *Journal of Economic Literature, 37*(1), 112–156.

Thomas, V., Wang, Y., & Fan, X. (2001). *Measuring Education Inequality: Gini Coefficients of Education.* World Bank Publications.

Thompson, C. (2011, July 15). How Khan Academy is changing the rules of education. *Wired Digital.* Retrieved from http://www.wired.com/magazine/2011/07/ff_khan/

UNDP. (1990). *Human development report, 1990.* New York, NY: Oxford University Press.

Unterhalter, E., & Carpentier, V. (2010). *Global inequalities and higher education: Whose interests are you serving?* New York, NY: Palgrave Macmillan.

Van Doren, C. (1992). *A history of knowledge: Past, present, and future.* New York, NY: Ballantine Books.

Vicari, S., & Troilo, G. (2000). Organizational creativity: A new perspective from cognitive systems theory. In G. von Krough, I. Nonaka, & T. Nishiguchi (Eds.), *Knowledge creation: A source of value* (pp. 63–88). London, UK: Macmillan.

von Krough, G., Nonaka, I., & Nishiguchi, T. (Eds.). (2000). *Knowledge creation: A source of value.* London, UK: Macmillan.

Warsh, D. (2007). *Knowledge and the wealth of nations: A story of economic discovery.* New York, NY: W. W. Norton & Company.

Weinberger, D. (2011). *Too big to know.* New York, NY: Basic Books.

Woods, N. (2005). The shifting politics of foreign aid. *International Affairs, 81*(2), 393–409.

World Health Organization. (2002, May 8). New formula for oral rehydration salts will save millions of lives. *WHO.* Retrieved from http://www.who.int/mediacentre

CHAPTER 8

A PHILOSOPHICAL DECONSTRUCTION OF LEADERSHIP AND SOCIAL JUSTICE ASSOCIATED WITH THE HIGH-STAKES TESTING AND ACCOUNTABILITY SYSTEM

Tawannah G. Allen, Fenwick W. English, and Rosemary Papa

ABSTRACT

In this chapter, the authors argue that the current high-stakes testing and accountability system used in public education is too narrowly defined, applies only to certain schools and to some students, and is not applicable to the larger social system in which schools are embedded. The system also promotes faulty assumptions regarding the purpose of high-stakes testing. These assumptions not only erode the practice of social justice, but they also contradict the philosophy of education conducive to student achievement and effective school

Educational Leadership for Ethics and Social Justice, pages 135–157

leadership. To this end, the chapter concludes with six recommended metrics to provide social justice within the testing and accountability system.

INTRODUCTION

Gunzenhauser (2003) defines the philosophy of education as a set of ideas and commitments about the purpose and value of education that guides our practice and helps us make choices. By understanding this philosophy, better choices are made regarding the who, what, where, when, and how of educating students, while also understanding the role of education in creating a society (Postman, 1995). Ongoing conversations with students attending public schools and their parents, building administrators, and our colleagues not only aids becoming reflective practitioners, but also permits the consideration of multiple educational perspectives. These conversations are influential as these members of society work together to identify and implement their philosophies of education and form their school community.

Postman (1995) questions what kind of public or society the public educational system creates. How this question is answered undergirds the response to how and why we educate children. Also imbedded in this question is how the current accountability system drives the written, taught, and tested curriculum (English, 2010) but also limits teachers' instructional creativity. Unfortunately, an outcome is school-based administrators being forced to abandon their own priorities and visions and adopt those driven by the high-stakes testing movement (Gunzenhauser, 2003).

High-stakes testing refers to the use of standardized testing measures as criteria for determining the quality of schools, promotion of children to the next grade and high school graduation, and teacher bonuses (Gunzenhauser, 2003). Birthed out of the behaviorist philosophy and the rise of neoliberalism, the high-stakes movement places strong emphasis on quantitative measures (Crotty, 1998). Accountability may be defined as the mechanism whereby those in political power use institutional schooling as the means to reinforce their privileged position in the larger society.

The form and use of political power to perform such domination must be disguised, especially within a democratic public sphere. Standardized testing is one of the means that presents such a disguise (Au, 2009). Similarly, the application of testing curriculum knowledge being passed off as culturally neutral and school routines that are homogenous with class differences round out how schools, despite their egalitarian rhetoric, work to keep the poor *poor* (Barry, 2005; Lucas, 1999), while also keeping those in privileged positions from recognizing their own interests in the perpetuation of a system that affords them maximum advantage, a concept Bourdieu called "*misrecognition*" (English, 2012; Webb, Schirato & Danaher, 2002, p. xiv).

The convenient and most utilized forms of assessment today are deeply flawed, socially unjust, and reinforce the gaps between the social "haves" and "have nots" (Au, 2009). In its current state, high-stakes testing and accountability systems have created philosophical conflicts, while also limiting the possibilities for educating students in the public education system (Gunzenhauser, 2003). Assessments commonly employed reflect the dominant perspectives of the cultural elites who have the political power to impose their notions of knowledge and culture on everyone else. Bourdieu and Passeron (2000) have identified this practice as "the cultural arbitrary" (p. 16). The political imposition of the cultural arbitrary perpetuates a form of "symbolic violence" (Bourdieu & Passeron, 2000, p. 31). One manifestation of such "violence" is the achievement gap that falls along socioeconomic, cultural, and racial fault lines with astonishing predictability, not only in the U.S. but internationally (Condron, 2011; Wilkinson & Pickett, 2010).

In this chapter, we briefly speak to how the current high stakes testing accountability system in public education is not only socially unjust but is also in direct contradiction of the philosophy and purpose of democratic education. Also discussed are the faulty assumptions of the high-stakes testing accountability system and their impact on building level leadership. The chapter concludes with a new set of accountability metrics, focused on social justice and leadership, in the high-stakes testing accountability system.

FAULTY ASSUMPTIONS OF THE CURRENT HIGH STAKES TESTING ACCOUNTABILITY MODEL

High-stakes tests and high school graduation exams tend to be found in states with higher percentages of African Americans and Hispanics and lower percentages of Caucasians (Amrein & Berliner, 2002). Proponents of high-stakes testing affix quantifiable measures as criteria for determining the quality of schools, promotion of children to the next grade, teacher bonuses, or as a method associated with school accountability (Guzenhauser, 2003). Other motivations for the use of assessments include a "return back-to-basics" classroom instruction, while also attempting to cast public schools in negative light (Kohn, 2000).

Despite the plethora of research regarding high-stakes accountability, little consideration has been given to its effects on leadership. Principals are regarded as the chief educational accountability officer within their buildings. These responsibilities provide continual pressures of their school possibly being labeled as "low performing, while running the risk of being 'reconstituted' or being taken over by the state. Additional consequences of not being able to improve their test scores, includes having teachers, or even themselves being replaced—essentially sending the entire faculty and administrative team to the 'institutional guillotine'" (Hanson, 2003, p. 3).

To be successful in the age of high-stakes testing and accountability commands exceptional leadership skills. Leadership must influence change or promote continuity in the long term. Hargreaves and Fink (2003) offer sustained leadership as being most advantageous when navigating the testing and accountability system. They define sustainable leadership as:

> Sustainable leadership matters, spreads and lasts. It is a shared responsibility, that does not unduly deplete human or financial resources, and that cares for and avoids exerting negative damage on the surrounding educational and community environment. Sustainable leadership has an activist engagement with the forces that affect it, and builds an educational environment of organizational diversity that promotes cross-fertilization of good ideas and successful practices in communities of shared learning and development. (p. 3)

More importantly, sustainable leadership is sensitive to how privileged communities can be tempted to skim the cream off the local leadership pool. It recognizes and takes responsibility for the fact that schools affect one another in webs of mutual influence (Baker & Foote, 2006).

In this respect, sustainability and succession are inextricably tied up with issues of social justice. It is about being responsible to the schools and students that one's own actions affect in the wider environment (Baker & Foote, 2006). It is about social justice.

While examining the high-stakes testing conundrum, we offer the following faulty assumptions (imperfect premises) as evidence of how the tenets of social justice and the philosophy of education have been misconstrued via the testing and accountability system.

Faulty Assumption 1: High-Stakes Testing Is an Accurate Reflection of Student Learning

The current educational climate supports using high-stakes testing to measure academic performance and student learning. Our current system does not afford an adequate balance of assessment and its use to improve student outcomes. Supporters of high-stakes testing believe that the quality of public education can be vastly improved by introducing a system of rewards and sanctions that are triggered by students' standardized test performance (Raymond & Hanushek, 2003). The No Child Left Behind Act of 2001 initialized the mandate of high-stakes testing of reading and math for all students in grades 3–8 (Amrein & Berliner, 2003). Through an accountability system designed with sanctions and rewards, the goal of No Child Left Behind was to increase student achievement to a level proficiency for all students (Nichols & Glass, 2006) so that all students would be reading at proficiency by 2014.

High-stakes testing has achieved prominence behind the notion of a failing U.S. public educational system. Its role was to assist in the transformation of a perceived broken educational system (Nichols & Glass, 2006). The unintended consequence of NCLB was the inability of rewards and sanctions to increase motivation and learning (Amrein & Berliner, 2003). Sheldon and Biddle (1998) conclude that when stakes are attached to testing, students become alienated from their natural self-directed learning, ultimately separating from their own learning experiences. An increase in dropout and higher student retention rates were additional consequences of high-stakes testing (Normore & Brooks, 2012). Neither of these outcomes have positive effects on student learning. Clearly the time has come to rethink the relationship between standardized assessment and student learning.

Faulty Assumption 2: Every Child Has an Equal Chance at School Success

If the premise is that every child has an equal chance at success in the educational system, then at the end of that system we should find an equal representation of all social classes (Kohn, 2000). This is certainly not the case in the U.S. or in most world educational systems. Bourdieu and Passeron (1979) found that in their study of French universities, lower SES classes were not present in the same numbers proportionate to their larger social position; that is, the middle and upper classes were over-represented in French universities. Similarly, in the U.S., the same trends are evident: Higher education is available more to parents of high income than to parents of low or, now, even middle income (Harding, Jencks, Lopoo, & Mayer, 2005).

The American dilemma is characterized also by the ever-widening wealth gap in which the rich are accumulating more assets while the middle and working classes are just getting by. Currently, the richest 1% hold about 38% of all privately held wealth in the United States, while the bottom 90% held 73% of all debt" (Wikipedia). Leonhardt (2005) put it this way:

> In fact, though, colleges have come to reinforce many of the advantages of birth. On campuses that enroll poorer students, graduation rates are often low.... Only 41% of low-income students entering a four-year college managed to graduate within five years, the U.S. Department of Education found in a 2004 study, but 66% of high-income students did. That gap had grown over recent years. (p. 89)

In short, the larger socioeconomic field is increasingly tilted towards the "haves" using their wealth, influence and political power to further reinforce and advance their own social positions. A recent article in *The Economist* (2012) indicated that the richest 1% of Americans are more politically engaged "than the average 99-percenters" (p. 32). Sixty-eight percent (68%) of the 1% make campaign contributions, "nearly half had contacted a member of Congress and a fifth had solicited contributions on behalf of a candidate" (p. 32). High-poverty students are not afforded the opportunity to participate in the political conversations regarding education, often resulting in the silencing of their issues or perspectives.

Faulty Assumption 3: School Discipline Policies Assist in Promoting Student Learning

One of the most common misconceptions within the American educational system pertains to school discipline policies. The assumption is that these policies are used to promote student learning for all students. The overrepresentation of minority students, particularly African American and Latino males, is not a new finding. As early as 1975, supporting documentation has been provided that minority students, particularly African American males, have been overrepresented in our most exclusionary discipline consequences (Children's Defense Fund). Other groups just as likely to be pushed out of school through these practices include children of poverty (Casella, 2003) and those with academic problems (Balfanz, Spirikakis, Neild, & Legters, 2003).

Offered as an explanation for the high expulsion rates for many districts is that some students do not fit into the norm of the school (Casella, 2003) or that school personnel do not desire to be in control of student behaviors (Noguera, 1995). Those who deviate from the established set of social norms or behavioral rules are subsequently labeled as troublemakers (Bowditch, 1993). Unfortunately, these students, our most vulnerable population, lack the cultural capital needed to navigate toward success within the set school climate (English, 2010). Their failure to acknowledge and follow the hidden curriculum of their school perpetuates their higher identification for disciplinary consequences (Weinstein, Tomlinson-Clarke, & Curran, 2004).

Although commonly used to deter inappropriate behaviors, suspension and expulsion are not effective in meeting the needs of students, especially those of the academic nature (Mayer, 1995). Students identified as struggling often miss valuable instructional time and are faced with compromised learning due to suspensions. Skills missed during periods of suspension are rarely recovered. Despite the possibility of high absenteeism due to suspensions, standardized assessments are used to gauge students learning (Lassen, Steele, & Sailor, 2006).

Faulty Assumption 4: There are No Significant Differences between Children

Testing accountability models that use simple input/output economic and/or efficiency models assume that children are all alike and if not, then, the differences between them are not significant. Such models are blind to socioeconomic and cultural differences as they employ one test which is administered to everyone. If there are differences, they are attributed to "natural" or genetic differences. Rothstein (2004) has noted, "Parents of different social classes tend to raise children somewhat differently" (p. 19).

Lareau (2011) has also commented on this faulty assumption:

> Individuals' social position is not the result of personal attributes such as effort or intelligence. In particular, he [Bourdieu] argues that individuals in privileged social locations are advantaged in ways that are not a result of the intrinsic merit of their cultural experiences. Rather, cultural training in the home is awarded unequal value in dominate institutions because of the close compatibility between the standards of child rearing in privileged homes and the (arbitrary) standards proposed by these institutions. (p. 362)

Delpit (1988) posits, "Children from middle class homes tend to do better than students from non-middle-class families, due to the culture of the school is based upon those in power" (p. 283). For example, Gougis (1986) has argued that "race prejudice in American society is an 'environmental stressor' that increases the emotional stress of blacks over and above that experienced by other groups in the U.S" (p. 147). Gougis also concludes, "Race prejudice is pervasive, persistent, and particularly adverse for blacks in American society" (p. 147). This prejudice is most evident within classrooms and is often predicated by the taught curriculum.

Faulty Assumption 5: Curriculum Knowledge is Neutral

Pierre Bourdieu (1984) observed that, "The 'eye' is a product of history reproduced by education" (p. 3). Children of the upper classes come to school with a repository of cultural experiences that are not those of children from the lower classes. Knowledge is a source of power. Bourdieu (1984) comments that "art and cultural consumption are predisposed, consciously and deliberately or not, to fulfill a social function of legitimating social differences" (p. 7).

The school is the legitimating source of authority in reinforcing social power, and it does so by treating the knowledge prized by the cultural elites as knowledge that must be acquired by everyone. That current concepts of curriculum knowledge favor certain subgroups of students is nearly irrefutable from a vast array of sociological studies (Bratlinger, 2003; Bernstein, 1990). As purveyors of education, Apple (2004) asserts, "We need to place the knowledge that we teach, the social relations that dominate classrooms, the school as a measure of cultural and economic preservation and distribution, and finally, ourselves as people who work in these institutions, back into the context in which they all reside" (p. 3).

Faulty Assumption 6: Student Test Scores are a Reliable indicator of Teacher Effectiveness

Expert educators and political watchdogs resonate with the falsity of tying teacher performance measures to student test scores. Diane Ravitch, a former critic of public education, decries the Arne Duncan drive to force public schools into connecting test scores to teacher evaluation practices. Ravitch (2012) states:

> Duncan's policies demean the teaching profession by treating student test scores as a proxy for teacher quality. A test that a student takes on one day of the year cannot possibly measure the quality of a teacher. (Officially, the administration suggests that test scores are supposed to be only one of multiple measures of teacher quality, but invariably the scores *outweigh every other component* of any evaluation program, as they did in New York City's recent release of the teacher ratings). (p. 2, emphasis in original)

She also says:

> According to an August 30, 2010 Economic Policy Institute report:
>
> Student test scores are not reliable indicators of teacher effectiveness, even with the addition of value-added modeling (VAM), a new Economic Policy Institute report by leading testing experts finds. Though VAM methods have allowed for more sophisticated comparisons of teachers than were possible in the past, they are still inaccurate, so test scores should not dominate the information used by school officials in making high-stakes decisions about the evaluation, discipline and compensation of teachers. (p. 1)

The authors of this report (Eva Baker, Paul Barton, Linda Darling-Hammond, Edward Haertel, Helen Ladd, Paul Linn, Diane Ravitch, Richard Rothstein, Richard Shavelson, and Lorrie Shepard) conclude with the following:

Evaluating teachers accurately is a critical piece of the effort to improve America's schools, and VAM methods are appealing in that they seem to offer an objective and simplified way of comparing one teacher with another. However, as EPI's report makes clear, "There is simply no shortcut to the identification and removal of ineffective teachers." The authors conclude that, "Although standardized test scores of students are one piece of information that school leaders may use to make judgments about teacher effectiveness, test scores should be only a small part of an overall comprehensive evaluation." (p. 8)

Faulty Assumption 7: The Motivations and Goals of Education Reformers Are All the Same

According to Papa and English (2011), the range of motivations for educational reformers is from true altruism to "cheap and quick educational fixes" (p. 43). The for-profit mindset is to be able to adapt, adopt, and scale (Papa, 2012) educational practices that will benefit the stockholders in the company, not the student learners. Today's market includes philanthro-capitalists and their foundations who act in the best interests of their shareholders, not for promoting a strong public education.

Most if not all educators enter teaching and school administration because they feel they can make a difference in children's lives. This belief, coupled with a support for public education, allowed the profession to be underpaid: this and the reality that it is a female-dominated profession. To educate for the common good and foster our country's young into caring, happy citizens who wish to contribute to the welfare of our country can only be achieved if we give ourselves the clarity to develop individuals who feel strong in who they are.

Today, we are failing our students and public schooling by the rhetoric of either the political party who is sided with the billionaires seeking to rape our country's youth or the educators who teach them for short-term profits with no attention to the long-term health of our nation's citizenry.

Faulty Assumption 8: Competition Is the Best for Student Learners

High-stakes testing leads to competitive short-term practices. Sahlberg (2011), in his description of successful educational change in Finland, made the observation that "all of the factors that are behind the Finnish success seem to be the opposite of what is taking place in the United States and much of the rest of the world, where competition, test-based accountability, standardization, and privatization seem to dominate." The Finnish way of educational change, he believes, should be:

> encouraging those who found the path of competition, choice, test-based accountability, and performance-based pay to be a dead end. The future of Finnish education described can moreover offer an alternative means to customized learning. The Finnish Way is to tailor the needs of each child with flexible arrangements and different learning paths. (p. 144)

Unlike the Finnish way, the marketization of public education began 30 years ago with the publication of Milton Friedman's (1962) *Capitalism and Freedom*. Bartlett, Frederick, Gulbrandsen, and Murillo (2002) define marketization as the intensified injection of market principles such as deregulation, competition, and stratification into the public education sector.

Faulty Assumption 9: Performance Pay Incentives Will Drive Productivity

Many anecdotes from private sector pundits and neoliberal consultants advocate connecting educator pay to student test performance. Commonly used in private business settings, performance-based or merit pay has transitioned into the public school sector (Ballou, 2001). Despite many misgivings from the private sector and warnings of the acidic effects such efforts will have on a profession dependent on collaboration, state legislators continue to enact laws that connect student test performance to teacher and administrator pay (Ballou, 2001).

We need only look to the same private sector to see the culture of corruption that pay for performance has produced among the top management of corporate CEOs:

> From 1978 through 2002, federal regulators initiated 585 enforcement actions for financial misrepresentation by publicly traded companies, naming 2,310 individuals and 657 firms as potentially liable parties. The legal penalties imposed on individuals and firms are substantial. For example, individuals were assessed $15.9 billion in fines and civil penalties, and 190 managers received jail sentences for financial reporting violations. Companies were assessed an additional $8.4 billion in fines and damages via class-action lawsuits. (Cools, 2005, p. B2)

Henry Mintzberg (2009) advocates eliminating pay for performance in the form of bonuses. Mintzberg's reasons are that it rests on the following false assumptions:

- A company's health is represented by its financial measures alone—even better, by just the price of its stock.
- Performance measures, whether short or long term, represent the true strength of the company.
- The CEO, with a few other senior executives, is primarily responsible for the company's performance.

Mintzberg indicated that:

> I believe that if you do pay bonuses, you get the *wrong* person in that chair [the CEO's position]. At the worst, you get a self-centered narcissist. At the best, you get someone who is willing to be singled out from everyone else by virtue of the compensation plan. Is this any way to build community within an enterprise, even to foster the very sense of enterprise that is so fundamental to economic strength? (p. R6)

A recent example was that of Michael Mendes, CEO of Diamond Foods, who was dismissed in the wake of accounting irregularities, which was going to force his company to restate the last two years of earnings and which sent the stock price down 37%. The Diamond Board was "untangling its financial reports, managing a heavy debt load, repairing frayed relations with growers, assembling a new management team and finding a way to boost sales and profit" (Karp, Lublin, & Glazer, 2012, B1.)

According to Tirozzi (2010), while corporate barons insist on pay-for-performance, business management literature is filled with "warnings about incentives that rely heavily on quantitative rather than qualitative measures" (p. 2). He warns that short-term results are emphasized rather than long-term results. He finds that corporate barons actually understand this for the corporate world. He cites "a May 2010 Economic Policy Institute report [that] estimates that only one in seven private-sector employees is covered by a bonus or merit plan, which account for just a fraction of total compensation" (p. 2).

SUMMARY

The current politics of educational accountability are blind to the philosophy and purpose of education, the enormous social class differences, and the impact such differences make on not just student achievement, but also school leadership. The focus has been only on schools and the repeated moniker of "failing schools" in the descriptions of what's wrong with the public education. Under current arrangements, the schools will continue to fail the nation's poorest and most culturally diverse students. Bernstein (1990) put it this way:

Summarizing so far, theories of cultural reproduction are concerned with messages, the messages or patterns of dominance. We are here referring concretely to what goes on in a school; the talk, the values, the rituals, the codes of conduct are biased in favor of a dominant group. These privilege a dominant group, so such codes of communication are distorted in favor of one group, the dominant group. But there is another distortion at the same time; the culture, the practice, and consciousness of the dominated group are misrepresented, distorted. They are recontextualized as having less value. Thus there is a double distortion. However theories of culture reproduction are essentially theories of communication without an explicit theory of communication. (p. 171)

It is clear that if accountability as a concept is to do anything but reinforce the current failures of schooling some students, it must employ a different set of metrics. It is to this issue we now turn.

NEEDED: A NEW SET OF ACCOUNTABILITY METRICS FOR SOCIAL JUSTICE IN THE HIGH-STAKES TESTING SYSTEM

We argue that high-stakes testing accountability is too narrowly defined; it applies only to the schools and to some students, and not to the larger social system in which schools are embedded, and it punishes those who control the least variance in educational systems.

We are cautioned by Wilkinson and Pickett's (2010) statement: "More unequal countries and more unequal states have worse educational attainment—and these relationships are strong enough for us to be sure that they are not due to chance" (p. 105). This statement undergirds our proposed metrics or recommendations, essential in cultivating a public educational system that promotes social justice and an educational philosophy inclusive of all stakeholders and participants.

Metric 1: Measures of Social Inequality Should be Stated with Other Performance Measures When Accountability Is Discussed

We believe that measures of social inequality lie at the heart of the achievement gap dilemma. We concur with Rothstein (2004), who wrote:

All it is reasonable to say is that most of the racial test score gap probably results from social class factors, but a small part may also result from a culture of underachievement. It is possible, indeed likely, that cultural factors play a larger role for older children, but it is also likely that if social and economic conditions were equal for black and white kindergartners, and black children were then as successful in the early years of school as whites, cultural values that are hostile to education might be less attractive to black students when they were older. (p. 56)

There are many measures of social inequality. We believe these must become part of the systematic approach to implement not only change in the metrics of accountability, but are also necessary in the realignment of the philosophy and purpose of education. We will name just a few metrics here.

The Gini Coefficient and Other Health and Social Issues

The Gini coefficient is a statistical measure created by an Italian statistician named Corrado Gini in 1912 (Hephaestus Books, n.d.). It is a measure of distributive inequality, with a value of zero representing total equality, and a value of one representing maximum inequality. It has been used as a measure of a nation's inequality. Gini coefficients have been developed by different agencies. For example, Gini coefficients have been computed by the World Bank, the United Nations, the OECD and the Central Intelligence Agency (Hephaestus Books, n.d.). Gini coefficients do not take into account black market activities and are computed before and after taxes and transfers. The larger the Gini coefficient is, the more unequal a society is.

To demonstrate how countries are rated using the World Bank Gini coefficients, we show the World Bank Gini and CIA coefficients (Hephaestus Books, n.d.) in Table 8.1.

The data from Table 8.1 show that no country with a Gini coefficient larger than 36 did better than the United States on the 2009 PISA reading test (Sahlberg, 2011). It also shows that the United States has the largest Gini coefficient of any in the exhibit. Indeed, Condron (2011), quoting studies by Smeeding (2005) and Wolff (2002), has noted that among the most affluent nations in the world, the U.S. "is the most economically unequal. That is, income and wealth are more unevenly distributed in the United States than in any other affluent society" (p. 47).

Wilkinson and Pickett (2010) placed children's educational performance as one of nine factors by which a nation's inequality could be indexed to its health and social problems and found that the United States had the highest inequality of any studied, along with the highest index of health and social problems. Among those problems were: "teenage births; homicides; imprisonment rates; obesity; life expectancy and infant mortality; level of trust, mental illness (including drug and alcohol addiction) and social mobility" (Wilson & Pickett, 2010, p. 19). These indices are the most

TABLE 8.1   A Condensed Table of World Bank and CIA Gini Coefficients: Selected Countries

Inequality Rank	WB Gini Coefficient	CIA Gini Coefficient	Country
1	74	70.7	Namibia
2	66	65.8	Seychelles
3	60	59.2	Haiti
4	58	57.7	Honduras
5	56	61.3	Central African Republic
6	52	51.7	Mexico
7	48	48.0	Peru
8	43	39.7	Turkey
9	42	42.2	Russia
10	41	45.0	United States
11	38	44.5	Iran
12	37	36.8	India
13	36	32.0	Italy
13	36	34.0	United Kingdom
13	36	36.2	New Zealand*
14	35	30.5	Australia*
15	34	34.2	Poland*
15	34	33.7	Switzerland*
16	33	28.0	Belgium*
16	33	32.7	France
16	33	32.1	Canada*
17	32	31.4	South Korea
18	31	30.9	Netherlands*
19	28	27.0	Germany
20	26	25.0	Norway*
21	27	26.8	Finland*
22	25	37.6	Japan*
22	25	23.0	Sweden

* denotes reading test scores higher than the United States on the PISA 2009

commonly referenced predictors for academic success within the American public educational systems.

We proffer that any discussion of educational accountability should take into account how the lack of a social safety net and wide disparities in wealth contribute to educational achievement. We also propose that as educational achievement is presented in the popular media, this connection should be acknowledged and used by state and federal agencies in releasing test score data. This dual use of contributory causes of low educational achievement, and especially the omnipresent achievement gap, should illustrate that schools alone cannot be blamed nor can they "fix" the gap. If we insist on using test data to compare ourselves to other nations, we must also responsibly show how their lower income inequality data influences their higher test scores. Further, we believe that such measures as performance pay are inappropriate methods to either improve or blame educators and/or educational leaders for test score performance (Smeeding, 2005).

Metric 2: Authentic Assessments Offer Greater Insight in Student Knowledge

We acknowledge the importance of using assessments. Stiggins (1987) discusses the benefits of assessing for learning. This process requires more than teachers facilitating more frequently administered assessments. Teachers should use the classroom assessment process as a continuous flow of information about student achievement, in terms of determining whether they are ready to advance to the next skill (Stiggins, 1987). When assessments are utilized as a measure for learning, the self-confidence of the learner is continuously promoted. When used as a measurement of achievement, assessments place unfair burdens on children of varied socio-economic status, while often not accurately depicting the acquired knowledge by students. Students of color are often penalized for not knowing the cultural nuances associated with success (English, 2010).

Our current system of accountability promotes the (mis)measurement of many students within the public education system. The central issue with standardized assessments is that the standardization is tailored to and for children of typical development, and use of such standard materials and procedures with children of diverse special needs makes little psychometric or common sense (Neisworth & Bagnato, 2004). Evidence supports a need of alternative strategies for assessing student learning. To this end, using authentic assessments offers a more holistic approach to indicating student achievement and learning. Authentic assessments are based on student activities that replicate real-world performances as closely as possible (Svinicki, 2004), while also requiring students to integrate knowledge, skills, and attitudes as professionals do (Van Merrienboer, 1997). Assessments are deemed authentic when we directly examine student performance on worthy intellectual tasks (Wiggins, 1998). Gulikers, Bastiaens, and Kirschner (2004) offer three important elements of authentic assessments:

> (1) Authentic assessments should be aligned to authentic instruction in order to positively influence student learning (Biggs, 1996). (2) Authentic assessments require students to demonstrate relevant competencies through a significant, meaningful, and worthwhile accomplishment (Resnick, 1987;

Wiggins, 1993). (3) Authenticity is subjective, which makes student perceptions important for authentic assessment to influence learning. (p. 69)

Clear differences can be noted between standardized and authentic assessments. Wiggins (1998) contends that typical tests have only correct answers, whereas authentic tests are aimed more at the quality of the response and its justification. Typical tests infer student understanding based on the correlation between what is tested and what is desired; authentic tests go directly to the desired outcome. Typical tests are more summative in nature, but authentic tests provide diagnostic information and feedback to students so that they can see where and how to make corrections. Authentic assessments promote student individuality, as no two assignments are alike. This benefit prohibits making cross-student comparisons but only allows the comparing of a student's efforts with his or her own previous efforts (Svinicki, 2004). The benefits of using authentic assessments are many, and it is certainly more consistent philosophically with the public education learning paradigm.

Metric 3: Diversity Must Have Strong Moral Conviction

Teachers and school leaders who enter the profession should possess a belief that educators must actively strive to eliminate injustices and inequities based on exclusive privileges conferred by social class position (Murphy, 2002). As human beings, we embrace the ethic of caring for the human family, which in education means putting the needs of our students first. The ethical compass for the teacher and school leader has provided a basis in preparation and ongoing professional development—the ability to act responsibly from a critical theory perspective and strive to empower students who have been traditionally marginalized (Shapiro & Stefkovich, 2005).

Through the eyes of the educator is the primary mechanism to reverse social inequity, and base ethical decision-making and actions accordingly. School reform efforts must continuously be measured by their design to close the achievement gap by de-institutionalizing racism and empowering people of color. Levin states, "The quest for educational equity is a moral imperative for a society in which education is a crucial determinant of life changes. Yet whether there is an economic return to the taxpayer for investing in educational justice is often not considered" (Levin, 2009, p. 5).

Metric 4: Public Education is the Common Good and is a Means to that End

John Rawls (1971) defines social justice as 'fairness.' "Justice," Rawls states, "is the basic structure of society . . . the way in which the major social institutions distribute fundamental rights and duties and determine the division of advantages from social cooperation" (p. 7). The discussion of fairness continues to be longstanding, while striving to ensure that schools are universally available and are expanding equal access to education (Resseger, 2013). Kozol also (n.d.) chronicles this discussion:

> During the decades after Brown v. Board of Education there was terrific progress. Tens of thousands of public schools were integrated racially. During that time the gap between black and white achievement narrowed. If we allow public funds to be used to support our relatively benign, morally grounded schools, we will have to allow those public funds to be used for any type of private school. This is the moral dilemma we find ourselves today. We are failing public education. Without a strong public education we lose our American sense of public service. We are failing the American sense of working for a common good and not for an agendized sense of self that schooling is only for preparing students for a globalized world. (p. 1)

As Kozol tells us, "Children are not simply commodities to be herded into line and trained for the jobs that white people who live in segregated neighborhoods have available" (n.d., p. 1). Democratic citizenship is best developed and accomplished in the public arena. Private schooling is selective and predicated on ideas that may or may not support a common good. The primary goal of public education is to develop citizenry that supports democratic practices. As Shapiro (n.d.) tells us:

> Democratic citizenship, in any era, is a complex task but it seems especially difficult at this time when international conflict and growing economic and social inequality are the rule and not the exception. The spirit of the New DEEL [Democratic Ethical Educational Leadership] is towards a liberating education enabling students from different social classes, ethnicities, races, and even genders, to make intelligent and moral decisions as future citizens. (p. 1)

Metric 6: The Need for Culturally Proficient Professionals

Understanding and acceptance of various cultures is often missing from classrooms across America. Defined as the rules for daily living or the rules that reflect the covert values of a particular group, culture fosters the ability to identify with those most like you, while distinguishing those who differ from you (Lindsey, Robbins, & Terrell, 2003). The lack of this knowledge can result in cultural conflicts between the students' culture and the schools' mainstream culture, resulting in threats to the engagement and participation of minority students (Franklin, 2000).

Culturally proficient professionals accept and respect differences, carefully attend to the dynamics of difference, and assess their own cultural knowledge and beliefs, while also expanding their own cultural knowledge and resources (Lindsey et al., 2003). All of this is done while diligently working to eradicate the presumptions of entitlement (Ball, 1998). This knowledge is utilized when planning and implementing instructional and management strategies to meet students' academic and social needs (Townsend, 2000).

Effective change in the culture and climate of schools can be realized when educational employees employ the five essential elements of cultural proficiency (Lindsey et al., 2003):

- Assesses culture—Becomes aware of their own culture, along with learning about the culture of others within their school or organization
- Values diversity—Appreciates the challenges diversity may bring and works to develop a learning community which embraces all cultures
- Manages the dynamics of difference—Recognizes that conflict is a normal part of life but manages conflict in a positive way
- Adapts to diversity—Is committed to continuous learning and is informed by the guiding principles of cultural proficiency
- Institutionalized cultural knowledge—Creates opportunities for groups to learn about one another while taking advantage of teachable moments to share cultural knowledge. (p. 25).

Ideally, school factors (i.e., leadership, climate, procedures, and policies) and cultural differences should be examined as true contributors to the longstanding disproportionate numbers of minority students being suspended or expelled (Fenning & Rose, 2007). The understanding of various cultures, in addition to the creation of collaborative discipline teams comprised of multiple stakeholders to examine discipline practices and decisions for all students, also warrants consideration (Fenning & Rose, 2007) when assessing the use of high-stakes tests to measure student achievement.

CONCLUSION AND IMPLICATIONS

Although we advocate for the aforementioned accountability metrics to be employed to provide social justice in the high-stakes testing accountability system, we are also in agreement that fundamental aspects of the accountability system must be the forefront of the decision-making process. The focal aspects of the accountability system include: "what do schools expect of students academically, what constitutes quality instruction and how students and teachers account for their work and learning" (Elmore & Furhman, 2001). The constraints of the current high-stakes testing accountability model lead to building-level administrators experiencing not only difficulties in discussing issues of student achievement, but also difficulties navigating policies and procedures that undermine their administrative leadership (sustainable or otherwise), all while attempting to implement an educational philosophy most conducive to their school culture. We believe that the inclusion of the new metrics will go a long way toward improving social justice and achieve it for all children.

REFERENCES

Amrein, A., & Berliner, D. (2002). *An analysis of some unintended and negative consequences of high-stakes testing.* Tempe, AZ: Arizona State University Education Policy Research Unit (EPRU).

Amrein, A., & Berliner, D. (2003). The effects of high stakes testing on student motivation. *Educational Leadership, 60*(5), 32–38.

Apple, M., (2004). *Ideology and curriculum.* New York, NY: RoutledgeFalmer.

Au, W. (2009). *Unequal by design: High-stakes testing and the standardization of inequality.* New York, NY: Routledge.

Baker, M. and Foote, M. (2006). Changing spaces: urban school interrelationships and the impact of standards-based reform. *Educational Administration Quarterly 42*(1), 90–123.

Ball, E. (1998). *Slaves in the family.* New York, NY: Ballentine.

Ballou, D. (2001). Pay for performance in public and private schools. *Economics of Education Review 20,* 51–61.

Barber, B., (1992). *An aristocracy for everyone.* New York, NY: Ballentine.

Barry, B. (2005). *Why social justice matters.* Cambridge, UK: Polity Press.

Bartlett, L., Frederick, M., Gulbrandsen, T., & Murillo, E., (2002). The marketization of education: Public schools for private ends. *Anthropology & Education Quarterly, 33*(1), 1–25.

Balfanz, R., Spirkakis, K., Neild, R. C., & Legters, N. (2003). High-poverty secondary schools and the juvenile justice system: How neither helps the other and how that could change. In J. Wald & D. J. Losen (Eds.), *New directions for youth development: Deconstructing the school-to-prison pipeline,* (pp. 55–70). San Francisco, CA: Jossey-Bass.

Bernstein, B. (1990). *The structuring of pedagogic discourse: Class, codes and control.* London, UK: Routledge.

Biggs, J. (1996). Enhancing teaching through constructive alignment. *Higher Education, 32,* 347–364.

Bourdieu, P. (1984). *Distinction: A social critique of the judgment of taste.* Cambridge, MA: Harvard University Press.

Bourdieu, P., & Passeron, J-C. (1979). *The inheritors: French students and their relation to culture.* Chicago, IL: University of Chicago Press.

Bourdieu, P., & Passeron, J-C. (2000). *Reproduction in education, society and culture.* London, UK: Sage.

Bowditch, C. (1993). Getting rid of troublemakers: High school disciplinary procedures and the production of dropout. *Social Problems, 40,* 493–509.

Bratlinger, E. (2003). *Dividing classes: How the middle class negotiates and rationalizes school advantage.* New York, NY: Routledge-Falmer.

Casella, R. (2003). Punishing dangerous through preventive detention: Illustrating the institutional link between school and prison. In J. Wald & D. J. Losen (Eds.), *New directions for youth development: Deconstructing the school-to-prison pipeline* (pp. 55–70). San Francisco, CA: Jossey-Bass.

Children's Defense Fund. (1975). *School suspensions: Are they helping children?* Cambridge, MA: Washington Research Project.

Cools, K. (2005, March 22). Ebbers Rex. *The Wall Street Journal,* B2.

Condron, D. J. (2011). Egalitarianism and educational excellence: Compatible goals for affluent societies. *Educational Researcher, 40*(2), 47–55.

Crotty, M. (1998). *The foundations of social research: Meaning and perspective in the research process.* London, UK: Sage.

Delpit, L. (1988). The silenced dialogue: Power and pedagogy in educating other people's children. *Harvard Educational Review, 58*(3), 280–298.

Economic Policy Institute. (2010). *Leading experts caution against reliance on test scores in teacher evaluations: Press release.* Retrieved from http://www.epi.org/press/news_from_epi_leading_experts_caution_against_reliance_on_test_scores_in_te/

Elmore, R. F., & Fuhrman, S. H. (2001). Holding schools accountable: Is it working? *Phi Delta Kappan, 83*(1), 67–72.

English, F. (2010). *Deciding what to teach & test: Developing, aligning, and leading the curriculum.* Thousand Oaks, CA: Corwin.

English, F. (2012). Bourdieu's misrecognition: Why educational leadership standards will not reform schools or leadership. *Journal of Educational Administration and History, 44*(2), 153–168.

Fenning, P., & Rose, J. (2007). Overrepresentation of African American students in exclusionary discipline: The role of school policy. *Urban Education, 42*(6), 536–559.

Franklin, J. H. (2000). *From slavery to freedom: A history of Negro Americans.* (8th ed.). New York, NY: Random House.

Friedman, M. (1962). *Capitalism and freedom.* Chicago, IL: University of Chicago Press.

Gougis, R. A. (1986). The effects of prejudice and stress on the academic performance of Black Americans. In U. Neisser (Ed.), *The school achievement of minority children: New perspectives* (pp. 145–158). Hillsdale, NJ: Lawrence Erlbaum Associates.

Gulikers, J., Bastiaens, T., & Kirschner, P., (2004). A five-dimensional framework for authentic assessment. *Educational Technology Research & Development, 52*(3), 67–86.

Gunzenhauser, M. G. (2003). High-stakes testing and the default philosophy of education. *Theory Into Practice, 42*(1), 51–58.

Hanson, E. M. (2003). *Educational administration and organizational behavior* (5th ed.). Boston, MA: Allyn and Bacon.

Hargreaves, A., & Fink, D. (2003). *The seven principles of sustainable leadership.* Toronto, ON: International Centre for Educational Change Ontario Institute for Studies in Education, University of Toronto.

Hephaestus Books. (undated). *Wealth inequality in the United States.*

Harding, D., Jencks, C., Lopoo, L., & Mayer, S. (2005). The changing effects of family background on the incomes of American adults. In S. Bowles, H. Gintis, & M. Groves (Eds.), *Unequal chances: Family background and economic success.* (pp. 81–99). New York, NY: Russell Sage Foundation.

Karp, H., Lublin, J., & Glazer, E. (2012, February 10). 'Big' was Diamond CEO's style. *The Wall Street Journal,* B1.

Kohn, A. (2000). *The case against standardized testing: Raising the scores, ruining the schools.* Portsmouth, NH: Heinemann.

Kozol, J. (n.d.). Retrieved from http://readslove.com/16125-jonathan-kozol/161723-during-the-decades-after-brown-v-board-of-education-there-was-terrific-progress-tens-of-thousands-of-public-schools-were-integrated-racially-during-that-time-the-gap-between-black-and-white-achieve.html

Lareau, A. (2011). *Unequal childhoods: Class, race, and family life.* Berkeley, CA: University of California Press.

Lassen, S., Steele, M., & Sailor, W., (2006). The relationship of school-wide positive behavior support to academic achievement in an urban middle school. *Psychology in the Schools, 43*(6), 700–712.

Leonhardt, D. (2005). The college dropout boom. In B. Keller & New York Times contributors (Eds.), *Class matters* (pp. 87–104). New York, NY: Times Books.

Levin, H. M. (2009). The economic payoff to investing in educational justice. *Educational Researcher, 38*(1), 5–20.

Lindsey, R., Robbins, K., & Terrell, R., (2003). *Cultural proficiency: A manual for school leaders* (3rd ed.). Thousand Oaks, CA: Corwin Press.

Lucas, S. R. (1999). *Tracking inequality: Stratification and mobility in American high schools.* New York, NY: Teachers College Press.

Mayer, G. R. (1995). Preventing antisocial behavior in the schools. *Journal of Applied Behavior Analysis, 28,* 467–478.

Mintzberg, H. (2009, November 30). No more executive bonuses! *The Wall Street Journal,* p. R3.

Murphy, J. (2002). Reculturing the profession of educational leadership: New blueprints. *Educational Administration Quarterly, 38*(3), 176–191.

Neisworth, J., & Bagnato, S. (2004). The mismeasure of young children: The authentic assessment alternative. *Infants and Young Children, 17*(3), 198–212.

Nichols, S., & Glass, G., (2006). High-stakes testing and student achievement: Does accountability pressure increase student learning? *Education Policy Analysis Archives. 14*(1), 1–56.

Noguera, P. A. (1995). Preventing and producing violence: A critical analysis of responses to school violence. *Harvard Educational Review, 65,* 189–212.

Normore, A. H., & Brooks, J. S. (2012). Instructional leadership in the era of No Child Left Behind. In L. Volante (Ed.), *School leadership in the context of standards-based reform: International perspectives* (pp. 41–67) New York, NY: Springer.

Papa, R. (2012). *The Walter Dewey Cocking lecture 2011: Activist leadership.* Invited address given at the annual meeting of the National Council of Professors of Educational Administration, Portland, August 2011. In G. Perreault and L. Zellner (Eds.), *Social justice, competition and quality: 21st century leadership challenges.*

Papa, R., & English, F. (2011). *Turnaround principals for underperforming schools.* Lanham, MD: Rowman & Littlefield.

Postman, N. (1995). *The end of education: Redefining the value of school.* New York, NY: Vintage Books.

Ravitch, D. (2012, March 8). Flunking Arne Duncan. *The New York Review of Books posted on Common Dreams.* Retrieved from https://www.commondreams.org/view/2012/03/08-8

Rawls, J. (1971). *A theory of justice.* Cambridge, MA: Harvard University Press.

Raymond, M. E., & Hanushek, E. A. (2003). High-stakes research. *Education Next, 3*(3), 48–55. Retrieved from http://www.educationnext.org/

Resnick, L. B. (1987). Learning in school and out. *Educational Leadership, 16*(9), 13–20.

Resseger, J., (2013). The public purpose of public education. *Message on Public Education 2013 United Church of Christ Justice & Witness Ministries.* Retrieved from http://www.ucc.org/justice/public-education/pdfs/Message-13-web-version.pdf

Rothstein, R. (2004). *Class and schools: Using social, economic, and educational reform to close the Black–White achievement gap.* New York, NY: TC Columbia Press.

Sahlberg, P. (2011). *Finnish lessons: What can the world learn from educational change in Finland?* New York, NY: Teachers College Press.

Shapiro, J. P. (n.d.). Ethics and social justice within the new DEEL: Addressing the paradox of control/democracy. *International Electronic Journal for Leadership in Learning.* Retrieved from http://www.ucalgary.ca/icjll/vol10/shapiro/

Shapiro, J. P., & Stefkovich, J. A. (2005). *Ethical leadership and decision making in education: Applying theoretical perspectives to complex dilemmas* (2nd ed.). Mahwah, NJ: Lawrence Erlbaum Associates.

Sheldon, K. M., & Biddle, B. J. (1998). Standards, accountability, and school reform: Perils and pitfalls. *Teachers College Record, 100*(1), 164–180.

Smeeding, T. M. (2005). Public policy, economic inequality, and poverty: The United States in comparative perspective. *Social Science Quarterly, 86,* 955–983.

Stiggins, R. J. (1987). Design and development of performance assessments. *Educational measurement: Issues and practice, 6*(3), 33–42.

Svinicki, M. (2004). Authentic assessment: Testing in reality. *New Direction for Teaching and Learning, 100,* 23–29.

The Economist. (2012, January 21). Who exactly are the 1%? pp. 31–32.

Tirozzi, G. (2010). Pay-for-performance myths: Message from the executive director. *News Leader, 57*(7), 2–7.

Townsend, B. (2000). Disproportionate discipline of African American children and youth: Culturally-responsive strategies for reducing school suspensions and expulsions. *Exceptional Children, 66,* 381–391.

Van Merrienboer, J. J. G. (1997). *Training complex cognitive skills: A four-component instructional design model for technical training.* Englewood Cliffs, NJ: Educational Technology Publications.

Webb, J., Schirato, T., & Danaher, G. (2002). *Understanding Bourdieu.* London, UK: Sage.

Weinstein, C. S., Tomlinson-Clarke, S., & Curran, M. (2004). Toward a conception of culturally responsive classroom management. *Journal of Teacher Education,* *55,* 25–38.

Wiggins, G. P. (1993). *Assessing student performance: Exploring the purpose and limits of testing.* San Francisco, CA: Jossey-Bass/Pfeiffer.

Wiggins, G. (1998). *Educative assessment: Designing assessments to inform and improve student performance.* San Francisco, CA: Jossey-Bass.

Wilkinson, R., & Pickett, K. (2010). *The spirit level: Why greater equality makes societies stronger.* New York, NY: Bloomsbury Press.

Wolff, E. N. (2002). *Top heavy: The increasing inequality of wealth in America and what can be done about it.* New York, NY: New Press.

CHAPTER 9

SOCIOLOGY AND SOCIAL JUSTICE

Prospects for Educational Leaders in the United States

Mark Berends
University of Notre Dame

ABSTRACT

Since the discipline's beginnings, sociologists have focused on issues of social justice in their study of social structures and processes related to inequalities among individuals and groups within and across societies. This chapter examines the roots of sociology, particularly the sociology of education, and its perspectives on social justice. In addition, it will provide specific examples from the sociology of education to inform educational leaders about those aspects of schools and schooling processes that have implications for social justice—for students, teachers, parents, and leaders.

Sociologists have always had an eye towards issues of social justice. In the study of the social structures and processes that influence individuals and groups, sociologists have long focused on inequalities and injustices within

Educational Leadership for Ethics and Social Justice, pages 159–177
Copyright © 2014 by Information Age Publishing
All rights of reproduction in any form reserved.

and across societies. For instance, sociologists who focus on education have pointed to international comparisons of student achievement in the U.S. compared to other nations, which reveal that our students lag behind countries such as South Korea, Finland, Hong Kong, Singapore, Canada, New Zealand, Japan, and Australia (Fleischman, Hopstock, Pelczar, & Shelley, 2010).[1] However, these international scores obscure the test score inequalities in the U.S. For example, if we examine the wealthiest schools or districts, the U.S. ranks near the top of the international comparisons (Carnoy & Rothstein, 2013; Gamoran, 2011). Moreover, the gap within the U.S. between students from wealthy and poor families appears to be getting worse over time. As Reardon (2011) shows, the academic achievement gaps between children from high-income and low-income families has been growing over the past 50 years. For cohorts with more reliable data, the wealthy-poor achievement gap was 30–40% larger in 2001 compared with students born in the 1970s. Finally, the racial-ethnic gaps in student achievement between students of color and majority white students reveal persistent inequalities over time (Berends & Penaloza, 2010).

In addition to these group inequalities, there is also an increasing percentage of high-poverty schools in the U.S., a disproportionate number of which are located in central cities, typically enrolling a high percentage of African American and Latino students. In 2012, about 19% of students in the U.S. attended a high-poverty school.[2] Higher percentages of Latino students (37%) and African American students (37%) attend high-poverty schools compared with non-Hispanic white students (6%) (Aud et al., 2012; see also Frankenberg & Orfield, 2007). Moreover, the percentage of high-poverty schools has increased since 2000, now at 17% of schools compared with 12% a decade ago (Rowan, 2011).

Within this contemporary context, it is important to point out that the discipline of sociology has a long tradition of conceptual and empirical contributions to the understanding of social justice with implications for educational leaders. Ever since it was institutionalized within higher education in the United States, sociology has attended to social justice in its individual and collective forms (Cohen, 1986; Feagin, 2001; Rytina, 1986). For instance, Albion Small, who established the first department of sociology in the United States at the University of Chicago and established the discipline's first professional journal (*American Journal of Sociology*), argued that sociology was not an end in itself but served to improve society and social relationships. As national and international crises persist, sociology is uniquely positioned. As a discipline, sociology is itself a broad interdisciplinary field and draws on ideas from other social sciences (economics, psychology, political science, and anthropology) as well as the humanities and the physical sciences. Sociology is pluralistic, providing a richness that "gives sociology a particularly good position as a science to examine the complexities and crisis of a socially interconnected world" (Feagin, 2001, p. 6).

In sociology, the primary definition of social justice is drawn from the political philosopher John Rawls, who, in *A Theory of Justice* (1971), proposed:

> Each person possesses an inviolability founded on justice that even the welfare of society as a whole cannot override. For this reason justice denies that the loss of freedom for some is made right by a greater good shared by others. It does not allow that the sacrifices imposed on a few are outweighed by the larger sum of advantages enjoyed by many. (pp. 3–4)

According to Rawls, the concept of social justice was based on the belief that historical inequities related to current injustices should be addressed until the actual inequities no longer exist; redistribution of wealth, power, and social status can benefit not only individuals, but also communities and societies, and those who hold significant power (e.g., government) have the responsibility to ensure a basic quality of life for all citizens. In his presidential address to the American Sociological Association, Joe Feagin's statement about the importance of sociologists examining social justice in future research agendas defined social justice in a way that parallels a Rawlsian theory of justice:

> [S]ocial justice requires resource equity, fairness, and respect for diversity, as well as the eradication of exiting forms of social oppression. Social justice entails a redistribution of resources from those who have unjustly gained them to those who justly deserve them, and it also means creating and ensuring the processes of truly democratic participation in decision-making. (2001, p. 5)

James Coleman (1990) also draws on Rawls' theory of justice as "a product of a particular kind of social structure, one in which *each person can reasonably visualize himself* [or herself] *as exchanging places with any other person in society*" (p. 10, emphasis in original). This statement brings us into thinking not only about social structure and the roles individuals have within it, but also to the governing norms of social structures and the opportunities that individuals have within such social structures.

In what follows, I review the roots of sociology, particularly the sociology of education, and its perspectives on social justice. In addition, I will provide specific examples from the sociology of education to inform educational leaders about those aspects of schools and schooling processes that have implications for social justice—for students, teachers, parents, and leaders.

SOCIOLOGY AND SOCIAL JUSTICE

The notion of social justice is reflected throughout the writings of sociology's "founding fathers," who lived in times of significant social change. For instance, Emile Durkheim pointed to the types of social solidarity that correspond with different types of society. Mechanical solidarity characterizes more traditional societies. Social cohesion is accomplished through the homogeneity of individuals who are connected to others through similar family ties, work, religious training, and lifestyle practices. By contrast, organic solidarity characterizes more modern, complex societies with increasing work specialization and division of labor. Social cohesion in such societies emerges from the more specialized work tasks and roles and the interdependence among individuals and organizations to accomplish their specified tasks, even though they may have different values and interests. Yet Durkheim argued that social inequality that results from the passing on of economic and social resources across generations can compromise organic solidarity. He wrote that organic solidarity and social justice required the elimination of such inequalities that were based on ascriptive mechanisms rather than meritocratic ones:

> If one class of society is obliged, in order to live, to take any price for its services, while another can abstain from such action thanks to the resources at its disposal which, however, are not necessarily due to any social superiority, the second has an unjust advantage over the first.... [The] task of the most advanced societies is, then, a work of justice.... [O]ur ideal is to make social relations always more equitable, so as to as-sure the free development of all our socially useful forces. (1893/1933, p. 387)

In his work, Durkheim wrote about the importance of education in creating moral values that provided the foundation for organic solidarity in society:

> Education is the influence exercised by adult generations on those what are not yet ready for social life. It's object is to arouse and to develop in the child a certain number of physical, intellectual, and moral states which are demanded of him by both the political society as a whole and the special milieu for which he is specifically destined. (1956, p. 28)

Picking up on his larger ideas about the interdependence of institutions in modern society, Durkheim, in his book *Moral Education* (1961), described the function of schools and their relationship to society. Schools serve as the intermediary between the family with its affective morality and the rigorous morality of life in society (Ballantine, 2001). According to Durkheim, society was the source of morality; education provided students the moral tools they needed to function in society; and society could be reformed through education. Morality, in Durkheim's view, included three elements: discipline (constraint of egoistic impulses), attachment (voluntary commitment to groups), and autonomy (individual responsibility).

Although we see the importance of meritocracy and the morality in Durkheim's work, with some hint that organic solidarity within society can be threatened, his overall body of work is functionalist, failing to see the greater conflicts that emerge among societal groups, structures, and processes. To address these types of conflicts in theoretical sociology, it is the work of Weber and Marx that furthers understanding about the importance of empirically examining social justice as it relates to societal inequalities.

As another "founding father" of sociology, Max Weber also focused on social changes in societies over time, emphasizing the processes of rationalization and secularization under the growth of capitalism in the 19th century. In *The Protestant Ethic and the Spirit of Capitalism*, Weber (1953) argued that Calvinism was influential in the rise of Western market-driven capitalism and the rational–legal form of the nation-state. Although Weber's work did not specifically focus on educational processes in school systems, his work was influential in the way sociology came to view bureaucratic organizations in modern times—characterized by division of labor, administrative hierarchy, rules and procedures, written record keeping, formal relationships among roles, and rational behavior (Hallinan, 2000). Moreover, according to Weber, education had a dual character in modern society (Arum, Beattie, & Ford, 2011). On the one hand, meritocratic selection processes that are part of modern organizations allowed individuals to advance themselves. Schools were an important institution for imparting socially relevant skills and knowledge to individuals, who by their merit achieve certain adult attainments (e.g., further education, occupations, income). On the other hand, education was also a mechanism for social closure in that higher status groups use education as a way of keeping outsiders from attaining access to scarce resources (e.g., high-status occupations). Schooling was important for providing credentials that serve an exclusionary role for privileged occupational positions (see also Collins, 1971, 1979).

Taking more of a conflict perspective within a context of the emergence of capitalism and the changing forms of social organization, Karl Marx highlighted how modern capitalism promoted social inequality and injustice. Marx viewed capitalism as responsible for the social conditions of exploited workers of lower social classes. As Ballantine (2001, p. 10) writes, "He contended that society's competing groups, the 'haves' and the 'have-nots,' were in a constant state of tension, which could lead to the possibility of struggle." The upper classes—"the haves"—controlled power, wealth, material, goods, access to the best education, and they had to address the constant challenge of the lower classes—"the have-nots"—who sought a larger share of societal resources. Marx viewed societal institutions, and particularly schools, as systematically perpetuating and reproducing existing social class structures (Marx & Engels, 1848/1998). In their application of sociology to schools, Bowles and Gintis (1976, 2002) described the ways in which schools were an instrument used by the dominant class to maintain social inequalities and the status quo, socializing students and allocating them to positions in the job market and social hierarchy—reproducing inequalities within capitalist societies.

Although there have been many other sociologists to address the challenges of the social justice that have had lasting implications within the discipline, it should be noted that not all such views received immediate attention. For example, in 1896, W. E. B. Du Bois became an assistant professor of sociology at the University of Pennsylvania. In Philadelphia, Du Bois (1899) was one of the first sociologists to empirically study the patterns of life in Black communities and assess the immorality of discrimination. His work made important contributions to the sociological study of social justice, focusing on family, community, social problems, class relations, and the historical study of slavery and reconstruction in spite of the fact that Du Bois could not get an appointment in prestigious White-run sociology departments, even with his high-quality research portfolio, Harvard PhD, and experiences working with leading European social scientists (Feagin, 2001). Du Bois' writings address themes and issues relevant for sociologists thinking about social justice today, as indicated in his last autobiographical statement:

> [T]he contradictions of American civilization are tremendous. Freedom of political discussion is difficult; elections are not free and fair. . . . The greatest power in the land is not thought or ethics, but wealth. . . . Present profit is valued higher than future need. . . . I know the United States. It is my country and the land of my fathers. It is still a land of magnificent possibilities. It is still the home of noble souls and generous people. But it is selling its birthright. It is betraying its mighty destiny. (1968, pp. 418–419)

SOCIOLOGY OF EDUCATION AND SOCIAL JUSTICE

Sociologists who study education have long been interested in the organization of schools, and its impact on the quality of social relationships that promoted social justice (see Dreeben, 1994; Hallinan, 2006; Karabel & Halsey, 1977; Schneider, 2003; Waller, 1932/1961). Further, sociologists have examined the structures and processes of education systems and the impact of these on social mobility and stratification.

The connection between education and social mobility was first developed by Sorokin (1927/1963), who pointed to societal channels of upward and downward mobility. Within societies, institutional structures and accompanying social process mechanisms channeled individual mobility from one social stratum to another. Schools were an important social institution in such sorting because of their mechanisms of testing that resulted in distributing individuals to different strata. Within Sorokin's functionalist approach, other channels of social mobility included the family as well as military, religious, government, and political institutions.

Although Sorokin laid out a broad conception of the importance of schools in the stratification order, his ideas remained latent for several decades until social stratification researchers such as Blau and Duncan (1967) examined structure and mobility of American occupations in their seminal work (Dreeben, 1994). The research of Blau and Duncan and their parsimonious quantitative models of how an individual's origins (family background) were related to adult attainments (education, occupation, and income) led to a research agenda that has had a significant impact on how we understand stratification structures and mechanisms not only in the United States but internationally (Grusky, Ku, & Szelényi, 2008; Sewell, Hauser, Springer, & Hauser, 2004; Shavit & Blossfeld, 1993).

In addition to studies of social mobility and stratification, sociologists have focused more specifically on the organization of schools, emphasizing the structure and processes that occur among and within different types of schools (see Dreeben, 1994; Gamoran, Secada, & Marrett, 2000; Schneider, 2003). A long line of researchers have examined the relationship between school factors and student achievement, looking especially at how the structure and processes of schools correlate with social stratification outcomes and educational, occupational, and economic opportunities. More recently, research has shown that, although there is variation among schools in student achievement, the differences among classrooms and teachers are critical for student achievement growth (Rowan, Correnti, & Miller, 2002). A central focus in this line of research is what goes on inside the black box of schools and how school and schooling factors contribute to both social inequality and productivity (see Hacker, 2003). Sociologists have argued for the importance of understanding the social relationships that occur within schools, particularly the interactions within classrooms, because these provide students with the most immediate socialization experiences (Bidwell, 1972; Bidwell & Friedkin, 1988; Oakes, Gamoran, & Page, 1992). For instance, Waller (1932/1961) argues that the give-and-take during classroom instruction constitutes the "nucleus" of the school (Waller, 1932/1961, p. 33); Parsons (1959, p. 297) writes that the classroom is "where the 'business' of formal education actually takes place"; and Bidwell (1972, p. 5) emphasizes studying the immediate social relations of students in schools and classrooms to discover "fairly sizable effects on students."

Many have followed in this tradition of examining the organization of schools to understand school effects. Gamoran et al. (2000) provide a summary of this approach:

> An organization is a system of linked relationships, not simply a collection of individuals or of isolated categories. . . . For this reason a sociological study of an organization calls for a study of relationships, centering on how relationships become ordered, how they change, and how they influence outcomes. What may prove intriguing across organizations are differences in the character of the linkages that prevail. (p. 59)

It was a sociologist from the University of Chicago in the late 1960s who brought research on the organization of schools to the forefront of sociology and educational policy, with significant contributions to how we understand social justice and educational opportunity. In *Equality of Educational Opportunity*, Professor James Coleman and colleagues in the late 1960s examined the extent that schools and families contributed to inequalities among students—highlighting different ways of empirically analyzing social justice and educational opportunities (Coleman et al., 1966).

In the post-World War II era, there was a growing awareness that education was a primary path for social mobility, but was there equal opportunity for all? During the 1950s and 1960s, research revealed that school and individual performance throughout the schooling years was important for adult outcomes such as educational and occupational attainments. Yet there was also an increasing realization of the inequalities within the United States education system, particular among different racial-ethnic and socioeconomic groups. For instance, writing about the late 1960s and the importance of the 1966 Coleman report, Karabel and Halsey (1977) write, "In a period in which riots in black [areas] threatened to unravel the social fabric of American life, inequality of educational opportunity was widely held to be intolerable and the Coleman study was designed to help bring it to an end" (p. 20).

With the passing of the federal Civil Rights Act of 1964, which outlawed many forms of discrimination against African Americans and women, particularly segregation in public institutions such as schools, there was a congressionally mandated study to empirically examine educational opportunities and inequalities among students and the schools they attend. As stated in response to Section 402 of the Civil Rights Act of 1964:

> The Commissioner shall conduct a survey and make a report to the President and the Congress, within two years of the enactment of this title, concerning the lack of availability of equal educational opportunities for individuals by reason of race, color, religion, or national origin in public educational institutions at all levels in the United States. (Coleman et al., 1966, p. iii)

Congressional leaders who sponsored the legislation wanted not only to find these inequalities, but to know specifically what to change, for many believed that schools attended by racial and ethnic minority groups were inferior to White schools in resources and student characteristics, and a large national study would reveal these differences and explain any academic achievement differences (or gaps) that were found. The study was mandated by Congress, and Coleman and his colleagues (1966) were hired to conduct it.

At the time, the *Equality of Educational Opportunity* study was the largest survey of schools ever conducted in the United States. The study was a nationally representative sample of schools, including 3,000 elementary and 1,180 high schools and 645,000 students in grades 1, 3, 6, 9, and 12. Information was gathered about students' social background characteristics, including father and mother's educational attainment, father's occupation, mother's labor force participation, family size, and possessions in the home. In addition, data were gathered on schools, including school size and location, per-pupil expenditures, teacher salaries, number of library books per student, age of textbooks, number of science laboratories, and curriculum-tracking policies.

The findings, however, surprised many. In their array of statistical models, one of the most important findings was that controlling for students' social background, the differences across schools in resources (e.g., facilities and curriculum) had little association with student achievement. Moreover, the family background measures accounted for a large proportion of the differences among students in their achievement scores. Of the school factors that were important, it was school social composition (socioeconomic and racial-ethnic) that was a stronger predictor of achievement when compared with other school factors.

As Coleman et al. summarized:

> Schools bring little influence to bear on a child's achievement that is independent of his background and general social context; this very lack of an independent effect means that the inequalities imposed on children by their home, neighborhood, and peer environment are carried along to become the inequalities with which they confront adult life at the end of school. For equality of educational opportunity must imply a strong effect of schools that is independent of the child's immediate environment, and that strong independent effect is not present in American schools. (1966, p. 325)

When reflecting on this major study and its findings, Coleman faced the nation's assumptions of the social order, differing notions of social justice, and varying definitions of educational opportunities. In short, he said: "Although there is wide agreement in the United States that our society accepts and supports the fundamental value of equal opportunity, when it comes to areas of specific application there is considerable disagreement over its meaning" (Coleman, 1968, p. 7). Such disagreement was common in the late 1960s and remains true today (Jean-Marie, Normore, & Brooks, 2009). The different meanings raise these questions: What does the equality of educational opportunity mean? And what has it meant? Coleman attempted to answer this question, emphasizing the importance of historical context; the family involvement in children's lives throughout the life course; and the changes in the family, the workplace, and society that led to radical changes in the late 1960s about how people in the United Stated viewed equality of educational opportunity.

Within this context, Coleman articulated several notions of equality of educational opportunity that were embedded in the Civil Rights Act of 1964 and the *Equality of Educational Opportunity* study, or the Coleman report, which was "to assess the 'lack of equality of educational opportunity among racial and other groups in the United States'" (Coleman, 1968, p. 14). The types of inequalities that were examined included: (1) differences in community inputs into the school (e.g., per-pupil expenditure, school facilities, libraries, teacher quality); (2) racial (ethnic) composition of the school (to assess the degree of integration or segregation); (3) "intangible" school characteristics (teacher morale and expectations as well as student interest, engagement, and behavior); (4) consequences of schooling for individuals with equal backgrounds and abilities (equality of results when examining student achievement and social and behavioral outcomes); and (5) consequences of schooling for individuals with unequal backgrounds and abilities (equality of results given different individual inputs, such as for students who are of different national origins are English language learners). These differing definitions of educational opportunity and inequality continue to be addressed by social scientists interested in not only the effects of families and schools, but also schooling processes, teacher effects, and the other processes that take place within schools over students' careers to affect educational opportunities and the consequent outcomes.

At the time, not everyone agreed with Coleman's findings, and there were several responses and replications (Jencks et al., 1972; Mosteller & Moynihan, 1972). Because Coleman found that only about 15–20% of the total variation in student test scores was between schools, researchers began to look within schools and the differences that occur between and within classrooms (Dreeben, 1994; Schneider, 2003). Thus, research focused on how schools separated students into different tracks (college preparatory, vocational, or general) or ability groups (e.g., honors, regular, and remedial groups), which opened the door to understanding educational inequalities and the structure of schools in new ways (Gamoran & Berends, 1987; Oakes, 2005; Oakes et al., 1992).

Over time, there has been a great deal of research on ability grouping and tracking (for reviews, see Gamoran 2010; Oakes et al. 1992; Slavin, 1987, 1990). Comparisons of secondary students who are grouped homogeneously to those who are grouped heterogeneously reveal that separating students by purported abilities and interests has no effect on their achievement levels (Slavin 1990). In contrast, comparisons of high-group students to low-group students reveal an advantage of high-group placement on academic achievement (Gamoran, Nystrand, Berends, & LePore, 1995). Apparently, this positive effect is offset by a negative low-group effect resulting in an overall effect of zero (Gamoran, 2010; Kerckhoff, 1986). Although some have questioned these effects (Betts & Shkolnik, 2000; Figlio & Page, 2002), the balance of evidence suggests that the learning gap between high- and low-group students increases over time (see Gamoran, 2010; Gamoran & Berends, 1987; Oakes et al., 1992).

In addition to research that looked inside school organizations, some claimed that Coleman did not measure the right things about schools, which would lead to differences in student learning opportunities and distinguish effective from ineffective schools. This effective schools research agenda blossomed in the 1970s and continues to the present, although much of the early work was fraught with poor quality research. Even so, reviews of effective research reveal several characteristics of effective schools that emerge from quantitative and qualitative research (see Bryk, Sebring, Allensworth, Luppescu, & Easton, 2010; Purkey & Smith, 1983). These characteristics included: (1) *instructional leadership* of principals not only to fulfill administrative roles of budget, facility, and staffing but also to be engaged in supporting teachers in their instruction, provide meaningful feedback to those responsible for instruction, and foster professional development; (2) *authority* and *autonomy* at the school level to make decisions about staffing, organization, and instruction; (3) *staff stability* to build consistency over time; (4) *curriculum articulation and organization* so that there is a coherent focus on academic subjects and that adoption of new programs is consistent for improving instruction across the school; (5) *school-wide professional development* that involves a sufficient amount of time to learn new skills and develop new expertise, engages the entire school, has a focus on the content of instruction, incorporates active learning activities, and is coherent with other school initiatives (Desimone, Porter, Garet, Suk Yoon, & Birman, 2002; Desimone, 2009); (6) *parent involvement* and support of students' academic learning at home and at school; (7) *school-wide recognition of success;* (8) *maximized learning time;* and (9) *district support.* In addition, Purkey and Smith (1983) pointed to the importance of school culture as they highlighted additional characteristics of effective schools that continue to be relevant today. These attributes include: (1) collaborative planning and collegial relationships; (2) sense of community; (3) shared mission, clear goals, and high expectations; and (4) order and discipline.

Although it is difficult to single out the importance of any one of these characteristics, researchers and educators have emphasized the system of these characteristics as they attempt to develop comprehensive school reforms (see Berends, Bodilly, & Kirby, 2002), instructional designs for schools (Cohen, Raudenbush, & Ball, 2003), charter schools (Berends, Goldring, Stein, & Cravens, 2010), and school district reform (Bryk et al., 2010).

SOCIOLOGY'S CONTRIBUTION TO UNDERSTANDING SCHOOL LEADERSHIP & PROSPECTS FOR THE FUTURE

Leadership is one characteristic that stands out among the attributes of effective schools research and lessons learned from development and implementation of various school reforms (Berends et al., 2002; Bryk et al., 2010; Goldring & Berends, 2009). The importance of principal leadership for school reform and improvement has been well established in educational research. Many studies have shown the importance of leadership in establishing effective school improvement efforts, both in terms of setting the school's vision and mission as well as providing instructional leadership (Berends et al., 2002; Spillane, 1996).

As schools continue to develop leaders, Murphy, Elliott, Goldring, & Porter (2007) point to the body of research supporting the importance of today's school leaders:

> An assortment of researchers over the last three decades has helped us see that not all leadership is equal, that a particular type of leadership is especially visible in high performing schools and school districts. This type of leadership can best be labeled "leadership for learning," "instructionally focused leadership" or "leadership for school improvement." The touchstones for this type of leadership include the ability of leaders (a) to stay consistently focused on the right stuff—the core technology of schooling, or learning, teaching, curriculum, and assessment and (b) to make all the other dimensions of schooling (e.g., administration, organization, and finance) work in the service of a more robust core technology and improved student learning. (p. 179)

Within all of this, however, is leadership for a purpose, which has significant implications for social justice in our schools. As stated at the beginning of this chapter, there is a problem of inequality within the United States education system, among families, schools, and most importantly students. Amidst the myriad school reform efforts—whether focused on district reform and closing low-performing schools, school-wide reforms, teacher evaluation and performance pay, or market-based reforms (charters and voucher programs)—school leaders face challenges when addressing the learning opportunities of students most in need (Bryk et al., 2010; Goldring & Berends, 2009; Murphy et al., 2007).

Effective leaders can facilitate a positive vision for schools that reflects high and appropriate standards for learning and promotes a culture of the educability of all students. Moreover, they can emphasize ambitious goals that stretch families, teachers, staff, and students and help put the supports in place to accomplish those goals. The articulation of such a vision can occur through personal modeling and clear, consistent communication with school participants, and researchers are beginning to put in place tools that help monitor the various conditions under which school leaders can be effective (Murphy, Elliott, Goldring, & Porter, 2010).

When Murphy and others worked with the Council of Chief State School Officers (CCSSO), they emphasized these points during the development of the Interstate School Leaders Licensure Consortium (ISLLC) Standards for School Leaders. Updated in 2008, the National Policy Board for Educational Administration (BPBEA) updated the ISLLC standards, which represent high-priority themes that education leaders need to address to promote the success of all students. These standards called for:

- Setting a widely shared vision for learning
- Developing a school culture and instructional program conducive to student learning and staff professional growth
- Ensuring effective management of the organization, operation, and resources for a safe, efficient, and effective learning environment
- Collaborating with faculty and community members, responding to diverse community interests and needs, and mobilizing community resources
- Acting with integrity, fairness, and in an ethical manner
- Understanding, responding to, and influencing the political, social, legal, and cultural contexts (CCSSO, 2009, p. 6)

As the rigor of research and the tools to examine school leadership develop over the next few years, the remaining question is whether such leadership will lead to increased learning opportunities and close the persistent gaps among students from different socioeconomic and racial-ethnic circumstances. Our data systems at the federal, state, and local levels have improved immensely to monitor such gaps. Rigorous research designs, including those that focus on school leadership, have also improved greatly over time to assess the impact of different processes and structures to support strong school leadership (Porter, Polikoff, Goldring, Murphy, Elliott, & May, 2010).

As these models of leadership are developed and implemented in the incoming years, an important avenue for future research is to examine not only their impact on school improvement and student achievement in general, but also whether these models improve the learning opportunities for those that have been left behind. If such models have not only an overall impact but also an impact on closing the gap between low- and high-performing students, we will then have made significant strides in developing leadership models for social justice. Time will tell if such leadership occurs and whether it has these types of effects.

FINAL THOUGHTS

In the future, sociologists have a great deal to examine in terms of educational opportunities, trends of opportunities and outcomes over time, and whether leadership can have an impact. As a student of Coleman, my beloved colleague Maureen Hallinan continued the Coleman legacy of examining issues of social justice and educational learning opportunities throughout her illustrious career. When addressing these issues, she also wrote about the importance of sociologists pursuing excellence and high quality research informed by theory. She had high hopes for the field of sociology and its contributions to further understanding about educational opportunity and the societal relationships within educational systems. As she writes:

> Sociology is a powerful discipline whose time has come. The characteristics of contemporary society, the newly acquired maturity and sophistication of the sociological perspective and the increasing body of theoretical and empirical scholarship available in sociology have created the context in which sociology can be the crown jewel of the social sciences. If we take advantage of this opportunity, we can make a significant contribution to contemporary society through our discipline. (Hallinan, 1997, p. 13)

Although written over fifteen years ago, the sentiments remain applicable today. There is more to learn in terms of persistent inequalities and educational opportunities. As leadership has the potential to ameliorate some of these social injustices, the challenge will be to conduct empirical research that is rigorous, is theoretically driven, and reveals the conditions under which leadership (and leadership for social justice) has an impact.

NOTES

1. The Program for International Student Assessment (PISA) is coordinated by the Organization for Economic Cooperation and Development (OECD)

and includes 65 participating countries. The PISA administers assessments in reading, mathematics, and science every three years to nationally representative samples of 15-year-old students in the participating countries. The assessments attempt to measure applied knowledge and literacy to address how well student nearing the end of compulsory schooling apply their knowledge to real-life situations.

2. The *2012 Condition of Education* defines a high-poverty school as one with more than 75 percent of students eligible for free or reduced-price lunches, and as of 2009–2010.

REFERENCES

Arum, R., Beattie, I. R., & Ford, K. (Eds.). (2011). *The structure of schooling: Readings in the sociology of education.* Thousand Oaks, CA: Sage.

Aud, S., Hussar, W., Johnson, F., Kena, G., Roth, E., Manning, E., Wang, X., & Zhang, J. (2012). *The condition of education 2012* (NCES 2012-045). U.S. Department of Education, National Center for Education Statistics. Washington, DC. Retrieved from http://nces.ed.gov/pubsearch/

Ballantine, J. H. (2001). *The sociology of education: A systematic analysis* (5th ed.). Upper Saddle River, NJ: Prentice Hall.

Berends, M., & Penaloza, R. V. (2010). Increasing racial isolation and test score gaps in mathematics: A 30-year perspective. *Teachers College Record, 112*(4), 978–1007.

Berends, M., Bodilly, S., & Kirby, S. N. (2002). *Facing the challenges of whole-school reform: New American Schools after a decade.* Santa Monica, CA: RAND.

Berends, M., Goldring, E., Stein, M., & Cravens, X. (2010). Instructional conditions in charter schools and students' mathematics achievement gains. *American Journal of Education, 116*(3), 303–335.

Betts, J. R., & Shkolnik, J. L. (2000). The effects of ability grouping on student achievement and resource allocation in secondary schools. *Economics of Education Review, 19,* 1–15.

Bidwell, C. E. (1972). Schooling and socialization for moral commitment. *Interchange, 3,* 1–27.

Bidwell, C., & Friedkin, N. (1988). Sociology of education. In N. J. Smelser (Ed.), *Handbook of Sociology* (pp. 449–471). Beverly Hills, CA: Sage.

Blau, P. M., & Duncan, O. D. (1967). *The American occupational structure.* New York, NY: Wiley.

Bowles, S., & Gintis, H. (1976). *Schooling in capitalist America: Educational reform and the contradictions of economic life.* New York, NY: Basic Books.

Bowles, S., & Gintis, H. (2002). *Schooling in capitalist America revisited. Sociology of Education, 75*(1), 1–18.

Bryk, A. S., Sebring, P. B., Allensworth, E., Luppescu, S., & Easton, J. Q. (2010). *Organizing schools for improvement: Lessons from Chicago.* Chicago, IL: The University of Chicago Press.

Carnoy, M., & Rothstein, R. (2013). *What do international tests really show about U.S. Student performance?* Washington, DC: Economic Policy Institute.

Council of Chief State School Officers (CCSSO). (2009). *Educational leadership policy standards: ISLLC 2008*. Washington, DC: Author.

Cohen, R. L. (1986). *Justice: Views from the social sciences*. New York, NY: Plenum Press.

Cohen, D. K., Raudenbush, S. W., & Ball, D. L. (2003). Resources, instruction, and research. *Educational Evaluation and Policy Analysis, 25*(2), 1–24.

Coleman, J. S. (1968). The concept of equality of educational opportunity. *Harvard Education Review, 38*(1), 7–22.

Coleman, J. S. (1990). *Equality and achievement in education*. Boulder, CO: Westview Press.

Coleman, J. S., Campbell, E., Hobson, C., McPartland, J., Mood, A., Weinfield, F., & York, R. (1966). *Equality of educational opportunity*. Washington, DC: U.S. Government Printing Office.

Collins, R. (1971). Functional and conflict theories of educational stratification. *American Sociological Review 36*, 1002–1019.

Collins, R. (1979). *The credential society*. New York, NY: Academic Press.

Desimone, L. (2009). How can we best measure teacher's professional development and its effects on teachers and students? *Educational Researcher, 38*(3), 181–199.

Desimone, L., Porter, A. C., Garet, M., Suk Yoon, K., & Birman, B. (2002). Effects of professional development on teachers' instruction: Results from a three-year study. *Educational Evaluation and Policy Analysis, 24*(2), 81–112.

Dreeben, R. (1994). The sociology of education: Its development in the United States. In A.

Pallas (Ed.), *Research in sociology of education and socialization* (pp. 7–52) Greenwich, CT: JAI Press.

Du Bois, W. E. B. (1968). *The autobiography of W. E. B. Du Bois: A soliloquy on viewing my life from the last decade of its first century*. New York, NY: International Publishers.

Durkheim, E. (1933). *The division of labor in society* (G. Simpson, trans.). New York, NY: Free Press. (Original work published 1893)

Durkheim, E. (1956). *Education and sociology* (S. D. Fox, trans.). Glencoe, IL: Free Press.

Durkheim, E. (1961). *Moral education* (E. K. Wilson & H. Schnurer, trans.). Glencoe, IL: Free Press.

Feagin, J. R. (2001). Social justice and sociology: Agendas for the twenty-first century. *American Sociological Review, 66*, 1–20

Figlio, D. N., & Page, M. E. (2002). School choice and the distributional effects of ability tracking: Does separation increase inequality? *Journal of Urban Economics, 51*, 497–514.

Fleischman, H. L., Hopstock, P. J., Pelczar, M. P., & Shelley, B. E. (2010). *Highlights from PISA 2009: Performance of U.S. 15-year-old students in reading, mathematics, and science literacy in an international context (NCES 2011-004)*. U.S. Department of Education, National Center for Education Statistics. Washington, DC: U.S. Government Printing Office.

Frankenberg, E., & Orfield, G. (Eds.). (2007). *Lessons in integration: Realizing the promise of racial diversity in American schools*. Charlottesville, VA: University of Virginia Press.

Gamoran, A. (2010). Tracking and inequality: New directions for research and practice. In M. W. Apple, S. J. Ball, & L. A. Gandin (Eds.), *The Routledge international handbook of the sociology of education* (pp. 213–228). London, UK: Routledge.

Gamoran, A. (2011, April). *The future of educational inequality: Will more accountability reduce the gaps?* Presentation at the CREO Seminar, University of Notre Dame, South Bend, IN.

Gamoran, A., & Berends, M. (1987). The effects of stratification in secondary schools: Synthesis of survey and ethnographic research. *Review of Educational Research, 57,* 415–435.

Gamoran, A., Secada, W. G., & Marrett, C. B. (2000). The organizational context of teaching and learning. In M. R. Hallinan (Ed.), *Handbook of the sociology of education* (pp. 37–63). New York, NY: Kluwer Academic/Plenum Publishers.

Gamoran, A., Nystrand, M., Berends, M., & LePore, P. C. (1995). An organizational analysis of the effects of ability grouping. *American Educational Research Journal, 24,* 687–715.

Goldring, E., & Berends, M. (2009). *Leading with data: Pathways to improve your school.* Thousand Oaks, CA: Corwin Press.

Grusky, D. B., Ku, M. C., & Szelényi, S. (2008). *Social stratification: Class, race, and gender in sociological perspective* (3rd ed.). Boulder, CO: Westview Press.

Hacker, A. (2003). *Two nations: Black & white, separate, hostile, unequal.* New York, NY: Simon & Schuster.

Hallinan, M. T. (1997). A sociological perspective on social issues. *The American Sociologist, 28*(1), 5–14.

Hallinan, M. T. (2000). Introduction: Sociology of education at the threshold of the twenty-first century. In M. T. Hallinan (Ed.), *Handbook of the sociology of education* (pp. 1–12). New York, NY: Kluwer Academic/Plenum Publishers.

Hallinan, M. T. (2006). Present status of sociology in the United States. *Journal of Applied Sociology, 48,* 1–17.

Karabel, J., & Halsey, A. H. (1977). Educational research: A review and an interpretation. In J. Karabel & A. H. Halsey (Eds.), *Power and ideology in education* (pp. 1–85). New York, NY: Oxford University Press.

Kerckhoff, A. C. (1986). Effects of ability grouping in British secondary schools. *American Sociological Review, 51,* 842–858.

Jean-Marie, G., Normore, A. H., & Brooks, J. (2009). Leadership for social justice: Preparing 21st century school leaders for a new social order. *Journal of Research on Leadership Education, 4*(1), 1–31.

Jencks, C., Smith, M., Acland, H., Bane, M. J., Cohen, D., Gintis, H., Heyns, B., & Michelson, S. (1972). *Inequality: A reassessment of the effect of family and schooling in America.* New York, NY: Basic Books.

Marx, K., & Engels, F. (1998). *The communist manifesto.* New York, NY: Penguin Group. (Original work published 1848)

Mosteller, F., & Moynihan, D. P. (1972). *On equality of educational opportunity.* New York, NY: Random House.

Murphy, J., Elliott, S., Goldring, E. B., & Porter, A. C. (2007). Leadership for learning: A research-based model and taxonomy of behaviors. *School Leadership & Management, 27*(2), 179–201.

Murphy, J., Elliott, S., Goldring, E. B., & Porter, A. C. (2010). Leaders for productive schools. In P. Peterson, E. Baker, & B. McGaw (Eds.), *International encyclopedia of education* (vol. 4, pp. 246–751). Oxford, UK: Elsevier.

Oakes, J. (2005). *Keeping track: How schools structure inequality,* (2nd ed.). New Haven, CT: Yale University Press.

Oakes, J., Gamoran, A., & Page, R. N. (1992). Curriculum differentiation: Opportunities, outcomes, and meanings. In P. W. Jackson (Ed.), *Handbook of research on curriculum* (pp. 570–608). New York, NY: Macmillan.

Parsons, T. (1959). The school class as a social system: Some of its functions in American society. *Harvard Educational Review 29,* 297–318.

Porter, A. C., Polikoff, M. S., Goldring, E. B., Murphy, J., Elliott, S. N., & May, H. (2010). Investigating the validity and reliability of the Vanderbilt Assessment of Leadership Education. *The Elementary School Journal, 11*(2), 282–313.

Purkey, S. C., & Smith, M. S. (1983). Effective schools: A review. *Elementary School Journal, 83,* 427–452.

Rawls, J. (1971). *A theory of justice.* Oxford, UK: Oxford University Press.

Reardon, S. F. (2011). The widening academic achievement gap between the rich and the poor: New evidence and possible explanations. In G. J. Duncan & R. J. Murnane (Eds.), *Whither opportunity? Rising inequality, schools, and children's life chances* (pp. 91–115). New York, NY: Russell Sage Foundation.

Rowan, B. (2011). Intervening to improve the educational outcomes of students in poverty: Lessons from recent work in high-poverty schools. In G. J. Duncan & R. J. Murnane (Eds.), *Whither opportunity? Rising inequality, schools, and children's life chances* (pp. 523–537). New York, NY: Russell Sage Foundation.

Rowan, B., Correnti, R., & Miller, R. J. (2002). What large-scale survey research tells us about teacher effects on student achievement. Insights from the *Prospects* study of elementary schools. *Teachers College Record, 104*(8), 1525–1567.

Rytina, S. (1986). Sociology and justice. In R. L. Cohen (Ed.), *Justice: Views from the social sciences* (pp. 117–152). New York, NY: Plenum Press.

Schneider, B. (2003). Sociology of education: An overview of the field at the turn of the twenty-first century. In M. T. Hallinan, A. Gamoran, W. Kubitsheck, & T. Loveless (Eds.), *Stability and change in American education: Structure, process, and outcomes* (pp. 193–226). Clinton Corners, NY: Eliot Werner Publications.

Sewell, W. H., Hauser, R. M., Springer, K. W., & Hauser, T. S. (2004). As we age: The Wisconsin Longitudinal Study, 1957–2001. In K. Leicht (Ed.), *Research in social stratification and mobility* (vol. 20, pp. 3–111) Greenwich, CT: Elsevier Scientific Publishers.

Shavit, Y., & Blossfeld, H. P. (1993). *Persistent inequality: Changing educational attainment in thirteen countries.* Boulder, CO: Westview Press.

Slavin, R. E. (1987). Ability grouping and achievement in elementary schools: A best-evidence synthesis. *Review of Educational Research, 57,* 293–336.

Slavin, R. E. (1990). Achievement effects of ability grouping in secondary schools: A best-evidence synthesis. *Review of Educational Research 60*(3), 471–499.

Sorokin, P. A. (1927/1963). *Social mobility.* [Reprinted as Social and cultural mobility.] Glencoe, IL: Free Press.

Spillane, J. P. (1996). School districts matter: Local educational authorities and state instructional policy. *Educational Policy, 10*(1), 63–87.

Waller, W. (1961). *The sociology of teaching.* New York, NY: Wiley. (Original work published 1932)

Weber, M. (1953). *The Protestant ethic and the spirit of capitalism* (Talcott Parsons, trans.). New York, NY: Charles Scribner's Sons.

CHAPTER 10

I'VE DONE MY SENTENCE, BUT COMMITTED NO CRIME

An Interdisciplinary Perspective on Violence Exposure, Urban Male Adolescents, and Educational Leadership

Nicole Limperopulos
Teachers College, Columbia University

ABSTRACT

The central purpose of this chapter is to provide educational leaders with critical insights into the pernicious effects that chronic violence exposure has on the physiological, psychological, and emotional development of urban male adolescents. The chapter will represent an interdisciplinary approach, calling upon essential theories in psychology, urban studies, education leadership, social justice, and adolescent development to illustrate the ways in which chronic violence exposure is contributing to the underachievement of African American and Latino males in urban settings. Furthermore, in an era characterized by high-stakes testing and accountability, this chapter seeks to catalyze educational leaders to leverage their positional authority to address social justice issues that continue to impact the lives of our urban male adolescents.

Educational Leadership for Ethics and Social Justice, pages 179–201
Copyright © 2014 by Information Age Publishing

INTRODUCTION

Social justice issues are rampant in urban communities. Young people in urban neighborhoods are witnesses, victims, and perpetrators of violence in may dimensions of their lives, and often initiate violence in the belief that such actions will protect them from more serious reprisals (Freudenberg, Roberts, Richie, Taylor, McGillicuddy, & Greene, 1999). In fact, among urban Black adolescents, witnessing violence and victimization were the strongest predictors of carrying weapons (Jenkins & Bell, 1994).

Although countless teens live safely within the confines of our nation's cities, studies have revealed that African American and Latino males are disproportionately impacted by the effects of violence exposure in urban environments. The following chapter is part of a larger study that focused on the effects of chronic violence exposure on urban male adolescents—effects that result in social inequity and injustice. In-depth interviews with urban male adolescents who reside and attend school in the South Bronx were conducted in an effort to better understand the ways in which they conceptualize their experiences with chronic violence exposure. Additionally, the first-hand accounts of violence exposure shared by study participants were augmented with robust descriptions of the South Bronx provided by members of the New York City Police Department and community organizations.

In the early 1990s, researchers discovered that despite a national decline in violent incidents, perpetration of lethal violence in urban areas continued to soar. Within this cauldron of incessant violence, researchers first identified the relationship between chronic exposure to community violence and the development of posttraumatic stress disorder, an anxiety disorder that usually occurs after a person experiences or witnesses a traumatic or violent event. While researchers' successfully revealed a silent epidemic that plagued the inhabitants of urban environments, the research concluded prematurely, and the subject area was essentially abandoned by the mid-1990s.

This chapter seeks to resurface and reexamine the effects of chronic violence exposure on urban male adolescents, while concurrently recognizing the educational and social justice implications that such a phenomenon has for school leaders. In order to do so, this chapter is organized in the following way. First, we examine the role that educational leaders play in helping to eradicate the underachievement of African American and Latino urban male adolescents. Next, readers are provided with a brief description of the origins of the study that informed the current chapter, which is followed by a case study in urban violence. An introduction of the urban underclass helps orient readers to the historic attitudes of racism and classism that have led to the insidious violence in the South Bronx. Then the chapter explores the effects of chronic violence on urban male adolescents, including posttraumatic stress disorder. Finally, the chapter explores increased faculty training and the development of an innovative program that specifically seeks to address the unique needs of urban male adolescents.

A CALL TO ACTION FOR EDUCATIONAL LEADERS

Over the past decade, as No Child Left Behind (NCLB) ushered in an era of high-stakes testing and accountability, the education community has witnessed a consistent decline in the academic performance of Black and Latino male adolescents. The pervasive underachievement of urban male adolescents emerges as a complex social justice problem that is deeply rooted in issues of race, class, equitable access to education, and violence. Educational leaders are called upon to address the needs of students who are least likely to succeed in the current educational climate. For if we, as an educational community, cannot successfully provide access to our most vulnerable students, then we have failed to provide all students with equitable access to a high-quality education.

Historically, school leaders have been trained to address the needs of special populations on the basis of academic needs. However, scaffolding instruction to meet the discreet needs of special education students and English language learners ignores the unique needs of male students of color who, in many settings, are a special population at risk for academic failure. In fact, "the literature is replete with evidence documenting the overrepresentation of male students of color in special education due to urban schools' inability to address the unique needs of said population" (Patton, 1998, p. 26).

Urban schools are called upon to serve as more than institutions that deliver a prescribed curriculum in each of the major content areas. In order to truly live up to the challenge of preparing students to meet the demands of a 21st-century global economy, urban schools must be willing to serve as pillars of support for urban male adolescents who are struggling to process their repeated exposure to violent events.

While many school leaders seek to close the achievement gap through the development of rigorous college preparatory curricula, doing so is putting the proverbial cart before the horse. In order to fully support students' academic achievement, it is necessary to usher in a paradigm shift that enables school leaders to conceptualize a school community that acknowledges and supports the unique needs of urban male adolescents. Therefore, in order to eradicate the underachievement of male adolescents of color, and subsequently ensure their academic success, it is imperative that school leaders (1) recognize that urban male adolescents who have been chronically exposed to community violence exhibit significant symptoms of the disorder that mental health experts identify as posttraumatic stress disorder (PTSD), (2) work collaboratively with various stakeholders to develop a rigorous training program that prepares teachers to understand the challenges faced by urban male adolescents, and (3) implement an innovative advisory program to offset the symptoms of PTSD that hinder male adolescents' academic performance.

Many urban administrators and teachers work tirelessly to provide their students with a high-quality education. Yet despite their best efforts, there exists an unprecedented rate of failure among urban male adolescents. The disconnect between teachers' efforts and urban male adolescents' failures hinges on the school personnel's unawareness of the significant impact that chronic exposure to community violence has on urban male adolescents' academic performance.

The vast majority of faculty members in urban schools are new teachers who have secured their positions through alternate-route programs. In most cases, these teachers are White, in their early 20s, and have attended affluent universities throughout the nation. These teachers have a rudimentary understanding of urban blight and are largely unfamiliar with the insidious violence to which their students are exposed. Unfortunately, the vast majority of young teachers in urban schools are ill prepared for the job for which they were hired. The struggle to balance a full course load, curriculum development, mandated state testing, and classroom management leaves young teachers exhausted and unable to do much more than repeat the process again the following day. However, the missing link for these young teachers is a comprehensive understanding of the effects that chronic exposure to community violence has on their students.

ORIGINS OF THE RESEARCH

At the end of the 2009 academic year, I sat with a group of urban adolescents who, along with spotless attendance records, possessed above-average levels of intelligence. All measurable indicators slated these students for academic success, yet they consistently underachieved, failing virtually all of their courses. As we sat and talked about achievement and failure, a student raised his hand. "Miss, don't you see? It is easier to accept failure when you don't try. If I don't care, it can't bother me."

If I don't care, it can't bother me. Those words have stayed with me, as I frequently think about a wildly talented group of urban adolescents who had quietly resigned themselves to failure. The very prospect of failure shattered my students' fragile self-esteem and forced them to disengage in order to protect themselves.

As a White middle-class woman, insidious violence, unspeakable loss, and abject poverty were not part of the reality that defined my worldview.

Although my students were haunted by the inescapable violence that plagued their community, the truth was, at the end of each day, I was able to get in my car and leave the tragic realities of the South Bronx behind in my rearview mirror. Yet working with my students spurred a desire to work toward greater equity and equality by understanding the experiences that defined their worldviews. In so doing, I was provided with a glimpse inside their tumultuous and frightening worlds.

It is rarely the case that we are provided with the opportunity to navigate the intricacies of two different racial groups and social classes. The privilege afforded to me by being able to view the world through my students' eyes, carried with it a moral obligation to take action. Once aware of the insidious violence and the subsequent effects that chronic violence exposure carries with it, I could not sit passively in the cocoon of my comfortable White middle-class life, closing my eyes to the harsh realities of life in the South Bronx—not if I wanted to contribute to a more just society for myself and my students. And so, my worldview has been forever altered.

THE SOUTH BRONX: A HISTORICAL PERSPECTIVE

Interviews with local residents, community-based organizations, and members of the New York Police Department revealed the convergence of a number of complex factors that have all contributed to the insidious violence that plagues the South Bronx. Stretching over 7.6 square miles, the South Bronx is bounded by the Cross Bronx Expressway to the north, the Bronx River to the south, Webster Avenue to the east, and Southern Boulevard to the west. Topless bars, abandoned lots, vacant buildings, and commercial warehouses punctuate the landscape. The South Bronx houses the highest number of methadone clinics, homeless shelters, and AIDS cases in the nation (U.S. Census Bureau, 2010).

At one time the South Bronx was a vibrant manufacturing center, housing a variety of industries. The availability of affordable housing, coupled with a multitude of employment opportunities, attracted working class and immigrant families to the neighborhood. However, industry declined and thousands of families were displaced when Robert Moses blasted through the Bronx in order to construct the Cross Bronx Expressway.

Once completed in 1972, the Cross Bronx Expressway created an invisible barrier that cordoned off the South Bronx from the rest of the borough. Properties located within close proximity to the Cross Bronx Expressway were quickly devalued, spurring a mass exodus of thousands of working class inhabitants. Vacancies created by white flight were soon filled by an influx of racial and ethnic minorities.

Declining property values, coupled with widespread vacancies, caused a total economic collapse that resulted in an arson epidemic in the South Bronx. When attempts to sell their properties failed, landlords and business owners began burning down their buildings in order to collect insurance money and flee the rising crime that was suffocating the neighborhood.

Recognizing the quality-of-life issues that emanated from urban blight, New York City began to rehabilitate abandoned tenement style buildings, designating them as low-income housing. Forty-six public housing complexes, comprised of 218 buildings that range from five to 29 stories, were erected within the borders of the South Bronx (New York City Housing Authority, 2005).

Forty-eight percent of residents in the South Bronx receive income support in the form of Medicaid, Supplemental Security Income, and/or Public Assistance (U.S. Census Bureau, 2010). Despite receiving government subsidies intended to defray the cost of living, the annual median household income in the South Bronx rests steadily at $23,043 (U.S. Census Bureau, 2010). The average total household expenditure in the South Bronx is $34,316, which illuminates the residents' inability to secure financial stability (U.S. Census Bureau, 2010). When considering that the average household expenditure is 33% greater than the average annual household income, it is not surprising that the South Bronx is the only congressional district in the nation with a poverty rate of 46.7% (U.S. Census Bureau, 2010). Furthermore, overwhelming unemployment rates in the South Bronx have resulted in a staggering 58.6% of children living beneath the poverty level (U.S. Census Bureau, 2010).

The South Bronx falls under the auspices of the 40th, 41st, and 42nd police precincts, and despite being the smallest in territorial in command, the precincts are charged with patrolling the largest concentration of low-income public housing projects in the nation (New York City Housing Authority, 2005).

Quality of life issues emanate from the high population density within the housing projects. Crawling with gangs, illegal guns, and drugs, the low-income enclaves quickly degenerated into havens of crime, leaving residents to grapple with a multitude of social justice issues. The presence of graffiti, litter, and broken windows in the public housing complexes demonstrates that the area is plagued with crime, in addition to poverty. Located just off the Cross Bronx Expressway, areas of the South Bronx provide people with easy access to prostitution, drugs, and arms deals. The housing project stairwells offer a protected cover, enabling people to engage in illegal transactions ranging from drug deals to gun sales.

The South Bronx is plagued by insidious gang warfare that emanates from the bloody feud between MHG (Most Hated Gangsters), TOB (Tricks on Bitches), and FM (Fresh Mob), rival gangs that have emerged out of the various housing projects as subsets of the notorious Bloods and Crips. Gang violence is largely responsible for the murders, rapes, robberies, and felony assaults that are reported each year. Social justice issues surrounding violence, advocacy, and justice have significantly hindered the success of gang intervention initiatives. The vast majority of gang members are minors who, due to the efforts of advocacy groups, will be arraigned and released within 24 hours of committing a crime.

The South Bronx is the manifestation of modern-day social and racial segregation. The absence of employment opportunities, coupled with crime and poverty, leaves the neighborhood's inhabitants with virtually no options for advancement. The income gap has become an unbridgeable chasm that has led to the socioeconomic destruction of low-income minority communities in the South Bronx. While the city has attempted to sow the seeds of revitalization, the South Bronx remains a far cry from a flourishing renaissance.

THE URBAN UNDERCLASS: A CONVERGENCE OF RACISM AND POVERTY

The widespread and pervasive violence that has come to characterize the South Bronx is largely an outgrowth of the convergence of historical and social attitudes of racism and poverty. The United States has been characterized as an "inegalitarian society in which the myth of equal opportunity has obscured the reality of submerged class conflict and racial discrimination" (Peterson, 1992, p. 10). Extremes of wealth and poverty have emerged side by side, and "some efforts to ameliorate these extremes developed in the wake of the Great Depression of the 1930s and the civil disorders of the 1960s" (Peterson, 1992, p. 623). However, remedying the paradox of persistent poverty requires politicians, educators, law enforcement officers, and private citizens to "recognize the crucial role of America's own apartheid in perpetuating urban poverty and racial injustice" (Massey & Denton, 1990, p. 16).

Structural changes in the American economy, beginning in the 1960s, led to the emergence of the urban underclass, "people, mostly black and living in urban areas, who were said to be outside the American class system" (Jargowksy & Bane, 1991, p. 235). "Uneven economic growth, increasing technology and automation and labor market segmentation" (Wilson, 1978, p. 154) had a disproportionate impact on young Black urban males who often lacked the skills to compete for jobs in a new service-sector economy (Marks, 1991). Additionally, the increasing suburbanization of industry affected Black males because many of them lived in urban areas, miles away from new entry-level jobs (Wilson, 1987). Ironically, the success of the Civil Rights movement further exacerbated the difficulties of the underclass. As integration allowed many middle-class Black families to move to the suburbs, urban Black communities often suffered the loss of role models, resources, and a level of social organization (Wilson, 1987).

The term "underclass suggests the lowly, passive, and submissive, yet at the same time, the disreputable, dangerous, disruptive, dark, and evil" (Jencks & Peterson, 1991, p. 3). Apart from the aforementioned personal attributes, it suggests "subjection, subordination, and deprivation" (Jencks & Peterson, 1991, p. 3). While the "deserving poor"—the blind, the deaf, the disabled—were placed within nationally funded programs that improved their welfare, the government was still reluctant to address the needs of the "undeserving poor": those marginal citizens who fell into the urban underclass (Peterson, 1992). A cover story in *Time Magazine* in 1977, described the underclass as:

> People who are more intractable, more socially alien, and more hostile than almost anyone had imagined. They seem to be stuck more or less permanently at the bottom. The underclass is made up mostly of impoverished urban blacks who still suffer from the heritage of slavery and discrimination. (*Time Magazine*, 1977, p. 18)

The editors of *Esquire Magazine* (1988) expanded on the racist and classist attitudes conveyed in *Time Magazine* when it reduced the underclass population to:

> Blacks trapped in cycles of welfare dependency, drugs, alcohol, crime, illiteracy, and disease living in anarchy and isolation in some of the richest cities on earth. In a ten-year period, the underclass has been transformed from surplus and discarded labor into an exclusive group of black urban terrorists. (Hamill, 1998, p. 98)

The effects of poverty led to the social, economic, and political isolation of the underclass. Peterson (1992) suggested that such isolation encouraged "marginal citizens to think of themselves as outsiders who share in neither the benefits nor the responsibilities of the social and political community" (p. 625). As a result, the underclass developed an "alternative status system that is defined in opposition to the basic ideals and values of American society" (Massey & Denton, 1992, p. 92). Therefore, many of the shortcomings typically associated with urban environments—teenage pregnancy, single-parent families, unemployment, drug abuse, violence—function as coping mechanisms for dealing with isolation in a harsh environment (Massey & Denton, 1992).

Today, the South Bronx is the epicenter of abject poverty, not only in New York City, but in the nation. Researchers and theorists' repeated underestimation of the "continuing significance of racism as the cause of inner-city poverty" (Massey & Denton, 1990, p. 62) represents the convergence of two social justice issues traditionally considered taboo by most White Americans: racism and poverty. However, Massey and Denton (1990) note that racism is not merely a relic of the past, and efforts to explain persistent poverty among the underclass cannot be divorced from race and class. Therefore, remedying underclass poverty requires more than strategic planning; it requires direct confrontation of race and classism in society.

As Marks (1991) points out, "it is not race per se, urban residence per se, nor even poverty that defines the underclass, but the combination of all three (p 453)." It is a mistake to believe that the perpetuation and oppression of the underclass requires outward expressions of hatred. Instead, privilege and indifference combine to create problem "as formidable as the presence of a group of people, largely concentrated in the nation's principal cities, who live at the margin of society" (Auletta, 1982, p. 24).

COMMUNITY VIOLENCE: A FACT OF LIFE FOR URBAN MALE ADOLESCENTS

Brookmeyer, Henrich, and Schwab-Stone (2005) cite research (e.g., Fitzpatrick & Boldizar, 1993; Jenkins & Bell, 1994; Osofsky, Wewers, Hann, & Fick, 1993; Richters & Martinez, 1993; Schwab-Stone, Kasprow, Voyce, Barone, & Shriver, 1995) when pointing out that "in the 1990s, community violence was characterized as a public health epidemic in the United States and numerous studies reported that urban adolescents were witnessing disturbingly high rates of violence in their communities" (p. 917). Community violence is somewhat unique in that it involves intentional, rather than unintentional perpetration of a malevolent act, and it is ongoing, as opposed to isolated in terms of the frequency with which it occurs. Community violence is most commonly described as acts by a person or a group of individuals intended to harm another person or group of individuals—such as being threatened, robbed, mugged, raped, shot, stabbed, or killed (Buka, Stichick, Birdthistle, & Earls, 2001). Further, community violence occurs in public (e.g., mugging), rather than in the home and involves nonsexual violence (Rosenthal, 2000).

For urban adolescents, violence is not a single phenomenon, but rather a continuum of behaviors and attitudes. The public nature of community violence not only makes it likely that one will observe violent acts, but it also increases one's risk of being a random or accidental victim. In Chicago, over half of the city's homicides occurred in a public way, thereby bringing literal meaning to the term community violence (Jenkins & Bell, 1997). Chronic exposure to community violence has had a debilitating affect on the urban male adolescents in the South Bronx. The absence of recent research, coupled with inhabitants' deep mistrust of the police, impedes accurate reporting, making it virtually impossible to pinpoint precise statistics regarding violent incidents in the South Bronx. With homicide, AIDS, and overdoses as the dominant causes of death in the South Bronx, residents only have a 1-in-20 chance of dying of natural causes (DuRant, Pendergrast, & Cadenhead, 1994). Black and Hispanic males, ages 15–19, have a homicide rate nine times higher than White males in the same category, making homicide the leading cause of death for Black and Hispanic males under the age of 25 in urban environments (DuRant et al., 1994). As one student explained to the researcher during class,

> If you make it to 18 in my hood, you are blessed. Once you make it to 18, you only have a few more years until you hit 21. Unfortunately, a lot can happen during those years, and too many people don't live to celebrate their 21st birthday. It's like they died before they even had the chance to live.

Being victimized or witnessing recurring community violence during the adolescent years results in symptoms typically associated with psychological trauma, including anger, anxiety, and dissociation (Rosenthal, 2000). In addition to serving as a key variable in violent behavior for urban adolescents, depression is one of the psychological consequences of exposure to violence. A study conducted by Freeman, Mokros, and Poznanski (1993) demonstrated the link between violence exposure and symptoms of depression, and Lynch and Cicchetti (1998) found that adolescents who reported clinically significant levels of depression also reported witnessing more violence and being victimized more than non-depressed youth. Chronic violence exposure produces feelings of hopelessness and depression, particularly when adolescents are forced to consider their own mortality. Each exposure to a shooting, stabbing, beating, and violent situation increases the depth and complexity of an adolescent's depression (Woodall, 2009). According to Woodall (2009), "Violence has become so commonplace, death so expected, that there exists a chilling sense of resignation among urban male adolescents" (p. 2).

McCart, Smith, Saunders, Kilpatrick, Resnik, and Ruggiero (2007) assert that "although all youth are affected by violence, there is a disproportionate impact on adolescents living in low-income urban neighborhoods" (p. 434). Citing statistics provided by the Bureau of Justice, McCart et al. (2007) report that "the average annual violent crime rate in urban areas is about 74% higher than the rural rate and 37% higher than the suburban rate" (p. 434). Studies have examined exposure to community violence among relatively high-risk populations, which are defined as economically disadvantaged, ethnic-minority, inner-city males. In these studies, as many as 97% of adolescents disclosed being a witness to some form of community violence, and as many as 70% reported being victimized (Fitzpatrick & Boldizar, 1993; Osofsky et al., 1993).

Adolescence is the age of highest risk for victimization, and surveys of urban youth indicate that by early adolescence many have had encounters with shootings, stabbings, and other acts of violence in their communities (Jenkins & Bell, 1994; Martinez & Richters, 1993; Osofsky et al., 1993). Overstreet, Dempsey, Graham, and Moely (1999) studied violence exposure among low-income children between the ages of 10 and 15 and found that 92% had heard guns fired in their neighborhoods; 83% knew someone killed by violence; 55% had witnessed a shooting; 43% had seen a dead body in their neighborhood; 37% had been victims of physical violence; and 10% had been threatened with murder.

THE EFFECTS OF CHRONIC VIOLENCE EXPOSURE ON URBAN MALE ADOLESCENTS

Chronic exposure to community violence has been linked to urban adolescents' antisocial behavior, including physical fights, gang involvement, delinquency, and the use of weapons (Durant, Cadenhead, Pendergrast, Slavens, & Linder, 1994; Farrell & Bruce, 1997; Gorman-Smith & Tolan, 1998; Hill, Levermore, Twaite, & Jones, 1996; Lynch & Cicchetti, 1998). Researchers have argued that repeated exposure to neighborhood violence leads to increased aggression and antisocial behavior (Farrell & Bruce, 1997; Garbarino, Dubrow, Kostelny, & Pardo, 1992; Gorman-Smith & Tolan, 1998).

Schwartz and Proctor (2000) note that "social learning perspectives suggest that urban youth acquire aggressive behaviors by witnessing violent interactions (p. 671)." Calling upon research conducted by Perry, Perry, and Rasmussen (1986) and DuRant et al. (1994), Schwartz and Proctor (2000) explain that "through observation of powerful aggressive role models, children develop the belief that the use of violence and aggression is associated with positive outcomes" (p. 671). Adolescents exposed to chronic community violence may also come to believe that aggressive and violent responses are normal and effective methods for handling conflict (Miller, Wasserman, Neugebauer, Gorman- Smith, & Kamboukos, 1999). DuRant et al. (1994) examined relationships between exposure to violence and the use of violence by 225 African American adolescents aged 12 to 19 years from housing projects in Augusta, Georgia. Violence exposure was the strongest predictor of violent behavior, including fighting and carrying or using a weapon (DuRant et al., 1994). Urban adolescents who perpetuated violence reported a diminished sense of purpose in life and a lower expectation of being alive at age 25 (Schwab-Stone et al., 1995).

Lorion and Saltzman (1993) note that urban adolescents are exposed to environmentally pervasive violence and their reactions hold more in common with the chronic adaptations of children living in war zones. These kinds of experiences lead to symptoms of anxiety, helplessness, futurelessness, numbness, difficulties concentrating, desensitization to threat, and participation in dangerous activities (Garbarino et al., 1992; Lorion & Saltzman, 1993). According to Schwab-Stone and colleagues (1995), "This pattern of pathological adaptation may serve to perpetuate its very cause—the reliance on violent actions to work out the problems of social living" (p. 1344).

For urban adolescents, chronic violence exposure and pervasive feelings of danger develop into a state of chronic threat, which in turn demands adjustments in personal behavior, internal affect state, and in the conceptualization of oneself in relation to society (Schwab-Stone et al., 1995). Additionally, exposure to violent incidents alters adolescents' norms regarding the appropriateness of aggressive behavior (Huesmann, 1988). Schwartz and Proctor (2000) note that chronic violence exposure is associated with the "development of cognitive belief systems that potentiate aggressive behavior" (p. 672). In particular, urban adolescents who chronically witness violence develop "efficacy beliefs for aggression (i.e., beliefs that one can successfully engage in aggression), positive expectancies regarding the outcomes of aggression (i.e., beliefs that aggressive behavior leads to positive outcomes), and evaluation of behavioral strategies as appropriate responses to ambiguous social stimuli" (Schwartz & Proctor, 2000, p. 672). Many adolescents who are chronically exposed to community violence are also living in poverty, facing environmental stressors, and attending overburdened schools, and such an accumulation of risk has been shown to jeopardize cognitive development (Garbarino et al., 1992; Sameroff, Siefer, Barocas, Zax, & Greenspan, 1987).

The emotional and behavioral symptoms often associated with exposure to community violence may interfere with learning, resulting in decreased academic performance (Masten & Coatsworth, 1998). Adolescents may withdraw or become aggressive in their attempts to cope with the repeated trauma of community violence, and these behavior changes can interfere with academic performance (Garbarino et al., 1992; Pynoos & Nader, 1988). Furthermore, Pynoos, Frederick, Nader, Arroyo, Steinberg, and Eth (1987) suggest that the intrusion of thoughts related to chronic violence exposure impacts the adolescent's ability to exercise higher-order thinking skills.

Schwartz and Gorman (2003) investigated the role of "depressive symptoms in the relation between neighborhood violence and poor academic outcomes" (p. 163). The emotional distress experienced by adolescents following violence exposure interferes with academic performance at school (Jenkins & Bell, 1997; Lorion, 1998; Overstreet, 2000). Dyson

(1990) reported on the academic functioning of six urban African American students who had experienced the murder of a family member. Based on a large sample of 2,248 sixth-, eighth-, and tenth-grade students, Schwab-Stone et al. (1995) found that the frequency of witnessing a shooting or stabbing significantly predicted poorer school achievement, defined in terms of grade retention and reported grades.

Schwartz and Gorman (2003) cite prior research conducted by Lynch and Cicchetti, (1998), Martinez and Richters (1993), Singer, Anglin, Song, and Lunghofer (1995), and Pynoos and Nader (1988) in noting that "the symptoms of depression and other forms of internalized distress associated with chronic exposure to community violence results in difficulties with intrusive thoughts, loss of energy, decreased motivation, and impaired concentration, which hinders adolescents' academic performance in the classroom" (p. 164).

Violent crimes resulting in the death of a family member or friend frequently elicit confusing and frightening grief and loss reactions (Osofsky et al., 1993). Grieving may also be complicated and impeded by rage and the desire to punish the perpetrator (Pynoos & Eth, 1985). "Parents' or caregivers' ability to deal with their own trauma or grief is critical to the outcomes of their children who are exposed to violent crimes" (Osofsky, 1995, p. 784). Unfortunately, "generations of the same family tend to suffer from undiagnosed mental health issues, such as anxiety and depression caused by the stresses of urban poverty, community violence, poor-quality schools, and limited access to health care" (Woodall, 2009, p. 4). As a result, Parson (1994) explains,

> Violence-based trauma often truncates the human connectedness and breaks the great chain of humanity that connects us all. As a consequence of both psychic trauma and the failure of the post-violence milieu to restore confidence, trust, and function in children, many of them become hardened to other people's needs and points of view, adopting an interpersonal anesthetic in the form of a cold, tough, aloof, and intimidating street-wise demeanor. (p. 163)

CHRONIC VIOLENCE EXPOSURE AND POSTTRAUMATIC STRESS DISORDER

Despite a national decline in murder and assault rates, the United States continues to lead the world in the highest crime rate among industrialized nations (Martinez & Richters, 1993). Efforts, on the parts of advocacy groups and politicians, to eradicate community violence have failed, leaving many urban adolescents to live in chronically violent neighborhoods.

Chronic exposure to community violence has deleterious effects on the social, emotional, and cognitive development of urban adolescents, and researchers have documented a strong and consistent relationship between exposure to community violence and the prevalence of posttraumatic stress disorder (PTSD) among urban inhabitants (Boney-McCoy & Finkelhor, 1995; Fitzpatrick & Boldizar, 1993; Horowitz, Weine, & Jekel, 1995; Kliewer, Lepore, Oskin, & Johnson, 1998; Overstreet et al., 1999). Garbarino et al. (1992) have argued that exposure to community violence challenges adolescents' beliefs about safety and predictability and that "danger replaces safety as the organizing principle" (p. 83) in the lives of many youth living in impoverished urban environments (Osofsky, 1995). Adolescents exposed to chronic community violence may feel that there is no safe haven in the community or at school, which can lead to adverse psychological and behavioral consequences, including depression, hopelessness, delinquency, risky sexual behavior, substance abuse, and PTSD (Freudenberg et al., 1999; Overstreet, 2000).

The term "posttraumatic stress disorder was coined in 1980, and first entered the Diagnostic and Statistical Manual of Mental Disorders (DSM-IV-TR) classification system as an anxiety disorder" (Laslie, 2005, p. 4). The creation of this diagnostic category helped define the relationship between experiencing trauma and the development of subsequent psychological problems. Laslie (2005) noted that "since the introduction of PTSD, there has been a definitional shift from a focus on the severity of the event a person experiences towards a focus on the patient's reaction to the event" (p. 4).

Chronic community violence, which frequently includes extreme violence and traumatic events, leaves urban adolescents in jeopardy of developing PTSD. The American Psychiatric Association (2000) describes traumatic stressors as events that are characterized by the following:

1. The person experienced, witnessed, or was confronted by an event that involved actual or threatened death or serious injury, or a threat to the physical integrity of self or others
2. The person's response involved intense fear, helplessness, or horror.

Based on her clinical work with youth who had experienced trauma, Terr (1991) emphasized four PTSD-specific symptoms that children consistently display, regardless of the source of the trauma: repeatedly perceiving memories of the event through visualization of the trauma, engagement in behavioral reenactments and repetitive play related to some aspect of the trauma, and trauma-specific fears. The fourth change chronicled by Terr (1991) is pessimistic attitudes about people, life, and the future, manifesting as a sense of hopelessness and difficulty forming close personal relationships.

Research ranging from clinical case studies to large-scale surveys indicates that urban youth who are exposed to violence suffer from psychological disturbances associated with PTSD. The initial trauma experience leading to the development of PTSD is believed to sensitize the brain to similar environmental and situational cues, leading to aggressive and violent responses to situations that resemble the initial trauma (Chemtob, Novaco, Hamada, Gross, & Smith, 1997; Kendall-Tackett, 2000).

Adolescence is commonly recognized as a stressful period: one where "vulnerability to stress is attributed to developmental changes including puberty, social role definition, cognitive development, school transitions, the emergence of sexuality, and the tasks of separation and individuation" (Berton & Stabb, 1996, p. 489). Normal developmental stress is exacerbated by chronic exposure to community violence. Berton and Stabb (1996, p. 489) cite Forehand, Wierson, Thomas, Armistead, Kempton, and Neighbors (1991) in acknowledging that "as the number of stressors increase, adolescent functioning deteriorates." Therefore, the "prevalence and severity of chronic and everyday stressors in the lives of urban adolescents predispose them to symptoms of psychological stress and the development of PTSD" (Stabb & Berton, 1996, p. 490).

Urban adolescents are at particularly high risk for experiencing clinical levels of PTSD and other related forms of psychological distress due to the high level of exposure to chronic stressors in their lives. The observed symptoms in traumatized adolescents are a function of both developmental level and changes to the individual's developmental course. Adolescents who are chronically exposed to violence are often changed by the experience, which can affect their psychological, moral, cognitive, and general personality development (Pynoos, 1993; Garabino, 1993). Independent decision-making coupled with the potential for greater risk-taking behavior leaves adolescents vulnerable to the traumatic stressors that are associated with community violence. As a result, important developmental changes, such as establishing their personal identities, may be short-circuited by chronic exposure to community violence (Jenkins & Bell, 1997). In fact, a major consequence of chronic violence exposure for adolescents is a "premature entrance in adulthood or premature closure of identity formation," which threatens to compromise the major psychosocial tasks of establishing trust and autonomy (Pynoos & Eth, 1985, p. 47).

Controversy has developed surrounding the diagnosis of attention deficit hyperactivity disorder (ADHD) in urban adolescents given the high rate of comorbidity between PTSD and ADHD (Biderman, Newcorn, & Sprich, 1991; Connor, Edwards, Fletcher, Baird, Barkley, & Steingard, 2003). Symptoms of PTSD that mirror ADHD exist primarily in the hyperarousal cluster area and include sleeplessness, irritability or anger outbursts, difficulty concentrating, hypervigilance, and exaggerated startle response (Weinstein,

Staffelbach & Biaggio, 2000). Perry (1997) suggests that the traumatized adolescents diagnosed with PTSD do not have an inability to attend to a particular task, but rather are hypervigilant to their surroundings. Such hypervigilance frequently results in difficulty filtering out external stimuli, which is similar to the ADHD adolescent who is often distracted by extraneous stimuli (APA, 2000). Given the wide variation in treatments for PTSD and ADHD, an improper diagnosis of ADHD does little to alleviate the symptoms of PTSD that are being experienced by the adolescent.

TRAINING TO BETTER SUPPORT THE NEEDS
OF URBAN MALE ADOLESCENTS

This study has illuminated the deleterious effects that chronic exposure has on the lives of urban male adolescents and results in educational inequity and social injustice. African American and Latino male adolescents living in the South Bronx are exposed to levels of violence that have been compared with active warzones. Unfortunately, little is being done to address the nefarious violence and the way that it has affected the lives of urban male adolescents.

Despite the fact that chronic exposure to community violence interrupts the normal developmental trajectory of urban male adolescents, resulting in the emergence of significant physiological, emotional, and psychological reactions, large urban school districts have proven unable to provide schools with the appropriate resources needed to support the unique needs of urban male adolescents. Furthermore, the vast majority of teacher and principal preparation programs fail to incorporate social justice learning modules—race, class, equity, accessibility, and violence exposure—into their curriculum. Therefore, it is incumbent upon educational leaders to leverage their positional authority to support faculty members in learning about the factors that impede urban male adolescents' academic achievement. We will never achieve a just and equitable society unless we ensure academic achievement for all of our students.

Over the past decade, countless attempts to implement new initiatives to decrease the achievement gap in urban schools have failed. Despite the promise that many initiatives held, the lack of training and support for administrators and faculty doomed the projects to failure. In order to address the enduring epidemic of the failure of our urban male adolescents of color, stand-alone professional development sessions simply will not suffice. Instead, educational leaders must support a paradigm shift that challenges faculty members to conceptualize the ways in which we address the needs of urban male adolescents. Therefore, administrators must commit to incorporating rigorous and ongoing training and support for faculty.

Monthly training sessions and weekly professional learning communities will augment extensive training sessions, delivered by trauma experts, each year in August. This type of continuous learning will provide faculty and administrators with the skills that they need to effectively deliver curriculum and support urban male adolescents in the school community.

CREW: AN INNOVATIVE ADVISORY PROGRAM TO SUPPORT URBAN MALE ADOLESCENTS

The pervasive violence that exists within the South Bronx is a silent epidemic that has claimed the lives of tens of thousands of urban male adolescents. By ignoring the existence of the heinous violence and the effects that such violence has on the lives of urban male adolescents, we, as a nation, are perpetuating the continuation of urban genocide.

From the perspective of study participants, life in the South Bronx has exacted a significant toll on their sense of hope and possibility for the future. Chronic exposure to community violence has robbed participants of the youthful exuberance and sense of unlimited possibility that exists within the heart of an 18-year-old. For these urban male adolescents, their perceived future contains a grim forecast: prison or death.

The South Bronx, which is characterized by high crime rates, abysmal poverty, and the lack of proper mental heath services, puts its young inhabitants at greater risk for developing PTSD. Working with adolescents in the South Bronx enabled me to witness, first hand, students' aggressive behavior, exaggerated startle response, debilitating depression, and suicidal ideation.

Over the past decade, in order to better connect students with individual faculty members, many urban schools have replaced homeroom with an advisory period.

While the move to advisory periods was intended to foster increased accountability for student learning and outcomes, the lack of a robust and meaningful curriculum reduced the initiative to little more than a free period for both teachers and students. Despite the lackluster results emerging from existing models of advisory, a newly conceptualized vision for the time previously devoted to advisory periods offers educational leaders with the opportunity to address the specific needs of urban male adolescents who have been chronically exposed to community violence.

Drawing from the literature on community violence and my experience as a teacher in and around the South Bronx, offsetting the effects of chronic violence exposure requires schools to provide urban male adolescents with opportunities to forge trusting and meaningful relationships, while simultaneously establishing a renewed sense of purpose for the future. The development of a program, titled Crew, which meets daily, offers educational administrators with a systematic method of addressing the needs of urban male adolescents who have been chronically exposed to community violence.

Ongoing training for members of the schools community, as previously discussed, will prepare faculty to serve as Crew advisors. Working collaboratively with trauma counselors and educational leaders, faculty members will administer a needs assessment to all incoming male freshmen in order to determine the presence of various physiological, psychological, and emotional symptoms caused by chronic violence exposure. The results of the assessment will, therefore, enable educational leaders to create homogenous Crews, which will be comprised of urban male adolescents who are experiencing similar symptoms as a result of violence exposure. These Crews will remain together from freshman through senior year, with the intent of alleviating the effects of chronic exposure to community violence by working collaboratively to achieve individual and collective goals.

Social workers, trained in trauma, will work alongside principals and teachers to develop a vertically aligned curriculum that centers on three annual goals for Crews over the four-year period. Given the varying needs of urban male adolescents, the team would be tasked with generating unique curricula, which would be turn-keyed in the schools.

Progress toward the goals will be evaluated quarterly, and faculty members will draw support from one another during weekly meetings. The Crews, administration, and faculty all represent professional learning communities (PLCs) that are working collaboratively to support urban male adolescents in the school community.

CONCLUSIONS

Throughout the nation, urban male adolescents are witnesses to, and victims of, unprecedented rates of violent crimes. When considering that violence exacts a disproportionate impact on urban adolescents living in low-income communities, it becomes imperative that educational leaders examine, analyze, and address the social justice issues—race, class, equality, crime, justice, power, and equity—that are inherently embedded within the context of this issue.

Chronic violence exposure has interrupted the normal developmental trajectory for the urban male adolescents who walk through the doors of our schools each day. The underachievement of Black and Latino males is a national epidemic that is fueled by the anxiety, anger, depression, and PTSD—symptoms of psychological trauma—that are triggered by repeated exposure to community violence. Education leaders are called to address the needs of students who are least likely to succeed in the current educational climate, and this includes the recognition of the deleterious effects of violence exposure on urban male adolescents. Unfortunately, little is being done in our urban schools to address the unique needs of our urban male adolescents.

Our African American and Latino male adolescents are gifted, intelligent, and talented; inside each young man lies the potential for discovering the cure for cancer, an alternative to our dependence on petroleum, or a resolution to the deadly conflicts that plague our world. However, without the commitment and determination on the part of our education leaders to address the effects of chronic violence exposure on urban male adolescents, we are contributing to the perpetuation of an urban genocide that continues to claim generations of our promising African American and Latino male adolescents.

My research has brought me back to the Bronx during the inter-war years, led me through white flight and the settlement of racial and ethnic minorities, the burning of the Bronx during the 1970s, and the violence, crime, and poverty that engendered a sense of hopelessness and despair for its inhabitants.

As I reflect back on my time working with urban adolescents, I am dismayed by the number of students that we have lost to community violence. While we might have been powerless to stop the untimely deaths of those we have buried, it is now our moral obligation to mobilize awareness and commitment among the educational community to support our African American and Latino males in realizing their full potential.

In the past, well-intentioned educators and others with an interest in education believed that we cannot improve our schools until society ends poverty and violence. I am forced to conclude that we will never end poverty and violence until our schools address the needs of our urban male adolescent students. Nearly 60 years after *Brown vs. the School Board of Topeka, Kansas,* it is long past time to rectify this injustice and establish real access and equity for all our children.

REFERENCES

American Psychiatric Association. (2000). *Diagnostic and statistical manual of mental disorders* (4th ed.). Washington, DC: Author.

Auletta, K. (1982). *The underclass.* New York, NY: Random House.

Berton, M. W., & Stabb, S. D. (1996). Exposure to violence and post-traumatic stress disorder in urban adolescents. *Adolescence, 31,* 489–498.

Biderman, J., Newcorn, J., & Sprich, S. (1991). Comorbidity of attention deficit hyperactivity disorder with conduct, depressive, anxiety, and other disorders. *American Journal of Psychiatry, 158*(5), 564–577.

Boney-McCoy, S., & Finkelhor, D. (1995). Psychosocial sequelae of violence victim-ization in a national youth sample. *Journal of Consultant Clinical Psychology, 63,* 726 –736.

Brookmeyer, K., Henrich, C., & Schwab-Stone, M. (2005). Adolescents who witness community violence: Can parent support and prosocial cognitions protect them from committing violence? *Child Development, 76*(4), 917–929.

Buka, S. I., Stichick, T. L., Birdthistle, I., & Earls, F. J. (2001). Youth exposure to vio-lence: Prevalence, risks, and consequences. *American Journal of Orthopsychiatry, 71*(3), 298–310.

Chemtob, C. M., Novaco, R. W., Hamada, R. S., Gross, D. M., & Smith, G. (1997). Anger regulation deficits in combat-related posttraumatic stress disorder. *Journal of Traumatic Stress, 10*(1), 17–36.

Connor, D. E., Edwards, G., Fletcher, K. E., Baird, J., Barkley, R. A., & Steingard, R. J. (2003).

Correlates of comorbid psychopathology in children with attention-deficit hyperac-tivity disorder. *Journal of the American Academy of Child and Adolescent Psychiatry, 42*(2), 193–200.

Durant, R. H., Cadenhead, C., Pendergrast, R. A., Slavens, G., & Linder, C. (1994). Factors associated with the use of violence among urban black adolescents. *American Journal of Public Health, 84,* 612–617.

Dyson, J. (1990). The effects of family violence on children's academic performance and behavior. *Journal of the National Medical Association, 82,* 17–22.

DuRant, R. H., Pendergrast, R. A., & Cadenhead, C. (1994). Exposure to violence and victimization and fighting behavior by urban black adolescents. *Journal of Adolescent Health, 15,* 311–318.

Farrell, A. D., & Bruce, S. E. (1997). Impact of exposure to community violence on violent behavior and emotional distress among urban adolescents. *American Journal of Preventative Medicine, 12,* 13–21.

Fitzpatrick, K. M., & Boldizar, J. P. (1993). The prevalence and consequences of exposure to violence among African-American youth. *Journal of the American Academy of Child Adolescent Psychiatry, 32,* 424–430.

Forehand, R., Wierson, M., Thomas, A. M., Armistead, L., Kempton, T., & Neigh-bors, B. (1991). The role of family stressors and parent relationships on ad-olescent functioning. *Journal of the American Academy of Child and Adolescent Psychiatry, 30,* 316–322.

Freeman, L., Mokros, H., & Poznanski, E. (1993). Violent events reported by nor-mal urban school-aged children: Characteristics and depression correlates. *Journal of the American Academy of Child and Adolescent Psychiatry, 32,* 419–423.

Freudenberg, N., Roberts, L., Richie, B., Taylor, R., McGillicuddy, K., & Greene, M. (1999). Coming up in the boogie down: The role of violence in the lives of adolescents in the south Bronx. *Health Education Behavior, 26*(6), 788–805.

Garabino, J. (1993). Children's response to war: What do we know? *Infant Mental Heath Journal, 14,* 103–115.

Garbarino, J., Dubrow, N., Kostelny, K., & Pardo, C. (1992). *Children in danger. Cop-ing with the consequences of community violence.* San Francisco, CA: Jossey-Bass.

Gorman-Smith, D., & Tolan, P. (1998). The role of exposure to community violence and developmental problems among inner-city youth. *Development and Psychopathology, 10,* 101–116.

Hamill, P. (1988, March). Breaking the silence. *Esquire,* pp. 91–102.

Hill, H. M., Levermore, M., Twaite, J., & Jones, L. P. (1996). Exposure to community violence and social support as predictors of anxiety and social and emotional behavior among African American children. *Journal of Child and Family Studies, 5,* 399–414.

Horowitz. K., Weine, S., & Jekel, J. (1995). PTSD symptoms in urban adolescent girls: Compounded community trauma. *Journal of the American Academy of Child and Adolescent Psychiatry, 34,* 1353–1361.

Huesmann, L. R. (1988). An information processing model for the development of aggression. *Aggressive Behavior, 14,* 13–24.

Jargowsky, P., & Bane, M. J. (1991). Ghetto poverty in the united states, 1970–1980. In C. Jencks & P. Peterson (Eds.), *The urban underclass* (pp. 235–273). Washington, D.C.: The Brookings Institution.

Jencks, C., & Peterson, P. (Eds.). (1991). *The urban underclass.* Washington, DC: Brookings Institution.

Jenkins, E. J., & Bell, C. C. (1994). Violence exposure, psychological distress, and high risk behaviors among inner-city high school students. In S. Friedman (Ed.), *Anxiety disorders in African-Americans* (pp. 76–88). New York, NY: Springer.

Jenkins E. J., & Bell C. C. (1997). Exposure and response to community violence among children and adolescents. In J. D. Osofsky (Ed.), *Children in a violent society* (pp. 9–31). New York, NY: Guilford Press.

Kendall-Tackett, K. A. (2000). Physiological correlates of childhood abuse: Chronic hyper-arousal in PTSD, depression, and irritable bowel syndrome. *Child Abuse and Neglect, 24*(6), 799–810.

Kliewer, W., Lepore, S. J., Oskin, D., & Johnson, P. D. (1998). The role of social and cognitive processes in children's adjustment to community violence. *Journal of Consulting and Clinical Psychology, 66,* 199–209.

Laslie, K. (2005). *Comorbidity of attention deficit hyperactivity disorder and posttraumatic stress disorder in low income urban youth.* Master's thesis, Louisiana State University, Baton Rouge, LA. Retrieved from http://etd.lsu.edu/docs/available/etd-04132005-140539/unrestricted/Laslie_thesis.pdf?&lang=en_us&output=json

Lorion, R. P. (1998). Exposure to urban violence: Contamination of the school environment. In D. S. Elliott, B. A. Hamburg, & K. R. Williams (Eds.), *Violence in American schools: A new perspective* (pp. 293–311). New York, NY: Cambridge University Press.

Lorion, R., & Saltzman, W. (1993). Children's exposure to community violence: Following a path from concern to research to action. In D. Reiss, J. E. Richters, M. Radke-Yarrow, & D. Scharff (Eds.), *Children and violence* (pp. 55–65). New York: Guilford Press.

Lynch, M., & Cicchetti, D. (1998). An ecological-transactional analysis of children and contexts: The longitudinal interplay among child maltreatment, community violence, and children's symptomatology. *Development and Psychopathology, 10,* 235–257.

Marks, C. (1991). The urban underclass. *Annual review of sociology, 17*, 445–466.

Martinez, P., & Richters, J. E. (1993). The NIMH Community Violence Project: II. Children's distress symptoms associated with violence exposure. *Psychiatry, 56*, 22–35.

Massey, D. S., & Denton, N. A. (1993). *American apartheid: Segregation and the making of the underclass.* Cambridge, MA: Harvard University Press.

Masten, A. S., & Coatsworth, J. D. (1998). The development of competence in favorable and unfavorable environments: Lessons from research on successful children. *American Psychologist, 53*, 205–220.

McCart, M., Smith, D., Saunders, B., Kilpatrick, D., Resnick, H., & Ruggiero, K. (2007). Do urban adolescents become desensitized to community violence? *American Journal of Orthopsychiatry, 77*(3), 434–442.

Miller, L. S., Wasserman, G. A., Neugebauer, R., Gorman- Smith, D., & Kamboukos, D. (1999). Witnessed community violence and antisocial behavior in high-risk, urban boys. *Journal of Clinical Child Psychology, 28*, 2–11.

New York City Housing Authority. (2005). NYCHA Housing Developments. Retrieved from http://www.nyc.gov/html/nycha/html/developments/dev_guide.shtml

Osofsky, J. D., Wewers, S., Hann, D. M., & Fick, A. C. (1993). Chronic community violence: What is happening to our children? *Psychiatry, 56*, 7–21.

Osofsky, J. (1995). The effects of exposure to violence on young children. *American Psychologist, 50*(9), 782–787.

Overstreet, S., Dempsey, M., Graham, D., & Moely, B. (1999). Availability of family support as a moderator of exposure to community violence. *Journal of Clinical Child Psychology, 28*, 151–159.

Overstreet, S. (2000). Exposure to community violence: Defining the problem and understanding the consequences. *Journal of Child and Family Studies, 9*(1), 7–25.

Parson, E. (1994). Inner city children of trauma: Urban violence traumatic stress response syndrome. In J. Lindy & J. Wilson (Eds.), *Countertrensderence in the treatment of PTSD* (pp. 157–178). New York, NY: Guilford.

Patton, J. M. (1998). The disproportionate representation of African Americans in special education: Looking behind the curtain for understanding and solutions. *Journal of Special Education, 32*, 25–31.

Perry, B. (1997). Incubated in terror: Neurodevelopmental factors in the cycle of violence. In J. D. Osofsky (Ed.), *Children in a violent society* (pp. 124–149). New York, NY: Guilford Press.

Perry, D. G., Perry, L. C., & Rasmussen, P. (1986). Cognitive social learning mediators of aggression. *Child Development, 57*, 700–711.

Peterson, P. (1992). The urban underclass and the poverty paradox. *Political Science Quarterly, 106*(4), 617–637.

Pynoos, R. S., Frederick, C., Nader, K., Arroyo, W., Steinberg, A., & Eth, S. (1987). Life threat and posttraumatic stress in school-age children. *Archive of General Psychiatry, 44*, 1057–1063.

Pynoos, R. S., & Eth, S. (1985). Developmental perspective on psychic trauma in childhood. In C. R. Figley (Ed.), *Trauma and its wake* (pp. 36–52). New York, NY: Brunner/Mazel.

Pynoos, R. S., & Nader, K. (1988). Psychological first aid: For children who witness community violence. *Journal of Traumatic Stress, 1*, 445–473.

Richters, J., & Martinex, P. (1993). Violent communities family choices, and children's chances: An algorithm for improving the odds. *Development and Psychopathology, 5*, 609–627.

Rosenthal, B. S. (2000). Exposure to community violence in adolescence: Trauma symptoms. *Adolescence, 35,* 271–284.

Sameroff, A., Seifer, R., Barocas, R., Zax, M., & Greenspan, S. (1987). Intelligence quotient scores of 4-year-old children: Social-environmental risk factors. *Pediatrics, 79,* 343–350.

Schwab-Stone, M., Ayers, T., Kasprow, W., Voyce, C., Barone, C., Shriver, T., et al. (1995). No safe haven: A study of violence exposure in an urban community. *Journal of the American Academy of Child and Adolescent Development, 34,* 1343–1352.

Schwartz, D., & Gorman, A. (2003). Community violence exposure and children's academic functioning. *Journal of Educational Psychology, 95(1),* 163–173.

Schwartz, D., & Proctor, L. (2000). Community violence exposure and children's social adjustment in the school peer group: The mediating roles of emotion regulation and social cognition. *Journal of Consulting and Clinical Psychology, 68(4),* 670–683.

Singer, M. I., Anglin, T. M., Song, L. Y., & Lunghofer, L. (1995). Adolescents' exposure to violence and associated symptoms of psychological trauma. *Journal of the American Medical Association, 273(6),* 477–482.

Terr, L. (1991). Childhood traumas: An outline and overview. *American Journal of Psychiatry, 48,* 10–20.

Time Magazine. (1977, August 29). The American underclass: Destitute and desperate in the land of plenty. *Time,* pp. 2–7.

U.S. Census Bureau. (2010). *American fact finder.* Retrieved from http://factfinder2. census.gov/faces/nav/jsf/pages/community_facts.xhtml

Van der Kolk, B. (2003). Posttraumatic stress disorder and the nature of trauma. In M. F. Solomon & D. J. Siegel (Eds.), *Healing trauma: Attachment, mind, body, and brain* (pp. 168–195). New York, NY: W.W. Norton.

Weinstein, D., Staffelbach, D., & Biaggio, M. (2000). Attention-deficit hyperactivity disorder and posttraumatic stress disorder: Differential diagnosis in childhood. *Clinical Psychology Review, 20(3),* 359–378.

Wilson, W. (1985). Cycles of deprivation and the underclass debate. *Social Science Review, 59,* 541–549.

Wilson, W. (1987). *The truly disadvantaged: The inner city, the underclass, and public policy.* Chicago, IL: University of Chicago Press.

Woodall, A. (2009, May 27). Violence in Oakland creates symptoms of post traumatic stress disorder. *Oakland Tribune.* Retrieved from http://www.insidebayarea. com/homicides/ci_9327607

ABOUT THE CONTRIBUTORS

Tawannah G. Allen, EdD, is an associate professor of educational leadership at Fayetteville State University (FSU). Prior to her role at FSU, she held central office and building-level administrative posts with several North Carolina public school systems. Her research foci include the academic success of minority males, strengthening professional development opportunities for teachers of minority students, mentorship for women in higher education, and turnaround principals for low-performing schools. Dr. Allen holds an EdD in educational leadership from the University of North Carolina at Chapel Hill. Her research has been presented at state and national conferences. She has authored numerous articles and book chapters.

George J. Petersen, PhD, has been a public school teacher, administrator, and university faculty member. Currently, he is a professor and dean in the Graduate School of Education at California Lutheran University. Prior to this appointment, he was a professor of educational leadership, chair of the department of graduate studies at the California Polytechnic State University San Luis Obispo and co-director of the University of California Santa Barbara and Cal Poly joint doctoral program in educational leadership. Dr. Petersen is the author or co-author of three books and over 100 book chapters, professional articles, research papers, monographs, and commissioned reports. Much of Dr. Petersen's scholarly work has focused on the executive leadership of district superintendents, their beliefs, roles, and work in the area of instructional leadership and policy. Dr. Petersen's work has been widely published and is internationally recognized for its quality and impact. In recognition of his scholarship and leadership in the

Educational Leadership for Ethics and Social Justice, pages 203–210
Copyright © 2014 by Information Age Publishing

field, he was the recipient of the University of California Santa Barbara's Gevirtz School of Education Distinguished Alumni Award in 2008.

Diane Rodriguez -Kiino, PhD, is an assistant professor of higher education leadership at California Lutheran University, where she teaches and advises doctoral students committed to executive leadership in postsecondary education. Prior to CLU she served as the director of campus diversity in the president's office of Santa Barbara City College, and she continues to consult and lecture on the issues of campus diversity and equity. She is a respected and successful grant writer and evaluator and has published on topics covering transfer students, women, and students of color in education. She currently serves as a senior researcher for the Research and Planning Group for California Community Colleges and an associate editor for the *Journal of Applied Research in the Community College*. Dr. Rodriguez-Kiino is 2012 fellow with the National Community College Hispanic Council. She holds an MEd in college student personnel services and a PhD in education policy with an emphasis on international intercultural education from the University of Southern California.

Mark Berends holds a PhD in sociology from University of Wisconsin-Madison. Dr. Berends is currently a professor of sociology at the University of Notre Dame, where he directs the Center for Research on Educational Opportunity (CREO) and the Research Center on Educational Policy (RCEP). He has written and published extensively on educational reform, school choice, the effects of family and school changes on student achievement trends, and the effects of schools and classrooms on student achievement. Prior to coming to Notre Dame, he was a professor at Vanderbilt, and before that, he was a senior social scientist at RAND. His research focuses on how school organization and classroom instruction are related to student achievement, with special attention to disadvantaged students and school reforms aimed at improving their educational opportunities. Currently, he is conducting several studies on school choice, including an examination of the Indiana Choice Scholarship Program, parent decision making and satisfaction in a lottery-based study of charter schools, and how in-school enabling conditions and classroom instruction are related to student achievement gains in charter schools and traditional public schools. He serves on numerous editorial boards, technical panels, and policy forums; he is the editor of *Educational Evaluation and Policy Analysis*; he is a former vice president of the American Educational Research Association's Division L, Educational Policy and Politics; and he is the AERA Program Chair for the 2014 annual meeting. His latest books are *Examining Gaps in Mathematics Achievement Among Racial-Ethnic Groups, 1972–1992; Charter School Outcomes; Leading with Data: Pathways to Improve Your School; The Handbook of Research on School Choice;* and *School Choice and School Improvement.*

Jeffrey S. Brooks , PhD, is professor and chair of the department of leadership and counseling at the University of Idaho. He is a J. William Fulbright Senior Scholar alumnus who has conducted studies in the United States and the Philippines. His research focuses broadly on educational leadership, and he examines the way leaders influence (and are influenced by) dynamics such as racism, globalization, social justice and school reform. Dr. Brooks is author of *The Dark Side of School Reform: Teaching in the Space between Reality and Utopia* (Rowman & Littlefield, 2006), and *Black School, White School: Racism and Educational (Mis)leadership* (Teachers College Press, 2012). He is also co-editor of the volumes *What Every Principal Needs to Know to Create Equitable and Excellent Schools* (Teachers College Press, 2012), *Confronting Racism in Higher Education: Problems and Possibilities for Fighting Ignorance, Bigotry and Isolation* (IAP, 2012), and *Anti-Racist School Leadership: Toward Equity in Education for America's Students* (IAP, 2012). Dr. Brooks is series editor for the Educational Leadership for Social Justice Book series (Information Age Publishing).

Bradley W. Carpenter, PhD, is assistant professor at the University of Louisville in the department of leadership, foundations, and human resource education (ELFH). A former public school teacher, assistant principal, and principal, Dr. Carpenter's research focuses on issues pertaining to the politics of school improvement reform policies; the ways in which school building leaders, parents, and communities participate in collaborative decision making; how professors within the field of educational administration facilitate conversations surrounding social justice, race, racism and race relations; and the possibilities that exist for education leaders asked to advocate for their children and their school communities at the state and federal levels of policy making.

T. Elon Dancy II is associate professor of higher education at the University of Oklahoma, where he also holds joint appointments in African and African American studies, women and gender studies, and the Center for Social Justice. His research agenda investigates the experiences and socio-cognitive outcomes of college students, particularly related to nexus of race, gender, and culture. With more than 50 publications to his credit, Dr. Dancy is the author of *The Brother Code: Manhood and Masculinity among African American Males in College.*

Sarah Diem, PhD, is an assistant professor in the department of educational leadership and policy analysis at the University of Missouri. Her research focuses on the social and cultural contexts of education, paying particular attention to how the politics and implementation of educational policies affect outcomes related to equity and diversity within public schools. She is also interested in the ways in which future school leaders are being prepared to address race-related issues that may affect the diverse students and communities they are called to serve. Dr. Diem received her PhD in educational policy and planning from the University of Texas at Austin.

Fenwick W. English is the R. Wendell Eaves Senior Distinguished Professor of Educational Leadership in the School of Education at the University of North Carolina at Chapel Hill, a position he has held since 2001. His record of publications includes 26 books and numerous book chapters, monographs, and referred journal articles. In addition, he has served as general editor for the 2005 *Sage Handbook of Educational Leadership*; the 2006 *Sage Encyclopedia of Educational Leadership and Administration* (2 volumes); and the 2009 *Sage Major Works Series in Educational Leadership and Administration* (4 volumes). Dr. English is also the author of recent texts including *The Art of Educational Leadership* (2008) released by Sage. He was a member of the executive committee of UCEA for seven years and served as President, 2006–2007, and later president of NCPEA 2011–2012.

Nancy Erbe, JD, LLM, is a professor in the interdisciplinary negotiation, conflict resolution and peace building program (NCRP) at California State University Dominguez Hills in the Los Angeles region. Dr. Erbe is a Senior Fulbright Specialist who lectured and conducted bicommunal dialogue in Cyprus. She has taught conflict and education, negotiation, ethics, conflict skills, and multicultural process to students from about 80 different countries and several professions (e.g., international studies and development, communications, social work, human resources, ombuds, law, nonprofit, education) for 18 years at schools including the Straus Institute for Dispute Resolution, the University of California Berkeley and the University of Oslo. She has also worked with development and conflict process in communities including the Balkans (during war), Cameroon, Cyprus, India, and Nepal as examples. Her most recent book is *Negotiation Alchemy: Global Skills Inspiring and Transforming Diverging Worlds* (Berkeley Public Policy Press, 2011). She is also the author of *Holding These Truths: Empowerment and Recognition in Action* (an interactive case study curriculum for multicultural dispute resolution) and a number of articles including one published by Harvard and several published with Sage as a contributor to its *Encyclopedia of Governance*. Her publication for educators with Southern Poverty Teaching Tolerance project was the most popular of that year. Dr Erbe has developed several curricula including a national nonviolence middle school curriculum funded by the U.S. Department of Justice. Prior to her academic career, she served as legal counsel to the Minneapolis Public Schools as a lawyer with Fredrickson & Byron with a focus on disciplinary and special education concerns.

Lynn Ilon, PhD, is a professor in the College of Education, Seoul National University in South Korea. She specializes in global knowledge economics and global learning systems and applies this specialization, generally, to poor countries. As such, her scholarly work centers of how to bring together the disparate worlds of rich and poor, global & local, applied & theoretical. Dr. Ilon has worked in the parallel worlds of academia and field world for decades having lived in the Pacific Islands (Micronesia, 3 years), the Middle East (Jordan, 1 year), Africa (Zimbabwe, 2 years; Zambia, 2 years), her native North America, and now South Korea (over 3 years). In addition, she has done field and other professional work in dozens of other countries spanning several regions of the world. Her work involves work for multilateral, bilateral, regional and World Banks and global and local NGOs. She is currently working on an innovative knowledge-economic design for an alternatively higher education institution in Southern Africa with a local NGO. Dr. Ilon holds degrees in anthropology (BA), educational research (MS), economics (MS), and international development education (PhD).

Gaetane Jean-Marie, PhD, is professor of educational leadership and chair of Leadership, Foundations & Human Resource Education at the University of Louisville. For the past seven years, she held a joint appointment in African and African American Studies while an associate professor of educational leadership at the University of Oklahoma. Her research focuses on leadership development and preparation, effective leadership for educational equity in K–12 schools, women and leadership in K–12 and higher education context, and urban school reform. To date, she has over 60 publications which include books, book chapters, and academic articles in numerous peer-reviewed journals. She is the co-editor of *Women of Color in Higher Education: Turbulent Past, Promising Future* (2011, Emerald Publishing) and *Women of Color in Higher Education: Contemporary Perspectives and New Directions* (2011, Emerald Publishing). Also, she is the editor of the *Journal of School Leadership,* book review editor of the *Journal of Educational Administration,* past chair/president of the Leadership for Social Justice AERA/SIG, and co-founder of Advancing Women of Color in the Academy (AWOCA).

JuYoung Lee is a PhD candidate in the College of Education, Seoul National University, South Korea. Her academic interest is the role of higher education in sustainable development in the era of knowledge economics. Especially she has focused on 'learning' as a mean and its implication in a shifting economic paradigm. Theoretically, she tries to expand her idea to bridge human capital theory and a higher level of learning in a new era. Formerly, she has worked as a chief aide for Member of National Assembly, Republic of Korea and a research assistant at economic research centers. She holds degrees in economics and Asian studies (BA) from

Mount Holyoke College (South Hadley, MA, U.S.), International Economics (MA) from Seoul National University (South Korea), and international Law (MSL) from Northwestern University School of Law (Chicago, IL, US).

Nicole Limperopulos serves as the associate director of the Summer Principals Academy at Teachers College, Columbia University, which is the largest university-based principal preparation program in the nation. In her role as Associate Director, she is responsible for operations oversight, fiscal management, and student recruitment. Dr. Limperopulos took an early leadership role in conducting a feasibility study and establishing partnerships that led to the successful launch of the Summer Principals Academy New Orleans. She also manages program accreditation, and led the Summer Principals Academy to secure full national accreditation through NCATE. Dr. Limperopulos completed her doctorate at Teachers College, and her research focuses on the effects that chronic exposure to community violence has on the lives of urban male adolescents. After completing an initial study on violence exposure in the South Bronx, Dr. Limperopulos is currently replicating the study in New Orleans, Chicago, Detroit, Washington, D.C., Miami, and Los Angeles. Prior to her work at Teachers College, Dr. Limperopulos spent eight years as a teacher in the New York City Department of Education. She holds an MA in history education from the City University of New York (CUNY), MEd in education leadership, and EdD in interdisciplinary studies from Columbia University.

Paula T. McWhirter, PhD, is a professor in the department of educational psychology at the University of Oklahoma. A Fulbright scholar, McWhirter completed her dissertation on intervention strategies with high-risk youth while training at a school-based community mental health center in Santiago, Chile. She completed her masters and doctoral degrees in counseling psychology from Arizona State University, a post-doctoral fellowship in statistics and research methodology from at the University of California at Los Angeles, and another post-doctoral position in the clinical neuropsychology department at Good Samaritan Regional Medical Center. Prior to accepting her current position at the University of Oklahoma, McWhirter served as clinical director for a comprehensive provider of behavioral health services for over 1,000 Medicaid-eligible children and their families, directing all aspects involving clinical policies, objectives, and initiatives and providing counseling consultation and supervision. Dr. McWhirter studies positive psychology approaches, interpersonal violence interventions, international issues in counseling psychology, and therapeutic factors within group and family/child counseling approaches.

Anthony H. Normore, PhD (Tony) is professor and department chair of educational leadership in the Graduate School of Education at California

Lutheran University, Thousand Oaks, California. Dr. Normore has published numerous books and journal articles in the area of leadership development, social justice, ethics, and global learning. He has published with Routledge/Taylor & Francis, Sage, Palgrave MacMillan, Teachers College Record, Springer, Sense Publishing, and Jossey-Bass. In summer 2013 he was a professor of ethics, law, and educational leadership for the Summer Leadership Academy at Teachers College–Columbia University (New York). Fluent in both English and French, Dr. Normore brings 30+ years of educational experiences that have taken him throughout North America, South Central Asia, Eastern Asia, UK, Continental Europe, and South Pacific. He co-edited a book *Leadership in Education, Corrections, and Law Enforcement: A Commitment to Ethics, Equity, and Excellence* (Emerald Group Publishing, 2011), which was central to his position as lead instructor of values-based leadership seminars to male inmates with the Los Angeles County Sheriff's department. In relation to this work, he has written and published with law enforcement personnel on publications such as *Education-Based Incarceration and Recidivism: The Ultimate Social Justice Crime Fighting Tool* (Information Age Publishing, 2012); *Leadership in Education, Corrections, and Law Enforcement: A Commitment to Ethics, Equity, and Excellence* (Emerald); *Maximizing Education Reaching Individual Transformation (M.E.R.I.T.): A Groundbreaking Leadership Development Program for Inmates in Los Angeles County Sheriff's Department* (*Law Enforcement Today*); and *Leadership Thinking: A Discipline of the Mind for the Effective Law Enforcement Supervisor* (*Journal of Authentic Leadership*). Dr. Normore serves on numerous steering committees including Center for Ethics and Educational Leadership (Penn State); Center for Values and Leadership (CLU); Leadership and Ethics Institute for Criminal Justice & Training/Police Academy (Golden West College); Education Based Incarceration (LA Sheriff's Department); and numerous professional editorial boards.

Rosemary Papa (formerly PapaLewis) currently serves as the Del and Jewel Lewis Endowed Chair in Learning Centered Leadership and professor of educational leadership in the College of Education at Northern Arizona University, since 2007. Her former positions in education include: P–12 teacher, principal, chief school administrator/superintendent, and various higher education positions including assistant vice chancellor, academic affairs, California State University system. Dr. Papa has a BA in history, MA in educational psychology, and an EdD in administration, curriculum, and instruction. Since 1987, she has been an active member of the National Council of Professors of Educational Administration since 1987. In 1991–1992, she served as the first female President of (NCPEA) and was the 2003 recipient of the NCPEA Living Legend Award, and she delivered the Walter D. Cocking Lecture both in 1999 and in 2011. In 2012 she became the first NCPEA International Ambassador and currently serves as the NCPEA Publications Committee Chair. In 2000 Dr. Papa founded and serves as editor of the *eJEP: Journal of Education Policy*, one of the first open-access, free, blind-peer-reviewed journals in the world. She has authored 80+ peer reviewed journal articles and 15+ books on learning and the learner, leadership, and multimedia impacts on learning. Her most recent books (edited/co-authored) include: 2011—*Technology Leadership for School Improvement; Turnaround Principals for Underperforming Schools; 2012 NCPEA Handbook of Online Instruction and Programs in Educational Leadership; Educational Leadership at 2050; 2013 Contours of Great Educational Leadership: The Science, Art and Wisdom of Outstanding Practice.* In 2012 she founded the Flagstaff Seminar: Educational Leaders Without Borders.

Genevieve Siegel-Hawley, PhD, is an assistant professor in the department of educational leadership at Virginia Commonwealth University and a research associate at the Civil Rights Project. She received her PhD in urban schooling from the University of California, Los Angeles' Graduate School of Education and Information Studies. Her research focuses on segregation, inequality, and opportunity in U.S. schools, along with policy options to promote an inclusive, integrated society.

Derik Yager-Elorriaga is a second-year PhD student in the counseling psychology program at the University of Oklahoma. He graduated Magna Cum Laude with his bachelor's degree majoring in psychology and a minor in neuroscience from Gettysburg College in 2012. While at Gettysburg College, Yager-Elorriaga served as a peer learning associate, an executive board member of the International Club, and a college conferences services coordinator. He received the Shand Research Fellowship, Psychology Department Honors, and was admitted into Psi Chi and Phi Beta Kappa Honor Societies. Yager-Elorriaga has studied the cognitive advantages among bilinguals and the relationship between ethnic pride and hope among ethnically diverse youth. Currently, he serves as a graduate research assistant for the University of Oklahoma K–20 Center, and his research focuses on positive psychology approaches to promoting individual and community wellbeing.

CPSIA information can be obtained at www.ICGtesting.com
Printed in the USA
BVOW09s2222121114

374852BV00004B/71/P